Christians in the City of Shanghai

Christians in the City: Studies in Contemporary Global Christianity

Series Editor: Dyron Daughrity

Christians in the City looks carefully at Christianity in many of the world's great cities. It draws on interdisciplinary methods including anthropology, ethnography, sociology, phenomenology, and history. The series marks a significant contribution to the growing body of scholarship on world Christianity, lived religion, material religion, urban studies, and globalization as it engages people on the ground, in their local setting. The cities covered are drawn from around the world: North America, Latin America, Africa, Asia, Europe, the Middle East, and Oceania.

Books highlight how Christianity is changing particular metro areas, as well as how those areas are impacting the Christian religion. Most major forms of Christianity are discussed: Pentecostalism, Roman Catholic, mainline Protestant, non-denominational megachurches, Eastern Orthodox, immigrant forms, and house churches. The net is cast wide in order to understand what is happening with Christianity as it engages the great urban centers of the world.

Forthcoming books:

Christians in the City of Hong Kong, Tobias Brandner
Christians in the City of Kinshasa, Fohle Lygunda li-M
Christians in the City of Rio de Janeiro, Graham McGeoch

Christians in the City of Shanghai

A History Resurrected Above the Sea

SUSANGELINE Y. PATRICK

BLOOMSBURY ACADEMIC
LONDON • NEW YORK • OXFORD • NEW DELHI • SYDNEY

BLOOMSBURY ACADEMIC
Bloomsbury Publishing Plc
50 Bedford Square, London, WC1B 3DP, UK
1385 Broadway, New York, NY 10018, USA
29 Earlsfort Terrace, Dublin 2, Ireland

BLOOMSBURY, BLOOMSBURY ACADEMIC and the Diana logo are trademarks of Bloomsbury Publishing Plc

First published in Great Britain 2024

Series design by Rebecca Heselton

Cover images © Denys Nevozhai/Edward He/Katherine Gu/Unsplash

A catalogue record for this book is available from the British Library.

Library of Congress Control Number: 2023934693

ISBN: HB: 978-1-3503-3004-7
PB: 978-1-3503-3005-4
ePDF: 978-1-3503-3006-1
eBook: 978-1-3503-3007-8

Series: Christians in the City: Studies in Contemporary Global Christianity

Typeset by RefineCatch Limited, Bungay, Suffolk
Printed and bound in Great Britain

To find out more about our authors and books visit www.bloomsbury.com and sign up for our newsletters

Contents

Figures

Preface

In the 1950s, a Chinese Adventist medical doctor, Caleb Hung-Ye Chu (Zhu Hongyi, 1913–92), was my father's family physician in Booneville, Kentucky. The *Courier-Journal* newspaper published an article about his life story and called him a medical missionary with "long, tapering, surgical fingers."[1] In Nanjing, Dr. Chu had been one of the three houseboys of the Generalissimo Chiang Kai-shek, the prominent Nationalist Party leader of the early twentieth century in Republican China. Chu came from a Methodist background but became a Seventh-Day Adventist due to the influence of a nurse, Elisabeth Redelstein from the Adventist hospital in Shanghai.[2] Madame Chiang sent Chu to a nursing school when Chu was 16 years old, and the General sponsored him to receive surgical training at the National Medical College in Lanzhou. After 1949, Dr. Chu and his family came to the United States through an American Adventist sponsorship. He was well-loved by the Appalachian community. Mrs. Chu hosted my father and family for meals and the Chu daughters were playmates of my three aunts. Dr. Chu and his family started my father's life-long interest in Chinese culture. Even though I have spent half of my life in three major cities in China, I have always joked about how my Scottish American father taught me to love Chinese cultures.

As for my own intrigue with Shanghai, it only happened after my first visit to the metropolis in 2007 while I was living in Xi'an City. On that fateful trip, I stumbled into major religious landmarks related to Shanghai's incredible history of Christianity. Xu Guangqi Memorial Park near St. Ignace Cathedral, Saint Nicholas Orthodox Church, the International Church, and the Jewish Refugee Museum (formerly Ohel Moshe Synagogue or *Moxi Huitang*) all captivated me and opened a fascinating world for me. They challenged me to confront all my presumptions about the history of Christianity in Shanghai.

Over the next fifteen years, I have returned to Shanghai again and again walking on both the narrow lanes (*lilong*) of the Old Shanghai *shikumen* and in the jungle of skyscrapers. I have sat on the wooden benches at Mu'en Memorial Church with local Christian women while singing and listening to sermons preached in the Shanghai dialect, and prayed with Shanghai Christian friends near the Huangpu River and in digital spaces. I have observed, participated, learned, and continued to witness the transformation of Shanghai as a global city and the changes of its religious landscape. I regret not having lived in Shanghai as a resident, but I am grateful for having been a guest in the city and having had friends who live in Shanghai as Christians and non-religionists.

Researching Shanghai Christianity has led to wonderful discoveries which have shocked me as a researcher and generated much gratitude and awe. Hopefully, my efforts in researching Shanghai will be informative in the history of Christian struggles and hopes in this amazing but under-appreciated global city.

Acknowledgments

I am grateful to Auntie Rosa Hwang of San Francisco and Samson Uytanlet of Manila, the Philippines, for making helpful connections for me to interview their friends and students. I appreciate my father, William Patrick, for reading my manuscript and being the soundboard. I am indebted to all my Chinese and Korean friends in Shanghai, for their incredible hospitality and support. Although I cannot name them for the sake of security, their identities and work are not forgotten.

Special thanks to the staff at Shanghai Guanfu Museum, for pointing out a significant artifact related to my research. Thanks go to Ayla Toussaint, director at the Loretto Heritage Center and Archives, and Amanda Beard, archive assistant, for bringing out valuable archival materials related to the Loretto Sisters in Shanghai. I also wish to thank Debra Bradshaw, director of the William Broadhurst Library at Nazarene Theological Seminary, for securing a few valuable German sources via interlibrary loans. My alma mater, Asbury Theological Seminary, also provided online access to many important digital books and JSTOR articles. Special thanks go to Dyron Daughrity, series editor of *Christians in the City*, Stuart Hay, and Lily McMahon at Bloomsbury, for their helpful work in the publishing process.

Although I have made most of the field trips alone, I am grateful to my grandmother Wilma and my mother Twana for accompanying me to the Loretto Motherhouse in Nerinx, Kentucky, ten miles away from where my grandmother grew up. The three-generation trip made my research more meaningful and personal. Emotional support from my brother Jason, sister-in-law Geran, and my little niece Kaarina of New York provides much encouragement. As a product of multiple cultures, my biological and adopted families nurtured and educated me with the desire to learn and to appreciate languages and cultures. Their faith, love, and perseverance compelled me to resonate with social justice and mercy issues. Even though I did not personally experience some of the historical struggles and sufferings of my ancestors, I could resonate with my Korean *Omma*'s family history and her Andong Kim clan's participation in Korean independence from Japan in the early twentieth century. During the Cultural Revolution in the 1960s, my biological family in China also lost factories in the coastal city of Tianjin. It is difficult to know how they remained hopeful. Their stories have become part of mine and they have given me perspectives to understand and perceive the world through the eyes of faith and compassion.

I could not have imagined writing this manuscript without all the works of others who have poured their lives into crossing many boundaries and forming faithful friendships. There is still so much to uncover and rediscover, I fully take responsibility for the deficiencies and flaws of my research. I hope other researchers in the future will also invest and expand our understandings of the place of Shanghai in World Christianity. Truly, it has been a transformative journey for me to have encountered Shanghai Christians.

Susangeline Patrick, PhD
Kansas City, Missouri
On the homelands of the Kaw, Jiwere, Nutachi, and Wahzhazhe Peoples

Abbreviations

ABCFM	American Board of Commissioners for Foreign Missions
CAOC	Chinese Autonomous Orthodox Church
CCA	Church of Christ in Australia
CCC	Church of Christ in China
CCM	Chinese Christian Mission
CCP	Chinese Communist Party
CE	Common Era
CES	Chinese Evangelical Society
CGM	Church of God Mission
CHMS	Chinese Home Mission Society
CIM	China Inland Mission
CLS	Chinese Literature Society
CMA	Christian and Missionary Alliance
CMS	Church Missionary Society
COA	Chinese Orthodox Association
COBS	Chinese Orthodox Brotherhood of Shanghai
FMS	Marist Brothers of the Schools
HHS	Society of the Helpers of the Holy Souls
KMT	Kuomintang/Guomindang/Nationalist Party
KPG	Korean Provisional Government
LSP	Congregation of the Little Sisters of the Poor (also PSDP)
LM	Legion of Mary
LMS	London Missionary Society
MEC, S	Methodist Episcopal Church, South
MEP	Missions Étrangères de Paris
OFASC	Orthodox Fellowship of All Saints of China
PEC	Protestant Episcopal Church USA

PRC People's Republic of China
PSDP Petites Sœurs des Pauvres
RGS Congregation of Our Lady of Charity of the Good Shepherd
RSCJ Society of the Sacred Heart
SAS Shanghai American School
SBC Southern Baptist Convention
SCS Shanghai College and Seminary
SDA Seventh Day Adventist
SL Sisters of Loretto
SMP Shanghai Municipal Police
TSMP The Sisters of Mary of the Presentation
TSPM Three-Self Patriotic Movement
UCCA Union for Chinese Catholic Association
UCMS United Christian Mission Society
USSR Union of Soviet Socialist Republics
WCTU Woman's Christian Temperance Union
WFMS Women's Foreign Missionary Society
WMU Women's Union Missionary Society of America
WSA Women's Suffrage Association
YMCA Young Men's Christian Association
YWCA Young Women's Christian Association

Series Introduction

Dyron B. Daughrity, Series Editor

Christians in the City is a fascinating and cutting-edge series that looks carefully at Christians in many of the world's greatest urban centers. It draws on interdisciplinary methods including anthropology, ethnography, sociology, phenomenology, and history. The series marks a significant contribution to the growing body of scholarship on world Christianity, lived religion, material religion, urban studies, and globalization as it engages people on the ground, in their local setting. The cities are drawn from around the world: North America, Asia, Africa, Europe, Latin America, and Oceania.

The Series' books highlight how Christianity is changing particular metro areas, as well as how those areas are impacting the Christian religion. Many different although often overlapping forms of Christianity are discussed in the volumes: Pentecostal, Roman Catholic, mainline Protestant, non-denominational, Eastern Orthodox, immigrant churches, megachurches, charismatic, evangelical, independent, and house churches. The net is cast wide in order to understand better what is happening with Christianity as it engages the great urban centers of the world. Christian organizations in the city—universities, private schools, and faith-based charities—will be explored as well.

The series features established as well as rising scholars. We have taken great care to choose authors who live in the cities under consideration, or at least have lived in those cities in the past. There is an intimacy that comes through in these volumes, and readers from those cities will recognize the streets, the sounds, the vibe, and the cultural accents that make cities unique. The volumes are written with crossover appeal—for audiences both inside and outside the academy.

Each volume contains interviews with leading figures from the city under consideration—as well as a broad array of laypeople—in order to gain a well-rounded perspective on these cities. There will be no shortage of material, as Christianity is not only the largest world religion in terms of adherents, but is also extremely widespread geographically, making it a diverse and complex religion that takes root in the soil of the cities it has been planted in.

The series will consist of monographs on 25 of the world's great cities, with carefully chosen, exceptional authors who have an intimate understanding of the city they write about. As the list of books in the series expands, a global balance will be maintained. The current list of cities/volumes that have either been contracted or are under consideration are:

- ***In North America*: New York, Los Angeles,* Boston, Houston,* Montreal***
- ***In Asia*: Shanghai,* Hong Kong,* Seoul, Delhi, Manila**
- ***In Africa*: Cairo,* Addis Ababa, Kinshasa,* Lagos,* Johannesburg,* Nairobi***
- ***In Europe*: Moscow, London, Athens**
- ***In Latin America*: Sao Paulo,* Rio de Janeiro,* Havana, Santiago, Mexico City**
- ***In Oceania*: Sydney***

  ****Books already contracted.***

This series has been several years in the making, and we are excited to see it now coming to light. Over half of the books are contracted, but the search continues for authors for the remaining volumes. We are open to proposals of other cities from potential authors.

Over half of the world's population lives in cities, and the expectation is that in coming years the number of people leaving the countryside for the city will only increase. Since its earliest days, Christianity was a religion of the city: Jerusalem, Alexandria, Antioch, Damascus, Corinth, Thessaloniki, and Rome. Established by the apostles themselves, that pattern continued. As Christianity expanded further, it gravitated towards cities: Aleppo, Edessa, Seleucia-Ctesiphon, Aksum, Etchmiadzin, and Constantinople.

The pattern continued, as the energy of the city attracted Christian missionaries, scholars, and laypeople in search of opportunity. As cities developed, Christians established bishoprics, cathedrals, and centers of learning in cities. Today, the great centers of Christian thought and influence are located chiefly in cities: Seoul, Addis Ababa, Rio de Janeiro, Dallas, Athens, Rome, and Moscow.

A series on Christians in the cities is timely, and promises to break new ground. There is an undeniable power in cities—a power to attract. And Christians continue to make their way, bringing with them manifold Christian practices, routines, rituals, and beliefs. In all of their diversity, they are united in one thing—they consider themselves Christians. And they live in the city.

For more information about this series, contact the Series Editor:

Dyron B. Daughrity
Professor of Religion
Pepperdine University
dyron.daughrity@pepperdine.edu

Introduction

Shanghai and World Christianity

How has Shanghai become a cosmopolitan face of World Christianity? This introduction sets up the reason for choosing Shanghai, the third largest global city, as a case study of World Christianity. I will introduce the topic, preview the seven chapters, and provide research methods and theoretical framework. Engaging primarily resources through library and archive research and ethnography, I will take an interdisciplinary approach, tracing and analyzing the history and anthropology of Shanghai Christianity. To many people's surprise, Shanghai has embodied the multifaceted aspects of the Catholic, Protestant, Orthodox, Indigenous, and Cosmopolitan Christian movements that will enlighten us about the past and equip us to envision a future. The goal of the research is to provide an updated and comprehensive history and analyze the fascinating stories of Christians in Shanghai. The book follows a topical order and is flexibly chronological within each chapter in order to highlight and analyze unique characteristics and aspects of Shanghai Christians.

For over 400 years, Shanghai has served as a hub of multifaceted Christian movements despite periodic social and political disruption. In the most recent thirty years, churches of many denominations, organizations, and non-affiliated individuals have rediscovered the memory of Christianity resurrected and Christians thriving in the global city. Todd Johnson and Gina Zurlo's third edition of the *World Christian Encyclopedia* identifies Shanghai as one of the "large urban areas [that] have significant minority Christian populations."[1] Both the distant and recent Christian past have not ceased to actively shape the present and the future of Shanghai Christianity. This book will explore two unique and neglected aspects of rediscovering and remaking historical memory. Historical contexts, figures, events, movements, institutions, and interpretations have all played significant roles in configuring the present perception of the past and the making of the future.

Another key question is in what ways have Christians interacted or shunned away from engaging adherents of other religions, philosophies, and the non-religious? Beyond the traditional ways of church planting and zealous evangelism which may be more appropriate in other contexts, what are some of the distinctive and innovative pathways people in Shanghai have engaged as *Jidu tu* (Christians) or *xing Yesu de* (a Jesus believer)? The stories of Christians in Shanghai effectively serve as a case study for Christians around the world to see how Christianity as a minority religion in a city has related to other religions and philosophies, and navigated incredible social, political, and economic changes. The stories of Shanghai Christians reflect features that are dynamically transnational, both Indigenous and Cosmopolitan, and social and politically diverse, paradoxical, and heterogeneous.

The Catholic story of Shanghai began in 1608. Sophisticated and high-positioned Ming Dynasty government officials encountered the astutely trained Jesuit missionaries from Italy, Portugal, and other European countries. The mutual and ongoing encounter generated the following four centuries of significant Catholic figures, such as Xu Guangqi (1562–1633) and Candida Xu (1607–80), the constructing of churches and sacred art, transforming the city through social services, and organizing large numbers of local women leaders and eventually Catholic schools and universities. Recent Catholics in both house churches and government-registered churches have been active in outreach to the elderly and the disabled, and fervently participating in wider society. Concurrently, I will extend two categories of Catholics to, first, the "old Catholics," descendants of Catholic families whose religious roots trace back to either the seventeenth century or the late eighteenth century. The second category is *wenhua jidutu* (cultural Christians), different from nominal Christians. They are intellectuals who do not necessarily identify as religious in an institutionalized church, but are cultural Christians who are attracted to certain philosophical or moral principles in Christianity. Understanding the changing historical contexts and the invariable Catholic spirit in Shanghai challenges Christians today.

Shanghai served as the missionary headquarters for more than a century from 1842 to the 1950s and Protestant missionaries continued and magnified the multicultural and multilingual layers of Christianity in the nineteenth and twentieth centuries in Shanghai. Serving to build self-supporting Chinese churches and local leadership, Protestant missionaries from various denominations and voluntary mission organizations participated in evangelism and discipleship, medicine, social welfare, and printing of Christian literature alongside their Chinese colleagues. Pentecostal and independent missionaries also contributed to the spread of the gospel. Some missionaries suffered in the Japanese internment camps in Shanghai during the Second Sino-Japanese War (1937–45). Subsequently, when Protestant missionaries returned to their home countries, they served as a bridge between Asia and the West and contributed to Europe and North America's learning about China and the academic field of sinology.

A surprising aspect of Shanghai Christian history is the Orthodox communities. The major Orthodox churches served as the social, cultural, and spiritual center of Russian Orthodox refugees in the early twentieth century. The Armenians found shelter in Shanghai after the Genocide and gathered as the Apostolic Church. Chinese Orthodox priests pastored in Shanghai, San Francisco, and Australia. Although the historical buildings of the churches have been destroyed or have been in nonreligious use for over fifty years, the Orthodox community in Shanghai has resurrected the churches' historical memory.

The modern history of Chinese-initiated Christian churches began in the early twentieth century. Wang Peizhen (1899–1971), Watchman Nee (Ni Tuosheng, 1903–72), and two hundred Chinese evangelists planted over seven hundred assembly places in Shanghai between 1927 and 1952. Indigenous Christian efforts extended to ethnic minorities, social reform, education, and business. After the chaotic decade of the Cultural Revolution (1966–76), Christians have persisted through the divergence of government-sanctioned church and house church. Beginning in the 1970s and 1980s, as more church properties were returned and restored, new gatherings of Christians have dotted the city landscape in the past thirty years. The history of Chinese churches sheds light on why and how Christians have created social and political changes and dialogued between gospel and culture.

The most unexpected but exciting history of Christians in Shanghai is the multicultural and multilingual churches across denominational lines. Japanese, Korean, Portuguese, Russian, and Cantonese Australian Christians contributed to the making of mosaic Christianity in early-twentieth-century Shanghai. In the twenty-first century, the vibrancy of Christians from all nations is visible. For example, Saint Peter's Catholic Church hosts mass in five languages: Chinese, English, French, German, and Korean. Other interdenominational churches only offer English for the international community in Shanghai. Due to technological advancement and the Covid pandemic beginning in 2020, many churches quickly switched to online worship, prayer meetings, and other gatherings via the chat application Weixin. The interactions between global and local will generate insights into multiculturalism, globalization, sinicization, and ecclesiology. The interreligious dialogues between Shanghai Christians and other religions and philosophies such as Buddhism, Daoism, Confucianism, Islam, Judaism, and other ideologies such as Nazism and freemasonry throughout history will also provide valuable reflections on the roles of Christians in a multireligious space.

This book synthesizes the lived Christian history of the past and the present. I will provide historical overviews of Catholic, Protestant, Orthodox,

Indigenous, and Cosmopolitan Christians. I will make the case why history in Chinese understanding is not a clear divide between the present and the future. That is also why new Christians from Shanghai and beyond are still seeking to recover, resurrect, and renew the historical memory of Shanghai Christianity.

Why Read this Book?

1. The urban Christian population of Shanghai City reflects a trend of World Christian distribution that has shifted from North America and Europe to the Majority World. As the largest Chinese city with 27 million city dwellers, urban Shanghai Christians provide an informative case of religion and secularism, gospel and culture, and Indigenous cosmopolitan and global reality in World Christianity.
2. As a super-modern city with the largest domestic migrant worker population and international community in China, Shanghai provides a key to understanding how Christian history is tightly connected to the past and the future. Shanghai Christian history allows us to explore the diverse and incredible growth of Christian churches and how they have navigated the challenges and opportunities of identity, community, and faith.
3. This book offers an interdisciplinary approach to studying the Christian history of Shanghai. Following conventional and unconventional ways of how Christians in Shanghai come to faith through social networks, broadcasting, art, music, film, and the internet, this book offers readers an opportunity to reflect on the holistic aspect of Christianity and the multidirectional ways of knowing God. In the postmodern age of North America and Europe, Shanghai perhaps will serve as a model for Christians around the world to find innovative ways of orthodoxy and orthopraxy.

Concept Statement

Shanghai represents a significant shift in Global Christianity as an urban and "glocal" religion. Readers will gain a historical and current understanding of the diversity and unity of Christians. Through historical documents, theology, the arts, and the stories of individual and communal Christians, we will be able to draw sources from the past and reimagine what it means to live in a pluralistic society as Christians.

My methods of study are both library/archive research, participant observation, and interviews. First, I have utilized primary and secondary resources from libraries and archives. Many online journals, digitized materials, and memoirs also provide valuable information about the history of Christians in Shanghai. Second, I have participated in church services online or in person when they are available and accessible. Third, I have interviewed Christians in Shanghai and people who have been formerly or are presently involved with Christians in Shanghai. They have provided valuable aspects of history that will be enriching.

I intentionally seek to reveal Christian women's work in Shanghai. A major disparity is the contrast between the plenteous mentions of participation by male Catholic priests and workers and the lack of women's participation in written documents. However, when examining the historical photographs, women not only showed up in these memorable moments, but they also represented most of the visual presence. For example, a photograph titled Mission Day at Sacred Heart Church had twenty women participants out of twenty-nine people. However, not even one name of the women was mentioned in the accompanying written records. The lack of written documentation of women's work raises further questions.

The geography of Shanghai has shifted its boundaries throughout the past 400 years. In the latest layout, Shanghai includes the seven central areas of Huangpu, Xuhui, Jing'an, Changning, Yangpu, Hongkou, and Putuo. Another eight districts are outside of downtown Shanghai including three suburban areas (Minhang, Baoshan, and Jiading) and five remote suburbs (Songjiang, Jinshan, Qingpu, Fengxian, and Chongming). Shanghai also includes one new urban development, Pudong New Area. I have limited my research to the central and urban areas except for Songjiang District due to its significance in seventeenth-century Catholicism. I have attempted to cover as many individuals and institutions as possible. However, with the extensiveness of Christians in Shanghai, there is still much to research in the future.

Historians from China and outside of China have conducted historical studies about China. It is important to state three main sources of written Chinese history: official court history, called *shi*; regional history, *zhi*; and family history, *pu*. Court historians with intensive training have maintained a continuity of major characters and events. Some preceding rulers also censored, altered, and even burnt some previous court history that could influence their reigns. However, court history remains a valuable source for later historians to critically study. Regional history concerns more about the records of a local city or county. It preserves more ordinary lives and events that court history would have no interest in and that are often ignored. Family history focuses on households but mainly records the male decendents due to the *Zhongnan qingnü* Confucian ideology of favoring the boy child. I have utilized a tripod of *shi*, *zhi*, and *pu*, looking to find significant reports but also examining how different historiographical approaches reported the same history.

I acknowledge that I am both an insider and an outsider on multiple levels in researching Christians in Shanghai. My multicultural upbringing in China and the United States has shaped the ways I interpret and analyze ideas and events. My education from my Australian teachers and my extensive interactions in the multiple worlds of Europe, Korea, and Central Asia also influenced the selection of materials. As a mission historian, I aim to bring out the diversity of Christian experiences and my linguistic skills and connections with the city help me pay attention to a more nuanced and critical understanding of Shanghai Christian stories. Simultaneously, I am not a scholar from Shanghai nor am I directly impacted by events or authorities from the city and I recognize my bias and limitations in my conceptualization and arrangement. However, Shanghai is a city I have visited multiple times to conduct field research in the past fifteen years. The drastic changes in the city constantly unveil new aspects and introduce ways into how the global city preserves, reconstructs, and develops historical and new memories of Christians. It is my intention to offer readers a rich and captivating history of Shanghai Christians.

1

Catholic Shanghai

This chapter covers a history of Shanghai Catholics, European Catholic missions, Catholic women, Chinese priests, and their works from the early seventeenth century until the early twentieth century. The rediscovering of Catholic Shanghai will focus on histories prior to the 1950s and the remaking of Catholic Shanghai will highlight the recent and diverse Catholic expressions in the metropolitan area after the 1970s. The details reveal that Catholicism in Shanghai was built by both foreign mission efforts and local Christians' active participations that spread and sustained the Catholic faith in Shanghai.

Catholic history of Shanghai can be traced through five different stages. The first stage (1608–1842) consists of both the early Catholic mission to Shanghai and how different Chinese Catholic families established a prominent presence in shaping the city's religious and social landscape. The second stage (1842–1912) comprises of various Catholic missions and Chinese Catholic activities in the context of semi-colonial[1] rule of the British, French, and Americans in Shanghai. The third stage (1912–54) contains the varied ways Shanghai Catholics engaged in publishing, education, medicine, and social charity in the context of the Republic of China's democratic movements and the city's struggles with diverse social-political circumstances.[2] The fourth stage (1950s–70s) denotes how Shanghai Catholics navigated the political currents and how Catholic churches diverged into different types of communities due to their sociopolitical and theological disagreements. The fifth stage (1970s–2022) explores the aspects of how Shanghai Catholics began to revive because of relaxed political control of religions and religious activities. The city witnesses both a resurrection of Catholic history in Shanghai and fast growth of new Catholics. At the same time, as a minority, Shanghai Catholics face new challenges but continue to thrive amid drastic changes in the twenty-first century.

Historical Background of Shanghai

A brief historical background helps to locate the context of Shanghai. The exact origin and date of Shanghai as a city is unclear. Although Liujia Harbor near Shanghai presents a maritime Silk Road connection via the fifteenth-century naval expedition led by Zheng He (1371–1433),[3] Shanghai as a global city rose to international fame in the 1920s and 1930s. Fang Xu recognizes both the merit and fault in the two competing narratives of Shanghai's cosmopolitan character and origin from Western settlers and Chinese historical records.[4] Since the semi-colonial period in the mid-nineteenth century, both Western and Chinese writers have described the city as a fishing village[5] prior to the rapid economic growth of the second half of the nineteenth century when the British, French, American, and other dominant powers began to settle in Shanghai after the Treaty of Nanjing in 1843 forcefully opened Shanghai as a port city. The description of Shanghai also entails how the British and French colonial powers rapidly transformed Shanghai into a global city in the 1920s mimicking the Cinderella story or how the ugly duckling became a beautiful swan.

The counternarrative comes from researchers such as Jeffrey Wasserstrom who contests what he names as the "Fishing Village Legend" as misleading and false.[6] The official Chinese record also emphasizes the long history of Shanghai and downplays the European and American imperial influence on making Shanghai a global city. For instance, in 2016, archaeological teams from the Shanghai Museum began to unearth about six thousand export ceramics and showed evidence that Qinglong zhen, a suburban town of Shanghai, acted as a significant port as early as the eighth century in the Tang Dynasty.[7] The new discovery conflicts with the narrative of Shanghai's humble beginning and attempts to elevate the city's significance even in the maritime Silk Road during the Tang (618–907 CE) and Song (960–1279 CE) dynasties. Qinglong town in the Qingpu District is currently about 40 kilometers from the center of Shanghai. The town acted as a hub for international trade with Japan, the Silla Kingdom in Korea, India, and Southeast Asia until the port moved to the nearby town of Wusong.[8] Shanghai's prosperity continued as a "market town" in 1074 CE and a "market city" in 1159 CE.[9] In 1113, the Northern Song (960–1127 CE) appointed *Shibo Si*, the Customs office in charge of imports and exports, in Huating (now Songjiang District in Shanghai). Located on the Yangtze Delta and the Grand Canal which links Shanghai with major Chinese cities further north, Shanghai acted as one of the seven international trading ports[10] and emerged as a city in 1291 during the Yuan Dynasty. The city had a population of 500,000 with a thriving network of waterways and businesses.[11]

In terms of early Christianity in nearby ancient Shanghai, no historical records indicate that Shanghai encountered Syriac Christians during the Tang, Song, and Yuan (1271–1368) dynastic periods. The archaeological discoveries of Qinglong town of Shanghai as an important port do not delineate that Syriac Christianity had a presence in Shanghai prior to the Chinese Catholics and Jesuit mission in the early seventeenth century. Shanghai closed off the import and export bureau in the late thirteenth century and throughout the Ming Dynasty (1368–1644 CE). In 1554, local Shanghainese constructed walls defending themselves from the frequent attacks of Japanese pirates.[12] The geographical advantages of being accessible to transportation by both land and water and the long-standing domestic and international trade made Shanghai's first encounter with Christianity in 1608 it possible for.

First Stage: Early Shanghai Catholics (1608–1842)

Shanghai's Catholic beginning originated from the Chinese Catholics who related to the early Society of Jesus in China. The best-known initiator of Shanghai Catholicism is Xu Guangqi (1562–1633), the Minister of Rites (equivalent to today's Prime Minister) and a Chinese Catholic returning from Beijing to Shanghai in 1608 which marks the official year of Christian history in Shanghai. Chinese Catholic women also played a significant role in promulgating the gospel in Shanghai. It is important to note that Xu did not arrive in Shanghai by himself, but with other Chinese Catholic *literati* such as Zhang Jingqiao (1569–1644), a Hebei native and a mutual friend of Jesuit missionary Matteo Ricci (1552–1610). Zhang left Beijing and arrived in Shanghai with Xu in 1608. Additionally, Xu issued an invitation to Italian Jesuit missionary Lazzaro Cattaneo (Guo Jujing, 1560–1640) to further Jesuit mission in Shanghai. Xu built a chapel known as *Jiujian lou* (Nine-room building)[13] in his Shanghai residence so they could celebrate mass.[14] As a result, the Xu family, the Shanghai Catholic women, the Zhang clan, and European Jesuits established a profound Catholic presence in Shanghai.

Chinese Catholic Scholars and their Families

The birth of Catholicism in Shanghai, however, had an unusual but remarkable beginning. When Xu's father Xu Sicheng's body was transported from Beijing to Shanghai in 1608, Xu and Cattaneo carefully planned the rituals because the funeral would be the first using the Catholic rites in Shanghai. According to Li Tiangang at Fudan University, Xu organized a countercultural funeral to be distinct from the Buddhist or Daoist rites. The funeral ceremony was solemn, instead of loud with wailing of the relatives and professional mourners. The Xu family dressed in black, instead of the customary white linen. After the funeral, two hundred people joined the Catholic Church which marked the beginning of Catholicism in Shanghai.[15]

The Catholic Xu Family

The collaboration of the Chinese Catholics and the European Jesuit mission serves as a key component of Shanghai Catholicism from 1608 until the end of the Rite Controversy in 1742. First, Xu Guangqi's conversion to Catholicism in the late Ming Dynasty was intertwined with the European Jesuit missionaries in China. Beginning in 1597, the Jesuits centered themselves in Portuguese-occupied Macau and spread their mission endeavors further to the mainland of China, Japan, and Southeast Asia.[16] The Jesuit seminary St. Paul's College provided language training for Jesuit missionaries to China and Japan, and enrolled European and Asian students to prepare them for priesthood or lay brotherhood. Shanghai was not a prominent mission station at first but became significant after Xu's retirement to his hometown.

Second, known as one of three pillars of Ming Catholicism, Xu was a Songjiang (now part of the Shanghai proper) native and Ming court official. After a long period of discussing doctrinal issues with Ricci in Shaozhou, Guangdong Province, and later in Nanjing, Xu voluntarily received baptism from Portuguese Jesuit missionary João de Rocha (1566–1623) as Baolu (Paul) in Nanjing (1603). Matteo Ricci stated that Xu's wife Lady Wu[17] and his father Xu Sicheng received baptism in Beijing.[18] An anonymous writer in the Qing Dynasty documented the origin and reasons for the spread of Christianity in a work entitled *Zhongguo Chuanjiao Yuanyou*. The account is significant because it also confirms that Xu Sicheng, the eighty-year-old father of Xu Guangqi, had confessed to being a Catholic and later the rest of the Xu household had adopted the Catholic faith.[19] Ming scholar Li Ruihe (1607–86), an official of Songjiang and friends with Xu and Jesuit missionaries, documented the building of the Shanghai Catholic church west of Xu's residence.[20]

Third, Xu's religious influence extended beyond his immediate family and household. He also set positive examples for others in the areas of his work as a competent scholar, a politician, and a scientist. Xu and Ricci mutually learned and influenced each other after they met again in 1604 in Beijing. Although the Ming court had Christian converts among the *literati*, some scholars in the court, such as Shen Que (?–1624), saw Christian ideology as a novel idea and a threat to the supposed stability of the Ming Dynasty. Under some scholars' active opposition and attacks, Xu assisted Ricci in mission work in Beijing and defended the Jesuit missionaries when the *Nanjing jiaoan* (a court case against Christian missionaries in Nanjing) occurred.[21] Xu also recognized the historical evidence from *Jingjiao* (Church of the East, Syriac Christianity) in Tang China and wrote about the significance of rediscovering the stone stele (781) in Xi'an.[22]

Furthermore, Xu's Christian faith produced ripple effects and influenced Chinese scholars in other regions. For example, the two brothers Han Sen (*c.* 1601–47) and Han Xia received tutelage under Xu from 1617 until 1619. The Han brothers later became two of the most significant Catholics in Shanxi Province. Han Xia authored important theological treatises such as *Shenshou yaolüe*, *Shengjiao xinzheng*, and *Bianjiao lun* which engaged Catholic theology and Chinese philosophy.[23] Sun Yuanhua (Ignacio, 1581–1633), a Shanghai native who studied mathematics with Xu Guangqi, also became a Catholic because of Xu's influence.[24]

The Shanghai Catholic Women

The Xu family became the most prominent Catholic family in seventeenth-century Shanghai. Nadine Amsler focuses on the female networks of the Xu family of Shanghai and analyzes how the high-status Catholic women had shaped Catholicism in Shanghai from *c.* 1630 to 1660.[25] Xu Guangqi's four granddaughters—Felicitas, Candida, Monica, and Martina Xu—all married non-Catholic husbands but maintained their Catholic identity through their strong bonds and mutual emotional supports.[26] Felicitas married into the Ai family, Candida the Xu family, and Martina the Pan. Three of the Xu sisters transformed their husbands' families into Catholics.[27]

The Xu Catholic women in Shanghai dedicated themselves to the Virgin Mary and began *Shengmu hui* (the Holy Mother Confraternity) with the founding Jesuit priest Pedro Ribeiro (Li Ningshi, 1572–1640) in 1636.[28] Gail King details how members of the confraternity soon included women and men. They practiced the works of mercy and followed *Shengmu hui gui* (Rules for the Holy Mother Confraternity).[29] By 1665, the works of the confraternities contributed to the vitality of the churches in the region with a report of sixty-six churches and over 50,000 Christians in Jiangnan.[30]

The Xu Catholic women used their own finances to build churches. Martina Xu, granddaughter of Xu Guangqi, married Pan Yaona, great-grandson of Pan Yunduan, governor of Sichuan and founder of the Yu Garden. Martina purchased *Shichun Tang* (Ever-Spring Hall), gifted it to the Catholic Church via Brancati, and dedicated it as *Jingyi Tang* (Worship the One Hall) which primarily served male Catholics due to the Ming Qing restriction separating female and male believers.[31] The Jingyi Church experienced a brief disruption between 1665 and 1671 when Catholicism was banned. After 1671, Jean-Dominique Gabiani and Philippe Couplet managed the church and restored service to the Catholic community.[32]

The Xu women formed their own congregation and met at *Shengmu Tang* (the Holy Mother Hall) which served solely as a women's church in the 1640s.[33] The creation of a women's church for Chinese Catholic women accommodated the Chinese aristocratic culture where high-class women usually socialized on gender-segregated terms. Xu Guangqi's first granddaughter-in-law, Flavia Yu,

FIGURE 1.1 *The exterior of the surviving Jingyi Tang, the seventeenth-century Old Catholic Church near the Yu Garden in Shanghai. Photo courtesy of Susangeline Patrick, 2019.*

wife of Peter Xu Erjiao, made a financial donation to the women's church and led a congregation of thirty women in the 1640s and 1950s.[34] Candida's daughter-in-law Philippa led the women's congregation in the 1680s.[35]

Additionally, Christian women in Shanghai dedicated themselves to charities. Candida Xu sponsored orphanages caring for abandoned children, hired wet nurses, and even bought land for the burial of the babies who did not survive.[36] Consecrated virgins such as Rosalie led prayers and services.[37] Unlike most of their European counterparts who were cloistered, they could participate in ministries beyond the confinements of convents.[38] Christian single, married, and widowed women all contributed to the sustaining of the Catholic faith in Shanghai.

The Zhangs and Other Catholic Families

The second most prominent Shanghai Catholics was the Zhang family from Hebei. The Zhangs have received little scholarly attention in Shanghai Christian historiography. However, they also established and spread their faith through families and social networks. The centrality of the home contributed to how the Christian faith passed from one generation to the next for over 400 years. The Zhang family descended from a Catholic convert, Zhang Jingqiao (1569–1644), whom the *Chuansha County Gazetteers* recorded as Xu Guangqi's "manager of land and property."[39] Originally from Hebei, Zhang paid a special visit to Matteo Ricci in Nanjing in 1600 and became one of the first *literati* class to convert to Catholicism. Zhang's friendship with Ricci and Xu grew from 1605 to 1608 and together they formed a vision to take the gospel to Jiangnan, south of the Yangzi River. Zhang's conversion had caused his clan to turn against him. Therefore, after Xu's father passed away in 1608, Zhang decided to resign from his official position and go to Shanghai with Xu.

Zhang built the foundation of Catholicism as he lived in Zhangjiawan from 1608 until 1640. In 1609, he invited another Jesuit missionary, Cattaneo, to preach to *dianhu*, the tenants who rented the land, and the *Chuansha County Gazetteers* recorded that "dozens of people received baptism right away."[40] Over the succeeding 400 years, the Zhang family eventually developed a Catholic village and a hub for Catholicism that influenced surrounding areas. The Yao, Fu, Feng, Xu, Yang, Jin, and Lian clans became Catholics as well. In 1744, the fifth generation of the Zhang family, Zhang Yujing, built the Sacred Heart Church in Zhangjialou memorializing Zhang Jingqiao's centennial. Among the recorded descendants, one branch had produced the most Catholic priests and nuns as at the beginning of the sixth generation.

Beside the prominent Xu and Zhang families, other Catholic families also preserved their faith and worshipped in their private oratories at their homes, such as the Rose Our Lady Church of the Fu family (*Fujia meigui shengmu Tang*), despite periodic anti-Christian struggles. In the 1937 Jesuit publication *A Guide to Catholic Shanghai*, Jesuit priest Peter Lefebvre reported: "In 1663 there were 40,000 fervent Christians; in 1703 . . . two churches and thirty chapels administered by three Fathers and one Coadjuster Brother."[41] Lefebvre omitted the names of the priests and the lay brothers; however, he mentioned three wealthy Catholic families with the names of "Ngai, Loh and Se"[42] in eighteenth-century Shanghai.

Additionally, the Zhu family became Catholics around the 1720s and were effectively expelled from the clan because Catholicism was still considered as an outrageous sin in the Qingpu District in Shanghai. Due to how different families or clans had been converted to the Christian faith, Catholicism functioned as a family religion. Different families built their own churches. The Immaculate Conception Church in Jinjiaxiang began between 1628 and 1643 as one of the earliest Catholic churches in Shanghai. Other Catholic churches served as family chapels facilitating the spiritual needs of the families and households in Shanghai.

The Chinese Rites Controversy

The Chinese Rites Controversy in the seventeenth and eighteenth centuries generated out of the different Catholic interpretations and approaches to

Chinese civic rites, particularly related to the veneration of deceased ancestors. Many scholars have discussed the issue from multiple perspectives about the devastating impact the Rites Controversy had on Chinese Catholicism. However, is it possible that we have overemphasized the negative impact of the Rites Controversy on Chinese Christianity? Chinese Catholics and the Jesuits in the seventeenth century established a well-structured policy adopting a favorable attitude toward Chinese culture, custom, and rites.

The Kangxi Emperor's Edit of Toleration in 1692 also protected Catholics. The Rites Controversy appeared to be a Roman problem, not a Chinese question, because the Chinese Catholics had already settled on the reconciliation between civic duties and religious ceremonies. The Jesuits debated with the Dominicans, Franciscans, and Augustinians in Rome, mainly about whether Chinese Catholics should participate in the rites of Confucius, using *Tian* (Heaven) or *Shangdi* (the Great Supreme Being) for God, or displaying ancestors' tablets. Even though there are no direct references of Chinese Catholics in Shanghai participating in the debate in Rome, a group of nineteen Chinese Christians answered the invitation of a Chinese Jesuit priest Blasius Liu Yunde and gathered in Nanjing in 1702 to draft a letter to the Pope in defending Christians in Fujian.[43]

Furthermore, even though Pope Clement XI's decree *Cum Deus optimus* in 1704 condemned the Chinese rites, the policy challenged the Kangxi Emperor who in return required all foreign missionaries to obtain a Qing imperial certificate stating that their policy accommodated Chinese culture in the same way the early Jesuit missionaries had established. The Rites Controversy reflects both a political struggle between the Pope in Rome, who extended religious control over Catholics in China, and the Qing imperial ruler, who saw Qing imperial sovereignty and authority above the universal ecclesiastical vision of Catholicism.

The Rites Controversy negatively impacted Shanghai Catholics in the eighteenth and early nineteenth centuries. The Yongzheng Emperor banned Catholicism in 1724 with a massive campaign of converting churches into other religious temples while ironically having Jesuit artists and scientists in his court. In Shanghai, the Old Catholic Church near the Yu Garden was converted to a Taoist Guandi Temple. The papal bull of Benedict XIV in 1742 prescribed an oath for all European missionaries to China condemning Chinese rites.[44] By the beginning of the nineteenth century, seven Chinese Catholic families, the Zhu, Lu, Zhou, Pan, Qin, Yao, and Shen, all sought refuge near Zhuxiang. In 1861, these Catholic families moved to the area near the Saint Francis Xavier's Church in a residential area called *Dongjia du* to avoid the violence of the Taiping Rebellion and they all survived the periodic tensions imposed by the Qing imperial court.

The European Jesuits in Shanghai

The seventeenth-century Jesuit missionaries in Shanghai found patronage among the gentry class of the Ming Dynasty, such as the Xu family. Although Cattaneo only lived in Shanghai from 1608 to 1610, short-term service was not uncommon among early Jesuit missionaries in Shanghai. Such an example is Jesuit missionary João da Rocha (1565–1623) who built a church in present-day Jiading District but mainly worked in Jiangxi and Hangzhou.[45] Early European Jesuit missionaries traveled extensively and missionized in other Chinese cities or towns, and even briefly explored the geography of neighboring Korea and Japan.

Mutual Friendship

The mutual friendship of the European Jesuit missionaries and the Shanghai Catholics made it possible for Catholicism to take root. The friendship was so long-lasting that later generations continued to share memories and emotional ties. Such is the case that when Xu was suffering a serious illness in 1633, German Jesuit missionary Johann Adam Schall von Bell (Tang Ruowang, 1591–1666) stayed with Xu, held a requiem service after Xu's death, and oversaw shipping Xu's body to Shanghai.

Jesuit missionary Francesco Sambiasi (Bi Fangji, 1528–1649) also maintained close friendship with the Xu family and his mission work involved Beijing, Jiading in Zhejiang, Shanghai, Korea, Kaifeng, Shanxi, Shandong, Nanjing, Macau, and Canton (Guangzhou). Xu Guangqi also recommended Sambiasi to be appointed to the Imperial Astronomical Bureau, and then the Southern Ming Dynasty Hongguang Emperor assigned Sambiasi as the ambassador to Macau in 1645 and the Yongli Emperor granted Sambiasi the title and rank of mandarin. Sambiasi's cartographic skills and knowledge linked Europe and China in the seventeenth century.[46]

The Jesuits in China generally pursued their language studies at St. Paul's Seminary in Macau and Thierry Meynard indicates that the original four-year Chinese study for the Jesuits began in 1624 but the program was not strictly implemented.[47] Language proficiency and familiarity with cultural customs would theoretically advance the Jesuit mission, so some Jesuits in Shanghai produced works in classical Chinese and some Chinese Catholics also acquired linguistic skills. Both cultural and religious learnings of the Jesuits and Catholics in Shanghai exhibited mutuality and reciprocity.

Candida's patronage of the Jesuit mission made it possible for new churches in the Jiangnan region. Her confessor, Flemish Jesuit missionary Philippe Couplet (Bai Yingli, 1623–93), wrote her biography in Latin and published a French translation titled *Histoire d'une Dame Chrétienne* (Story of a Christian Lady) and named her "*l'Apôtre de la Chine* [the Apostle of China]"[48] in 1688 in hopes that Catholic women in Europe would emulate Candida as a Christian model and support the Jesuit China mission through prayers and finances.

Jesuit priest Francesco Brancati (Pan Guoguang, 1607–71) headed the churches in Shanghai from 1637 until 1665 and maintained a long relationship with the Xu family. Brancati corresponded with Candida Xu via letters and acted as her spiritual director for twenty-one years.[49] When the Jesuit mission needed financial support, Candida generously supplied the necessities and even extended her alms to the Fujian Dominicans when they visited Shanghai.[50] Another Jesuit missionary, Girolamo de Gravina (1603–62), also received funds from Xu while he missioned in Hangzhou, Shanghai, and Changshu and François de Rougemont and Wu Li fostered a good friendship through the visual arts.[51]

Apart from working with the Chinese gentry class, European Jesuit missionaries such as François Noël (Wei Fangji, 1651–1729) primarily missioned among lower classes such as laborers and artisans in many parts of China.[52] In his letter to his patron, the Duchess of Aveiro, Noël reported baptizing 120 people in his brief time in Shanghai.[53]

Intercultural Accommodations

The Jesuits in seventeenth-century Shanghai encountered three significant issues with the first being related to Catholic converts' marriage. Although they prescribed monogamy and insisted that Chinese Catholic men should divorce their concubines, they understood the difficulty of finding suitable Catholic husbands for Chinese Catholic women, especially when the Catholic population was sparse. In the case of the four granddaughters of Xu Guangqi, all of them married non-Catholic husbands, although these did eventually convert to their wives' Catholic faith. The Jesuits made exceptions for the Catholic gentry families in Shanghai. For Xu's granddaughter Candida Xu, Couplet provided a combined Catholic and Buddhist ceremony with Candida bowing to the image of Christ and her husband to a statue of Buddha.[54]

Chinese customs in the seventeenth century sometimes prevailed in the Jesuit attempt to implement Catholic elements to marriage ceremonies between Chinese Catholics and non-Catholics. The Jesuits reported that Xu Guangqi'a nephew Fulgence read a confession during the matrimony. Nadine Amsler describes the Jesuits being unable to prescribe or prohibit Chinese Catholics from consulting astrologers for an auspicious date or displaying ancestral tablets.[55] The Rites Controversy centered on the issue of Jesuit accommodation to Chinese culture, exposed the conflict between Rome and Beijing, and somewhat restricted a potentially wider spreading of the Catholic faith.

The second significant issue is how translated books have served as vehicles of Christian theology in Shanghai Catholicism. The reciprocity and mutuality in how the Chinese Catholics and European Jesuits related to one another are profoundly reflected through translations of books and even how Christian charities conducted themselves in Shanghai. Instead of a converting model of the Chinese, the European Jesuits adapted and accommodated the Chinese culture which they deeply respected and critically reviewed. Translating books from European languages into Chinese and vice versa corresponds with the philosophy of mutual learning.

Third, the seventeenth-century Catholic faith in Shanghai was also a missionary religion. Chinese Christians acted as priests and missionaries due to the early Jesuit open attitude and practice of native priesthood. Wu Li (Wu Yushan, *c.* 1632–1718), a famous late Ming Dynasty Chinese painter, became a Christian through the Jesuit mission. From 1685, the first Chinese Dominican bishop, Luo Wenzao (Gregory Lopez, *c.* 1616–91), ordained three Chinese priests, including Wu who later began preaching as a missionary in the Shanghai area and served for over thirty years. Indigenous priesthood in seventeenth-century Shanghai was a remarkable practice because its role was significantly reduced in the nineteenth century and was only to surface again in the 1920s and 1930s. From 1724 until 1842, both missionaries and local Catholic priests and laity turned their activities underground.

The Jesuits exercised the first and major Catholic influence in Shanghai as the primary missionary organization. In 1703, Vice-Provincial and Jesuit

FIGURE 1.2 *Wu Li's painting (to the far left) displays at the Shanghai Museum. Photo courtesy of Susangeline Patrick, 2019.*

Antoine Thomas (An Guo, 1644–1709) submitted a detailed report on the Jesuit China mission to Rome. Thomas listed three Jesuit priests, one lay brother, and a grand total of 80,000 Christians with 1,500 yearly baptisms, 52 churches and 24 oratories in the Shanghai area.[56]

Second Stage: Shanghai Catholics in the Semi-Colonial Era (1842–1912)

The second stage of Shanghai Catholicism began with the survival story of Chinese Catholics despite a century of official banning of religion (*Jinjiao*). Although Portuguese bishop Cayetano Pires Pirera (Bi Xueyuan, 1769–1838) had held office as Bishop of the Diocese of Nanking (now part of Shanghai) since 1804, the Qing court only allowed him to stay in Beijing as a court official with the title of *Qin tianjian*, in charge of astronomy and calendar-making from 1823 until 1826. Pirera took care of Beijing church affairs from 1827 until his passing in 1838 whereupon all the responsibilities of Shanghai Catholic churches fell on the Indigenous priests and laity.

In 1839, Chinese priests Wang Ruowang and Zhang Ximan led ninety-eight Catholics in Zhangpuqiao, Songjiang, and drafted a letter to the Pope petitioning for bishops and missionaries.[57] The following year, Pope Gregorius XVI ordered Italian missionary Louis de Besi (Luo Boji, also known as Bishop Lodovico Maria Besi, 1805–71) to move from Shandong to take charge of the church affairs of the Jiangnan region. Then de Besi reached out to the Jesuits to assist his work and three French Jesuit missionaries, Claude Gotteland (Nan Gelu, 1803–56), François Estève (Ai Fangji, 1804–48), and Benjamin Brueyre (Li Xiufang, 1808–80), arrived in Wusong near Shanghai in 1842, as soon as the Vatican restored the Society of Jesus. Gotteland headed the Xujiahui mission and Estève and Brueyre actively engaged in mission as apostolates.[58] By 1844, Joseph de la Servière reported approximately 16,000 Catholics in Shanghai.[59]

The Old Catholics and the New Missionaries

After the devastation of the Taiping Rebellion (1850–64), the Catholic communities in Shanghai recovered and restored their ecclesiastical functions. Paul Mariani argues that it was the "old Christians" who helped the later Jesuits to resurrect their mission.[60] However, the relationship between the Jiangnan Christians and the European missionaries revealed thorny conflicts as de Besi and these Jesuits aimed to reform Jiangnan Christians by issuing instructions and prohibitions about the sacraments and liturgies. As Huang Xiaojuan points out in the local and foreign Catholic conflicts, Jiangnan Christians critiqued de Besi's reform and drafted an open letter titled *Zhaoran gonglun*, which, conversely, Gotteland refuted with *Wubang lun* (On Slander).[61] The bitter resentment would remain as part of Shanghai Catholic history in the following decades.

It is important to contrast the two major differences between the first-stage Catholic mission in Shanghai and the second one. First, Catholic mission in the mid-nineteenth century had political protections based on European colonial efforts at making Shanghai one of the unequal treaty ports. It meant that missionaries could own land, build churches, and were free to proselytize. Anthony Clark emphasizes that the nineteenth-century French mission enterprise *Propagation de la Foi* (Society for the Propagation of the Faith), a missionary organization based in Lyons, provided generous financial resources to French missionaries in China, and French missionaries perceived themselves as the force of French civilization who carried on the mantle as *fille aînée* (oldest daughter) of Rome.[62] Furthermore, the rise of British and American imperial and colonial powers competed with the French. The symbiotic relationships between missionaries and their governments eventually became problematic for the Chinese Christians in the early twentieth century.

Second, Jesuit mission in nineteenth-century Shanghai no longer assumed Christian monopoly. Catholic missionaries from many nations worked in Shanghai, including the Belgian missions in 1865, Steyl Missions in 1872, Marist in 1891, and Augustinian in 1904.[63] Catholics also shared their mission field with the abundant Protestant activities. With the new arrivals of Protestant missionaries in Shanghai in the mid-nineteenth century, Catholic–Protestant rivalry emerged and persisted in Shanghai with occasional collaboration between the two major mission groups.

Catholic Churches (1842–1912)

To the returned Jesuits in Shanghai, the repatriation of confiscated churches marked the external manifestation of the religious influence from the early Jesuit mission. The new missionaries eagerly repatriated the previous church properties and built new churches in Shanghai which marked a sense of Catholic global expansion post-French Revolution (1789–99). To fulfill these two expectations of restoring and recreating Shanghai Catholicism, Jesuit priest Mathurin Lemaître (1816–63), the Pro-Vicar Apostolic of Kiangnan (Jiangnan), petitioned the Qing imperial government to return the properties of the old Jesuit churches in 1847. The returning of Catholic properties occurred gradually as Jingyi Church was restored in 1862.

Additionally, the Jesuits also received three plots of land, including an area called Yangjingbang (now East Yan'an Road) which later developed into another Catholic enclave. Saint Ignatius Cathedral was built in 1847 on the land of the Catholic Xu family.[64] Later, in 1914, a Gothic cathedral was rebuilt near the tomb complex of the Xu family (now Xu Guangqi Memorial Park) and the French Concession extended to the Xu family village (Xujiahui) as a result.[65] A second new Catholic church in this period was the Jesuit-initiated Saint Francis Xavier's Church (Dongjiadu Cathedral, 1847–1966). Spanish Jesuit priests designed the building after the Jesuit mother church in Rome.

Catholic churches served as religious sites and shelters for refugees due to periodic social or political upheavals. The Little Knife Rebellion in 1853 forced 20,000 Chinese refugees to enter the International Settlement by 1857. Desjacques Marin (Duo Ruolan, 1824–84) began to pastor the mixed

FIGURE 1.3 *Saint Ignatius Cathedral in Xujiahui, Shanghai. Photo courtesy of Susangeline Patrick, 2019.*

congregation: 92 European Catholics and 180 Chinese Catholics. Marin subsequently opened the General Hospital (Gongji Hospital after 1877) to provide care for the wounded refugees in 1864.

A third new Catholic structure, Yangjingbang Saint Joseph's Church (*Sheng ruose Tang*) in Huangpu District, was built in 1860 with part of the church fund from the treaty compensation. In 1866, Jesuit missionary Basuiau Hippolyte oversaw the church and founded the *Société de Sainte Cécile* (Society of Saint Cecilia), famed as the first chamber orchestra in Chinese history.[66] In addition to music, French Jesuits contributed significantly to the renaissance of Christian-themed art. The Jesuit orphanage at Tushanwan (1864–1960s) in Xujiahui became the cradle of Chinese-Western painting, sculpture, and press.

The Jesuits built another significant fourth church known as Sheshan Basilica. After purchasing a plot of land from a former Buddhist monastery in 1863, the Jesuits constructed a small chapel, a retired missionary residential quarter, and a statue of the Madonna in place of the Maitreya Hall. In 1870, the burning of churches during the Taiping Rebellion in other cities had caused the Jesuits to seek protection. Father Gu Zhengsheng promised to form a church in honor of the Virgin Mary following the design of French Jesuit Léon Mariot (Ma Liyao, 1830–1902). Unlike all the other three major new Catholic churches in Gothic styles during this period, the Sheshan Basilica demonstrated a synthesis of Chinese and European architectural styles. These old and new Catholic churches served both the Chinese and European Catholics. They developed further into Christian centers and mediated spiritual formation around worship and pilgrimage, and advanced learning in the arts and sciences.

Catholic Women's Work (1842–1912)

Wei Mo points out that the most radical change for Catholic mission in Shanghai in the second half of the nineteenth century was the "feminization" of mission as the Jesuits invited the Helpers of the Holy Souls (*Auxiliatrices des âmes du Purgatoire, Zhengwang hui*, HHS) to take over leadership from the Chinese Catholic women and they began to develop the Notre Dame Complex in 1855.[67] I also argue that the new "feminization" of mission was built on replacing the de facto Indigenous Catholic women's leadership from the seventeenth and eighteenth centuries, as already evidenced in de Besi's reform when he deemed the church leadership of the Christian virgins and women inappropriate.[68] Indigenous leadership for Chinese Catholic women would resurge in the later 1920s and 1930s.

Late-nineteenth-century Catholic women's mission to Shanghai revealed varied degrees of ethnocentrism and superiority. Most European missionary orders of women excluded Chinese women or refused to admit local women in their ranks as full members. As a result, foreign Catholic missionary orders began to segregate local congregations for local Catholic women. For example, in 1855, a French Jesuit bishop made efforts to create a congregation exclusively for Chinese women known as the Chinese chapter of The Sisters of Mary of the Presentation (SMP). The HHS sisters trained the Chinese TSMP in Shanghai beginning in 1867.[69]

Other French Catholic women religious orders also began to work in Shanghai, mainly in education, hospitals, and charitable works. French nuns from Daughters of Charity (*Ren'ai xiunü Hui*) became involved in nursing and cared for Chinese patients at the General Hospital soon after 1877.[70] Another French group, Congregation of the Little Sisters of the Poor (PSDP, *Petites Sœurs des Pauvres, Anpin xiao zimei hui*) began in Shanghai in 1904.[71]

These four major French women religious orders evolved later, in the early twentieth century.

Catholic Publishing (1842–1912)

Catholic publishing thrived because the returning Jesuit missionaries to China in the mid-nineteenth century established their headquarters in Zi-ka-wei (Xujiahui), Shanghai. Catholics primarily focused on producing Christian-themed texts including literature and Bible translation. Lamin Sanneh, in his seminal work *Translating the Message*, emphasizes the essential theme of the translatability of the gospel in the global expansion of Christianity.[72] Translating Christian texts and circulating them through the aid of modern printing provided access for wider audiences in Shanghai and beyond. Three aspects of Catholic printing became notable.

First, Shanghai *Cimu Tang* engaged the traditional Chinese woodblock printing techniques and published early-seventeenth-century Jesuit theological works in China. Aleni's *Xingxue cushu* (A General Introduction of Human Nature) and other theological works in classical Chinese saw a revival in nineteenth-century Shanghai.[73] Christopher Reed examines the centrality of Shanghai in Chinese print workers adopting printing technology from Catholic and Protestant missions in the nineteenth century.[74] Innovative printing methods facilitated the Jesuits' historical interest of publicizing the knowledge of Syriac Christianity in the Tang Dynasty.[75] The California Jesuits also published *Catholic Review* which circulated among Shanghai Catholics.

Second, the French Jesuit connection to Xujiahui made Shanghai a center of publishing in the French language. Jesuit missionaries first established *Imprimerie de la Mission Catholique* (The Catholic Mission Printing Press) as the largest Catholic printing agent in Xianxian, Hebei Province, in 1874. As the French church-founded schools educated pupils to achieve competency in the

French language, the Catholic printing press also trained workers to manage the press. The Shanghai branch eventually rivaled the Xianxian printing press (Hebei Province) in publishing devotional materials to assist Catholic learning.

A third category of Catholic printing focused on promoting knowledge of Chinese culture and customs among Catholic missionaries both in China and in other francophone regions around the world. Chinese Jesuit priest Simon Kiong's *Quelques mots sur la politesse chinoise* (A Few Words on Chinese Politeness) introduced the complex symbols and meanings of Chinese customs, including the unwritten rules of the ritualistic and social usage of fans.[76] The efforts of printing books about Chinese cultures continued to generate French interest in and learning about China.

Catholic Education in Shanghai (1842–1912)

French Jesuits in the late nineteenth century heavily invested in education. Their new educational interest stands in sharp contrast to the early Jesuits in Shanghai. Paul Rule argues that the lack of Jesuit missionaries, funds, and the disturbance of the Rites Controversy are the reasons that the earlier Jesuits did not build large-scale Catholic institutions in Shanghai.[77] However, the Shanghai Jesuits after 1842 found financial and political support from the French state.

The first category of education investments was a library and observatory. The Jesuits first opened the Xujiahui Library (*Bibliotheca Zi-Ka-Wei*, 1847–1956) in 1847. The library hosted books in Chinese and other languages. Prior to 1955, Jesuit seminary students in Shanghai used the library as they consulted both rich scholarly sources in European and Chinese languages and the library served as one of the most important learning centers in China. The Jesuits also built two observatories near Saint Ignatius Church and the Sheshan Cathedral. Scientific investigations also facilitated students' learning.

The second category is primary and secondary education. In 1850, the French Jesuits built *Collège San Ignace* (Saint Ignatius High School) in response to the refugee children affected by the 1849 flood in Jiangnan. Parents could not afford to raise them and therefore sent the children to the Catholic church in Xujiahui. Saint Ignatius School began with thirty-one students in 1850 and trained boys who later became important contributors of the late Qing reform. For example, Chinese Jesuit Ma Xiangbo (1840–1939) studied and later taught at Saint Ignatius, and then founded Aurora University in 1903, Fudan Public School (now Fudan University) in 1905, and the Catholic University of Peking (later Fu Jen Catholic University). The school added the Chongsi building in 1918 that remains to this day. A branch of the Saint Ignatius School moved to

Taiwan during the Chinese civil war in the 1940s and is now known as *Xuhui Zhongxue* (Xuhui High School).

Catholics also provided access for Chinese girls to be educated. Saint Joseph's Church (1860) operated schools such as *Ruose Shuyuan* (Saint Joseph Academy), a middle school for girls. During that time, only high-status girls and women received classical education at home or from private tutors. The invention of the academy admitted girls from the lower class and was revolutionary for the historical period. The vice-superior of the Jesuit residence at Xujiahui, Louis Taffin (1810–64), had a desire to train Chinese students to do more catechistical work. Taffin also directed two girls' schools to train "virgins" and "widows."[78] French Catholic nuns also operated Jingyan Primary School from 1867 and changed its name to Chongde Girls' School in 1898. Additionally, HHS nuns opened another girl's school called *Qiming nüxiao* in 1904. Plenteous parochial schools functioned alongside churches to provide Bible literacy, French learning, music, and even embroidery classes.

A third category of Catholic educational contribution is higher education. The Jesuits founded Saint Francis Xavier's College (1874–93) and in 1893, the Jesuits invited some Marist Brothers of the Schools (FMS) to work at the college.[79] Aurora University was another major institution which enrolled students from diverse backgrounds. Liu Na'ou (1905–40), a Taiwan-born writer, had studied at the French program at Aurora University (*Zhendan daxue*)[80] after his education at Aoyama Gakuin, a Japanese Christian school in Japan.[81] These different individuals converged their diverse backgrounds and experiences in cosmopolitan Shanghai when a new modern identity was being born in the 1920s and graduates from Jesuit-related higher institutions became significant reformers of modernity. Additionally, the French Jesuits opened Jiangnan Seminary at Xujiahui in 1877. The campus was located between the Xujiahui Observatory and the Tushanwan Orphanage and, up to the 1940s, about three hundred Jesuits received theological training at the seminary.

Catholic Hospitals and Charitable Works (1842–1912)

The French Catholics mainly organized two hospitals between 1842 and 1912. French Jesuits founded the first Shanghai Catholic hospital, the General Hospital, in 1863 and assigned the nuns from Daughters of Charity to operate it. The French Jesuit bishop Próspero París (Yao Zongli, 1846–1931) founded a second Catholic hospital named *Hôpital Sainte Marie* (*Guangci Yiyuan*, Saint

Maria Hospital) in 1907. Saint Maria Hospital became the largest hospital in Asia in 1914 and Bishop París charged Daughters of Charity to oversee the hospital. The Shanghai government took the hospital over in 1951 and renamed it multiple times; it is now Ruijin Hospital attached to Jiaotong University Medical School in Shanghai. The Catholic Church organized the Aurora University Medical School beginning in 1903 and eventually added Sacred Heart Hospital (unknown date).

Catholics in Shanghai dedicated themselves to various kinds of charitable works and they provided homes for orphans and the elderly in the nineteenth century. The French Jesuits in Shanghai described infanticide in China and disseminated news about the practice in France. For example, Father Claude Gotteland addressed a fellow Jesuit priest, Father Guidée, in a letter from December 9, 1846. Gotteland discussed infanticide in China as barbarism.[82] Poverty and cultural beliefs in astrological signs caused some parents to abandon their healthy or deformed unlucky babies.[83] Foreign missionary-founded orphanages raised Chinese anxiety and concerns for imperialism in the mid-nineteenth century.[84] Shanghai official Shen Bing and other *literati* and local elders shared the concerns for social welfare and therefore made efforts at preventing female infanticide.[85]

Nuns at the Ruose Girls' Orphanage cared for Eurasian children and in 1906, *Anlao Hui* from France set up a home for the elderly. At first, the home accepted twenty-seven elderly women near the Dongjiadu Catholic church until the Catholic nuns moved to a new location at 39 Nanshi Jichang Street. The home for the elders received both women and men numbering 3,128 until 1929 and 1,685 elderly people registered for baptism. Prior to 1953, approximately 350 elders were living in the home with 28 nuns who cared for their physical and spiritual needs. French nun Marie de St. Eugénie managed the home affairs as the head of the elderly home. D. E. Mungello compares the nineteen-century French Catholic mission and the British and American Protestant mission in China and observes the Catholic emphasis on the weak and helpless children while the Protestant imagery of physical and spiritual strength dominated the Protestant works.[86]

Third Stage: Shanghai Catholics in the Republic Era (1912–54)

Shanghai continued to receive many missionaries from Saint Columban's Missions (1920) and Recollects (1924).[87] A surprising mission is the Russian Catholic mission beginning in 1928. Catholic churches, education, and charitable works continued to expand and impact the social life in Shanghai.

Catholic Churches (1912–54)

The Xujiahui Complex continued to thrive and expand in the Republic Era. The Jesuits in Shanghai also demolished the original Sheshan Basilica in 1923 seeking a more sizable construction in the Songjiang District. Belgian Jesuit architect missionary Alphonse De Moerloose (He Gengbo, 1858–1932) designed the plans, and Portuguese Jesuit architect missionary François-Xavir Diniz (Ye Zhaochang, 1869–1943) supervised the nine-year project. The church dedicated to Mother Mary hosted a rich collection of Mariology iconography with the bronze Madonna and Child (Our Lady of Zosè) statue atop the bell tower and fourteen Stations of the Cross on the path to the church on the hill. Other churches also emerged including the Church of the Good Shepherd (1933–53) and the Sacred Heart of Jesus (*Yesu shengxin Tang*) in Hongkou. A new Catholic construction, Saint Peter's Church (*Sheng Boduolu Tang*), was initially built in 1933 as a chapel for students from Aurora University. The original church resembling the Byzantine-style church consisted of five chapels with a central dome.

Modern Chinese Catholic priesthood followed a long tradition of ordination of local priests. Prior to the founding of the Catholic Patriotic Association (CPA) in the 1950s, many Chinese priests' ordination ceremonies were revealed from historical photographs in Xujiahui in the 1930s.[88] Chinese priests began to take over the leadership of Saint Francis Xavier's Church in 1933. After 1937, many church members moved near Saint Peter's Church.

Catholic Education in the Republic Era

Catholic education in the Republic Era focused on building primary/secondary education and higher education. A major paradigm shift is that Catholic higher education began to open up to women. The American Sisters of the Sacred Heart founded the Aurora College for Women and Saint Mary's School (now Fushi Square near Zhongshan Park) continued to admit both Catholic and non-Catholic girls.

The Marist Brothers, a Roman Catholic order from France, operated a boys' school called St. Joan of Arc's College and admitted a substantial student population of White Russians from poor backgrounds and Catholic students from mixed Macau Portuguese and Chinese parentage in the 1940s.[89] The founder of Casa Ricci in Macau, Spanish Jesuit Luis Ruiz Suárez (1913–2011), studied in Shanghai in the 1940s.

Jesuit missionaries from the California Province joined their fellow mission endeavors. George Dunne (1905–98) arrived in Shanghai in 1932 and pursued language studies in Xujiahui for two years. Dunne fostered an intellectual apostolate and advocated a synthesis of democracy and Christianity in China.[90] The Zi-Ka-Wei (Xujiahui) Major Seminary trained Chinese Jesuits beginning in 1923 and Aurora University educated students from 1903 to 1952. Students enrolled at Aurora came from multiple nations and cultures.

Catholic political activism also became a new theme in Republic of China Shanghai. Between 1900 and 1952, Shanghai experienced more social and political turmoil and Catholics continued to navigate a series of changes. Robert de Besange (1878–1946), a French Jesuit priest, created a safety zone for Chinese refugees to Shanghai during the second Sino-Japanese War in 1937.[91] Catholic schools and universities, however, generally feared retaliations from the authorities and therefore restricted the student body from participating in any public protests or demonstrations.

Catholic Women and Charitable Works (1912–54)

During the Republic Era, Catholic missionaries operated in holistic ways such as the Italian Salesians opening a school, a seminary, Saint Joseph's Hospice, and a farm in Shanghai in 1924.[92] In 1935 alone, Catholic missionaries added three more hospitals in Shanghai: Franciscan Missionaries of Mary Hospital, the Maryknolls' Mercy Hospital, and a German Augustinian group known as Brothers of Mercy of Trier who opened Mercy Hospital in Shanghai in 1935.[93] Daughters of Charity in Shanghai ran a hospice of St. Joseph.

Catholic nuns from Europe and North America worked with marginalized communities. Nuns from the Society of the Sacred Heart (RSCJ) arrived in Shanghai in 1926 and French nuns Concetta Nourry, Sarah Fitzgerald, Florence Manley, and Sarah St. Arnaud from Canada operated a women's college.[94] Sisters from the apostolic Congregation of Our Lady of Charity of the Good Shepherd (RGS) arrived in Shanghai in 1933 and provided a shelter for women and young girls[95] and Sisters of the Good Shepherd (*Shanmu xiunü hui*) founded a convent in Shanghai in 1933 and cared for abandoned children. They also ministered to people who transported passengers with rickshaws and people who were coolies.[96] The Sisters of Social Services operated in Shanghai from 1946.[97]

The Maryknoll Sisters, also known as Foreign Mission Sisters of St. Dominic, began their work in Shanghai in 1935. They admitted native women as sisters and worked at the Mercy Hospital for Mental Diseases caring for female patients. The Maryknoll Sisters cared for the people with psychological health issues and occasionally fellowshipped with the Sisters of Loretto (SL).[98]

The Shanghai Legionaries of the Legion of Mary (LM) focused on hospital visitations, catechisms, and apologetics, particularly the Catholic education of young students. As a unit of the larger Marian movement,[99] SL from Kentucky formed a school in Shanghai in 1933.[100] The Loretto motto *Fides Mores Cultura* (Faith, Morals, Culture) reflected its commitment to education. Two American Lorettine sisters, Mary Jane McDonald and Maureen O'Connell, were among the nine Lorettine sisters and one lay teacher.[101] Another teacher, Grace Clare Shanley (1893), originally from Colorado, taught at the Loretto school in Shanghai after serving in Hanyang embroidery school for two years.

SL ran a school for foreign girls in Shanghai in 1933.[102] The Loretto school first had 71 female students from the Holy Family School which was founded by HHS, but by 1937 Peter Lefebvre described the school as inadequate to host the growing student enrollment, which had reached 194.[103] The school enrolled students from multicultural backgrounds boasting thirty-seven ethnicities although most of them were born in Shanghai. Alumni later spread to many corners of the world. Mildred Josephine O'Leary Katemopoulos (1925–2013) emphasized the self-worth and faith that the Lorettines instilled in students. The Lorettines provided education for the girls of the upper and upper-middle class of the International Community in Shanghai. In 1942, the Japanese army in Shanghai interned fourteen Lorettines and ninety-six Women Religious at the Religious of the Sacred Heart until the end of the war in 1945.[104] SL also admitted native-born sisters into the order: Isabel (Ying Hwa) Huang became the first Chinese Sister of Loretto who later died by execution in China in 1956. I shall discuss the stories of Shanghai Lorettines in the United States in Chapter 7 as I investigate the theme of Shanghai Christians beyond borders.

Catholic Broadcasting (1912–54)

During the Republic Era, the Jesuits utilized new technologies in their evangelization and established three programs and one broadcasting station. The Californian Jesuits first began a radio program called *The Catholic Hour.* Located at no. 445 Paoma ting Road (now Wusheng Road), the program continued for half an hour every other week until the Pacific War interrupted it. After the Second World War, the program resumed and broadcast every week. The second program began in December 1938, featuring the celebration of mass by the expats from *Junwang Tang* at eleven o'clock every Sunday. French Jesuits Qiao Dian'ai and Fu Chenglie from Aurora University began the third program in French, *La Radio Catholique* (Catholic Radio), in March 1943, broadcasting for half an hour on Sunday evenings. The Shanghai Catholic bishop Hui Jiliang founded Huangzhong Broadcasting Station, and Chinese Jesuit priests and some lecturers from Aurora University hosted regular talks. The main purpose was to explain Catholic doctrines, Catholic news, music, and medical knowledge.

Fourth Stage of Catholic Shanghai: 1954–1970s

The change of political regime in 1949 initially met with optimistic Christian anticipation for the future of the church. Two reasons permitted a relative peaceful three years (1949–52) for the religious communities under the new Chinese Communist Party (CCP) rule. First, the 1945 defeat and surrender of the twelve-year Japanese occupation had now permitted Shanghai to rebuild from the rubble, and the intermittent battles between the CCP and the Nationalist Party ended with the Nationalists retreating to Taiwan. The new Chinese government focused on rebuilding after the destruction of war.

Second, the new Chinese government of 1949 only gradually moved from religious tolerance to utilizing powers to demand sole loyalty of religious adherents including Christians. Such loyalty could be achieved through the formation of the Patriotic Movement nationwide. Otherwise, the new power had to crush religions because the orthodox ideology of communism viewed religion as opium and a means of psychological control. In hindsight, the Shanghai Christians and foreign missionaries anticipated, and experienced, a surge of revitalization of and enthusiasm among the Christian communities before they met repression in 1952.

The Vatican and the New China

Although the CCP is popularly depicted as anti-religious, the animosity between the Vatican and the CCP peaked in the 1950s for two major reasons. First, the Vatican perceived the Nationalist Party as pro-religious and allied with the Nationalists in the 1930s and 1940s. The perception was formulated based on the Vatican's long-standing opposition to Karl Marx's thoughts. Therefore, the Holy See launched an anti-communist campaign in the 1940s:

> In 1946 the Vatican sent Archbishop Antonio Riberi (1897–1967) to China as the Holy See's first internuncio. Riberi supported the Nationalists, which the Communists knew, and in 1947 he forbade all Catholics in China from involvement in any Communist organization. He also mobilized the Legion of Mary in 1948 in China to combat Communist forces, and from his home in Shanghai Riberi launched a publication campaign against the new Communist government.[105]

These openly aggressive activities worsened Vatican–China relations in the 1950s and caused China to expel Riberi and other Catholic missionaries. Between 1952 and 1978, the CCP followed an ancient strategy of *Qinzei xian qinwang* (Capture the king if you want to defeat the enemy). Therefore, the

Party focused on arresting priests and Christian leaders. Columban missionaries Father Aedan McGrath (1906–2000)[106] and Father Joseph Seng from the LM were arrested in September 1951. Chinese Catholics also came under suspicion of supporting other governments.

Li Weiguang in Nanjing declared that Catholics should adopt the three-self principles (self-sufficient, self-preaching, self-pastoring) but the Vatican failed to acknowledge the validity of the principles. In 1952, the Pope issued an open letter to the Chinese church expressing his empathy for Chinese Catholics under the new Chinese government. However, two years later, the Pope opposed the three-self principles and declared that Chinese Catholics could not bear the title of Catholics if they lacked the characteristics of Catholicism.

The essential repression of Catholicism in China revolved around the question of Chinese Catholic allegiance to pope or country. In the early 1950s, Catholics in Shanghai experienced a watershed moment along with other religious groups which resulted in mass arrests and expulsion. Religious and cultural oppression intensified during the Cultural Revolution (1966–76) as all religions, even Confucianism, were seen as part of the *sijiu* (four old things) which hindered social progress. Historians continue to uncover, understand, and reconstruct this complex history due to a lack of historical records.

The Catholic Patriotic Association Church

A major strategy that the CCP adapted as the second phase was to domesticate religions, including Christianity in Shanghai. In 1957, the new Chinese government mandated Catholics to register with the Catholic Patriotic Association (CPA), an agency created to strictly monitor Catholic activities, church affairs, and the appointments of bishops. The Chinese government demanded the severance of ties between Roman Catholics and the authority of the Pope.

Chinese Catholics initiated two responses. Some Chinese Catholics resonated with the accusations of imperialism because local congregations prior to the 1950s struggled with the authority and control of foreign leadership. Most local Catholic communities only gained high-level leadership when the Chinese government expelled foreign missionaries in the 1950s. The responses among the Catholic communities diverged. Some signed letters of confession under the pressure of the CCP. Others provided lists of names to the CCP when they knew the Chinese Catholics who had left the country. From this perspective, some Catholics in Shanghai chose to support the Patriotic movement and CPA, and they organized their first national meeting in 1957. They began to select bishops without the permission of the Vatican.

The Underground Church (1950s–1970s)

The other response was Catholics who decided to ally themselves with the Vatican and they opposed the new Chinese government and other Catholics who consisted of the Patriotic movement. Without government permission, the Vatican-appointed bishop Peter Joseph Fan Xuanyan (1907–92) of Baoding, Hebei Province, ordained three new bishops. Jesuit historian Paul Mariani analyzes how the Shanghai Catholics had resisted the suppression of the CCP.[107] On the other hand, some Christians saw registering with the new government as a compromise to political powers. Their resistance also diversified. Some Christians armed themselves and clashed with the government, and others resisted peacefully but with drastic demonstrations of their Christian faith. For example, a group of fifty young students signed a blood letter for Bishop Gong (Kung) Pinmei.

Suffering and Enduring (1950s–1970s)

Shanghai Catholics forced underground suffered tumultuous years from 1952 to 1978, and even some Catholics who joined the CPA also could not escape the religious cleansing of the Cultural Revolution. Clergy from both Patriotic Catholics and the resisting Catholics suffered imprisonment and/or farms as a form of labor reform. Most Catholic churches suffered restrictions and damage; the Sheshan Basilica sustained damage during the Cultural Revolution. The fate of Shanghai Catholics took another turn in 1958 when local parishes and services were driven into private spheres. The two hundred priests and nuns in Xujiahui Convent made a living by manufacturing umbrella handles and pillowcases in the 1960s and early 1970s. The government gradually allowed Chinese Catholic groups to reconstitute themselves. Missionaries and Chinese Catholics who survived the Cultural Revolution often shared their stories of how God provided for them through miracles. For example, while McGrath was in solitary confinement, a bird often warned him whenever the prison guards would arrive.[108]

Although the three-self principles did not err in theory, the People's Republic of China (PRC) government used it as a tool for political and social control causing Chinese Catholics to be isolated from the universal church. However, this posture should also be interpreted from the perspective of the official Chinese government which saw religious activities as having the potential to either prosper or disrupt the core value of social harmony. Having witnessed dynastic changes and frequent political changes, the Chinese government viewed national loyalty as important for all religious and non-religious entities in China. Therefore, the Catholic Church in China maintains a rather complex relation with the Chinese government and how it relates to the Vatican.

Stage Five: Revival of Catholicism in Shanghai (1979–2022)

Shanghai Christians witnessed a drastic change in the Chinese government's attitude and action toward religious communities. Beginning in the late 1970s, three major changes have taken place in Shanghai. The first change is the returning of formerly confiscated church properties and making former Christian sites protected historical markers. For example, the government returned the confiscated Sheshan Cathedral property to the Shanghai Catholic Diocese in 1981 and the Sheshan Basilica congregation repaired and replaced some of the statues and church art in the early twenty-first century. Another significant land marker, Saint Peter's Church, was rebuilt in 1995. Today, the church still reflects its multicultural origin with masses celebrated in five languages: Chinese, English, French, German, and Korean. The liturgical art in the church sanctuary reflects a Nordic-style Jesus and saints. In the early twenty-first century, the Chinese TSMP reorganized into the Qibao Convent in Minghang District which became home to about forty Chinese sisters and novices. The Xujiahui Major Seminary (1923–40s) was preserved and restored as part of the Xuhui District Hui Exhibition Hall in 2003. After three years of restoration conserving the original integrity of the building, the renovated Jesuit seminary chapel was celebrated with guests in 2016.[109]

Second, Catholic liturgical celebrations have also been restored. For example, pilgrimage to the Sheshan Basilica formed the tradition beginning as early as 1874. Pope Pius IX (1792–1878) granted Plenary Indulgence[110] to pilgrims to Sheshan during the Marian month of May. As a result, large numbers of Catholics would travel via land or boat from other parts of China to pray and attend mass at the holy site. The practice of Catholic pilgrimage has been re-established since 1978. Another smaller-scale pilgrimage is around the Saint Ignatius Church in Xujiahui. During my field trip to Shanghai in 2007, I met a group of elderly Catholics who were making their pilgrimage journey.

The third change is the gradual rehabilitation of previously imprisoned priests and nuns. After 1979, some bishops and priests began to gain freedom and, in the 1980s, the third council meeting was held in Beijing. Sheshan Cathedral was the first church to reopen to the public. These unprecedented events also marked the attitude of reconciliation-seeking between the Chinese government and the Christian communities outside of mainland China. For instance, on March 25, 1985, the National Bureau of Religious Affairs invited a

FIGURE 1.4 *A Christian pilgrimage in the Xujiahui area of Shanghai. Photo courtesy of Susangeline Patrick, 2008.*

delegation under John Baptist Wu Cheng-chung (1925–2002), the first Bishop of Hong Kong to have obtained a week-long visit to Beijing and Shanghai. Although the Vatican and the PRC government have not established diplomatic relations, Shanghai Catholics have negotiated how they relate to church and state within the prevailing social and political tensions and opportunities.

2

The Protestant Century and Holistic Mission

This chapter investigates how Shanghai acted as a hub for Protestant mission activities in the nineteenth and early twentieth centuries and as a bridge for retired missionaries to take their experiences enriching their home countries. From 1817 until the 1950s, both foreign and local Protestants focused on evangelization, providing education and medical services, charities, and publishing Christian literature. The rediscovering section of the chapter will trace the historical memory related to a century of Protestant mission. Like the Catholic experience from Chapter 1, Protestant mission and Chinese Protestants in Shanghai also confronted challenges posed by the Cultural Revolution in the 1960s and 1970s. After Shanghai lifted the ban on religions in the 1970s, Chinese Christians[1] and Protestant missionaries from outside of China have rekindled the dormant interest in mission, dealing with a whole new metropolitan reality of Shanghai. I will underscore the Indigenous and Cosmopolitan Christians in Chapters 4, 5, and 7.

I will broadly divide the Protestant mission history of Shanghai into two general periods of early Protestant mission (1817–42) and Protestant missions in the semi-colonial context and the Republic of China (1842–1912 and 1912–1950s).[2] I underline the contrast between colonial churches and voluntary missionaries from varied Protestant denominations, fellowships, and mission organizations. Throughout this chapter, Protestant missionary motivations, brief biographies, and characteristics of missionary activities will weave into the narrative and analysis of the Protestant mission in Shanghai.

First Stage: Early Protestant Mission (1817–42)

When Protestant missionaries from England explored the possibility of Shanghai as a mission field in the early nineteenth century, Shanghai Catholics persevered despite the periodic ban. Although early Protestant missionary activities prior to 1842 mainly occurred in southern China centering around Macau, Hong Kong, and Canton (Guangzhou), London Missionary Society (LMS) missionary Rev. Walter Henry Medhurst (1796–1857) was the first Protestant who arrived in Shanghai in 1817.[3] The second Protestant missionary, Right Rev. William Jones Boone (1811–64) from the Protestant Episcopal Church USA (PEC), reached the city in 1837.[4] A year later, LMS missionary Dr. William Lockhart (1811–96) stationed in Shanghai.[5] These temporary visits enabled Medhurst, Boone, and Lockhart to discern missional potentials. The Qingpu religious case (*Qingpu jiaoan*) of 1848 occurred when LMS missionaries Medhurst, Lockhart, and William Muirhead (1822–1900) missionized in Qingpu County (now District) near Shanghai. All three pioneer missionaries would contribute to the founding of the first Protestant printing press called the London Missionary Society Press (*Mohai shuguan*) in 1842 and Lockhart would be a medical missionary in Shanghai until his departure for England in 1857.[6] Their early short-term exploratory experimentations paved the way for the later Protestant missionaries to establish more permanent missions.

Second Stage: Protestant Mission During the Semi-Colonial and Republic Eras (1842–1950s)

In the early nineteenth century, the East India Company structured a complete system to use Indian labor for cultivating opium and then illegally smuggled opium from India into China. Heavy drug trafficking perpetuated rampant social and health problems. China's efforts to eliminate the trade ended with the first Opium War (1839–42) as Qing China signed the Treaty of Nanjing (August 29, 1842) with Britain, marking a turning point in Shanghai's history. The unequal treaty subsequently opened Shanghai as a trading port city obligated to British colonial powers.[7] The following Treaty of Bogue in 1843 further established British extraterritorial privileges in China. The Second Opium War (1857–9) ended with the Treaty of Tianjin from which Britain, France, Russia, and the United States extracted concessions from the Qing government and economic rights.

The unequal treaties forced the Qing government to allow foreign Protestant missionaries to purchase land, build churches, and freely participate in the social reform of the city. For Protestant Christians in Europe and North America, China as a mission field from the outsider's perspective appeared to be a daunting task in the mid-nineteenth century. The opening of port cities, therefore, presented an opportunity for mission. At first, a few Protestant missionaries and mission organizations ventured into cities including Shanghai and rural areas. Their pioneer missionary service inspired and heightened the later mission enthusiasm at the turn of the twentieth century.

The consolidation of foreign settlements in Shanghai had a degree of segregating effect on Christian interactions in Shanghai. Hongkou District in Shanghai became the American Settlement due to the oral agreement made between Boone and the mayor of Shanghai, Wu Jianzhang, in 1848 and quickly merged with the British Settlement to form the International Settlement.[8] With France's establishment of the Shanghai French Concession in 1849, the city of Shanghai was loosely divided into three areas of the Old City,[9] the International Settlement, and the French Concession with changing boundaries in the succeeding decades. It is against this historical background that Protestant mission began in Shanghai.

Foreign Protestant Missions (1842–1950s)

In the mid-nineteenth century, Protestant missionaries in Shanghai faced three main challenges. They first encountered a triple linguistic issue to overcome. Shanghainese is part of the Wu dialect in the Jiangnan region (south of the Yangzi River). Missionaries also had to learn Mandarin and *Wenyan wen* (the classical written Chinese literary style). Robert Morrison (1782–1834), the first Protestant missionary to China, had published a grammar book and a Chinese–English dictionary in six volumes[10] which helped missionaries prepare for linguistic skills. However, learning resources on Shanghainese were not readily available.

A second reality Protestant missionaries faced in the nineteenth century was the length of their sailing journey to Shanghai. To provide a perspective on how traveling has changed from 1855 to 2019, I will compare the journey of Channing Moore Williams (1829–1910) with my field trip. Williams boarded the ship from New York in November 1855, sailed around South America and then stopped at Rio de Janeiro and Sydney, and the trip lasted eight months. The 1855 world did not have other alternative means for Williams to reach Shanghai from New York. My 2019 air flight from Boston to Shanghai took less than thirty hours with a day layover in Hong Kong. My trip is 194 times shorter than the trip Williams made in 1855–6. If I were to sail from New York to Shanghai, a modern ship would take two months to travel 13,903 nautical miles. The long journey in the nineteenth century was not a simple reason to stop missionaries from traveling to what they viewed as their calling from God, but the distance was significant because of their physical separation from their original familiarity provided by a network of family and friends. Interactions with other missionaries thus imparted fellowship and comfort.

The third factor was that health problems challenged Protestant missionaries and their endurance in Shanghai. For example, American missionaries who worked with Boone, the first Episcopalian missionary and Bishop of China and Japan based in Shanghai, had a 50-percent survival rate between 1845 and 1855. George Smith listed American Episcopal Church (AEC) missionary Rev. W. Woods and LMS Rev. R. Fairbrother who arrived in Shanghai in 1845 but both had left China due to failing health or "domestic causes."[11] Jessie Lutz propounds mental struggles and loss of beloved ones as a significant issue nineteenth-century Protestant missionaries faced.[12] These three challenges remained significant in how Protestant missionaries carried on their work in Shanghai regardless of their denomination and fellowship in the nineteenth and early twentieth centuries.[13]

From the mid-nineteenth century, Protestant missionaries from various denominations such as American Presbyterians, Anglicans, American Methodists, the British Inland Mission, United Christian Mission Society (UCMS), and Seventh Day Adventists all involved themselves in evangelization and social concerns. Most of these mission-initiated churches adopted *Tang* (Hall) in their names, reflecting a long tradition of inculturation inherited from the Society of Jesus in seventeenth-century Shanghai. Different Protestant denominations negotiated where to build the churches against the background of the colonial powers dividing Shanghai into different settlements.

Late-nineteenth-century Protestant missionaries organized four types of churches in Shanghai including colonial churches, mission churches tied to denominations, volunteer missionary organizations, and independent/Pentecostal churches. Colonial churches almost exclusively catered to the foreign communities who were concerned with maintaining European and American privilege. For Shanghai, the pattern of colonial church was uniquely Protestant in the semi-colonial era. Catholic churches in Shanghai in the previous and contemporary historical periods did not formulate European churches. The second type of Protestant churches in nineteenth-century Shanghai focused on mission and evangelization. Their foundation, organization, structure, and functionality all pivoted on the Great Commission of Jesus from Matthew 28: 19–20, "Go therefore and make disciples of all nations, baptizing them in the name of the Father and of the Son and of the Holy Spirit, and teaching them to obey everything that I [Jesus] have commanded you. And remember, I am with you always, to the end of the age."[14] Volunteer missionary organizations crossed the restrictions of denominational lines and emphasized mission works over the model of church planting. Independent and Pentecostal churches tasked themselves with faith works and all Protestant missionaries heavily relied on multiple means to fulfill such a vision. In the following sections, I will detail the varied church building activities from 1842 to the 1950s.

British Colonial Church

After 1842, British Anglicans first worshipped at the British Consulate in Shanghai, and later in a small temporary chapel at a private British residency. The British Anglican-founded Trinity Cathedral exemplifies a type of colonial church. Although multiple unfortunate incidents followed the initial founding of a permanent Anglican parish building with the first pastor drowning, the second pastor falling from the church roof, and a typhoon severely damaging the building in 1862, the British Anglicans built a large red-brick building, Holy Trinity Cathedral (*Sheng Sanyi Tang*), in 1869. Located in the Shanghai International Settlement, Trinity only served the British Anglicans who were businesspeople and sailors. Trinity maintained its British connection from the beginning until the 1950s.

From the church design to the furnishing and ecclesiastical functions at Trinity, everything was unapologetically British. British architect George Gilbert Scott (1811–78) designed the Gothic Revival-styled building. A junior architect William Kidner modified Scott's design because of the congregation's limited budget. The church also intentionally faced Jerusalem which was a British convention of the nineteenth century. In 1875, the Church of England appointed William Russell as bishop in the Diocese of North China. In 1914, Trinity had the largest organ in Asia supplied by a British firm of organ builders called J. W. Walker & Sons Ltd. The church remained a prestigious place for the British and Eurasian elites and their celebrations such as the wedding of Frances Blanche Madar and William Thomas Manley (1893–1960) on April 28, 1923.[15] Anglican missionaries from Britain also used the building, as was the case of Kenneth Graham Bevan (1893–1993) who became an Anglican missionary to China in 1925. Bevan was consecrated as a bishop at Trinity in 1940 and served as the Bishop of Eastern Szechwan (Sichuan) from 1940 until 1950. The notorious East India Company connected merchants and the social elites from India, Singapore, and Hong Kong to Shanghai.

The British Anglican mission practiced segregation between the English-speaking British Anglicans and the Chinese-speaking local Christians of Shanghai. Trinity served the British expats resulting in another Anglican mission church, Saint Paul's, serving Chinese Christians. It is difficult to determine the full reasons for such segregation. However, cultural ties served as an important motivation for colonial churches. Anglican pastors such as John Hobson came directectly from England. The English language remained important to the identity of the church linked to British culture and politics.

The Britishness of Trinity also excluded American Anglicans in the 1930s. In 1912, several Anglican provinces including the Church of England, the Episcopal Church of the United States, and the Anglican Church of Canada merged as the Anglican-Episcopal Province of China (*Zhonghua sheng gonghui*). After the Berlin Conference in 1930, Trinity came under the religious authority of the Zhejiang District, instead of the Jiangsu District, because the British Anglicans desired to distinguish themselves from the American Anglicans who had established in the Jiangsu District. Trinity church affairs including births, baptisms, weddings, and funerals all registered and reported to the British government. The tight relation between the British Anglicans and the British government suggests the British Anglicans' attitude of self-preservation in their national identity.

To analyze the British colonial churches in Shanghai further necessitates an assessment of the unique identity of the Shanghailanders who viewed themselves as defenders of the Christian faith. Robert Bickers points out that Christian imperialism firmly informed the Shanghailanders' consciously masculine and militant self-image.[16] Shanghailanders also revived the imagery of medieval crusaders as anti-Christian activities reached a new height in Shanghai in the 1920s. When the Nationalist government expelled foreign missionaries in the interior of China in 1926, which resulted in an influx of missionaries to Shanghai,[17] Shanghailanders reinforced their view of Shanghai as a holy city to be defended. Colonial churches acted drastically different from mission churches.

Mission Churches in Shanghai

Mission churches focused on building missional connections with the local people in Shanghai. Overall, Protestant missionaries maintained a strong connection with their sending mission organizations, or home churches, or mission boards in the United States or Britain. They maintained a transatlantic and transpacific connection intellectually, financially, and emotionally through letter correspondences. In 1844, two years after Shanghai's status as a port city, the Britain-based Church Missionary Society (CMS) sent George Smith (1815–71) and Irish missionary Thomas McClatchie (1814–85) to Shanghai. Another CMS Anglican missionary, John Shaw Burdon (1826–1907), taught English and studied classical Chinese texts.[18] Two American Episcopal Church missionaries Rev. R. Graham and Rev. E. Syle stationed in Shanghai in 1845.[19]

Mission churches are distinct from colonial churches in three ways. First, mission churches showed interest in integrating faith and Chinese culture. Furthermore, the line between a strictly foreign mission-initiated church and Indigenous- or Chinese-initiated church is at times difficult to distinguish. The primary reason is that large numbers of missionaries and Chinese Christians sought partnership. For example, although connected with the American Presbyterians, *Qingxin Tang* (Pure Heart Hall, also known as the First Presbyterian Church of Shanghai) first gathered at Chinese pastor Lou Liren's home in 1860. Most of the early church members came from Qingxin Middle

School and Qingxin School for Girls which were Presbyterian mission-related. From 1919 to 1923, the church became more formalized and moved to *Dafo chang* (now Dachang Street). Church members also endeavored to integrate Chinese cultural elements to indicate a degree of Christian sinicization. For instance, the exterior resembled a folded fan which revealed their intention to adapt local culture.

Second, most Protestant mission churches such as the First Presbyterian had church leadership and congregation from both foreign and local origins. It does not mean that either foreign missionaries or local Christians in Shanghai did not dispense or encounter ethnocentrism. In church organizations and missional activities, foreign missionaries and Chinese Christians relied on one another. A significant reason for the cooperation was that the primary focus of Protestant missions in Shanghai was evangelism and churches were the places to dispense salvation to the local people.[20]

Third, Protestant missionaries worked in circumstances with intermittent anti-Christian events. The 1900 Boxer Incident marked the heightened angst against European colonialism, missionaries were attacked and many died as martyrs. Shanghai, however, was not the location of the main activities of the Boxers. William Cooper (1858–1900), a British missionary from the China Inland Mission (CIM), was one of the only two martyrs associated with Shanghai. Cooper worked for the Shanghai CIM headquarters for nineteen years and died in today's Baoding City, Hebei Province. Cooper spoke at the CIM annual meeting and urged participants to pray fervently for the church in China: "Join the Prayer Union and pray for these native brothers and sisters that God would make them burning and shining lights in the midst of the awful darkness; and that they may preach the gospel all over China."[21]

The other martyr was Flora Constance Kelly Glover,[22] also a British CIM missionary. Glover worked in Lu'an (Changzhi City, Shanxi Province) for three years before the self-organized militant Boxers drove her and her family to Wuhan. She gave birth to a daughter Faith who died days after. Glover died from exhaustion in Shanghai.[23] These are the only two incidents related to missionaries in Shanghai during the Boxer Rebellion. Protestant missionaries would encounter more anti-Christian movements in the Republic Era in the 1920s.

American Presbyterians

Motivated by sharing the gospel with people in China, American Presbyterian missionaries joined the force in Shanghai. J. M. W. Farnham and wife, J. A. Silsby and wife, H. G. C. Hallock, Miss M. A. Possey, Miss E. Silver, Miss E. A. Lindholm, George E. Partch and wife, G. F. Fitch and wife, C. W. Douglass and wife, James Williamson, and J. Trevor Smith and wife were from the American Presbyterian Mission.[24]

The American Presbyterians carried on the tradition of openness to Chinese culture. In addition to their first Qingxin Church, they expanded by building a second church *Silou Tang* (Lowrie Memorial Church) to honor the memory of the first American Presbyterian missionary to China, Walter Macon Lowrie (1819–47). In 1925, the church relocated to Hongkou District and changed its name to *Hongde Tang* (Fitch Memorial Church) in remembrance of American Presbyterian missionaries George F. Fitch (1845–1923) who headed the American Presbyterian Mission Press and Mary McLellan Fitch (1848–1918). The church building applied the Chinese palace style with flying eaves. The new Fitch Memorial church building of 1928 fully embraced a Chinese style in its exterior and reflected contemporary Christian indigenization efforts of the 1920s and 1930s. During the turbulent years of the Japanese occupation of Shanghai, the church pastor Jiang Shixu, his wife, and a few congregation members died as martyrs in 1932. Qingxin Church and Fitch Memorial Church became significant places of worship for American and Chinese Presbyterians in Shanghai until the 1950s.

British Congregationalist

Shanghai Union Church was built to accommodate British expatriates who did not worship at Holy Trinity Cathedral on Jiujiang Road. British Congregationalist missionary Walter Henry Medhurst opened his home for Christians to gather in 1864. In 1885, the church relocated when the size of the house church congregation increased. *North China Daily News* in 1886 reported how the members faced the task of building a church without large financial backing. Members, including the Sunday School children, donated articles for fundraising. British architect W. M. Dowdall designed the church facilitating its social functions.

Union Church also became a landmark for building interdenominational and international missionary connections and hosting significant events. For example, the Door of Hope (*Jiliang suo*) was birthed out of the prayer meeting of American missionary Cornelia Bonnell (1874–1916) and five other American and European Protestants at Union Church in 1900,[25] and British philosopher Bertrand Russell gave a speech in Union Church in 1920 when he was lecturing in China and Japan for a year. Union Church experienced multiple trials including the Japanese bombing of the western aisle in 1937 and being used as offices for a lamp factory after the Chinese government took over the churches.

American Episcopal

The American Episcopal Church's Foreign Mission established the bishopric in Shanghai. From 1844 to 1950, six missionary bishops served the American

Anglican diocese of Shanghai: William Jones Boone (the father), Channing Moore Williams, Samuel Isaac Joseph Schreschewsky, the Shanghai-born William Jones Boone (1846–1891, the son), Frederick Graves (1858–1940), and William P. Roberts. The only Chinese assistant bishop was Mao Ke Chung. American Episcopal Church Mission listed eighteen missionaries in Shanghai at the beginning of the twentieth century. F. R. Graves (medical doctor and pastor) and wife, F. L. Hawks Pott and wife, C. F. McRae, C. S. F. Lincoln, S. E. Smalley and wife, F. C. Cooper and wife, G. B. Palmer, M. P. Walker, Mrs. G. F. Mosher, Mrs. L. P. Fredericks, Miss Williette Eastham, Miss S. L. Dodson, Miss Lillis Crummer, and Miss C. Warnock all served via medicine or education.[26]

Some Episcopal missionaries involved themselves with multiple roles and responsibilities. American Episcopal missionary Cameron Farquhar McRae (Mai Ganlin, 1873–1954), taught at St. John's University, and pastored at St. Luke's Hospital[27] (now Tongren Hospital) in 1908. McRae built several churches including Zhusheng Tang (Christ All Saints Church) in 1925. Located in the French concession, the building embodied a Romanesque style. Although the American Episcopal Church had thriving missionary activities, they did not focus on church planting.

American Methodist

American Methodist missionaries began multiple churches in Shanghai. The first church, Moore Memorial Church (*Mu'en Tang*), was built in 1887 with an

FIGURE 2.1 *Mu'en Tang (Moore Memorial Church, 1887) stands near the People's Park and shopping malls in Shanghai. Photo courtesy of Susangeline Patrick, 2019.*

endowment from Mr. and Mrs. Lyman Royster Moore of Kansas City, Missouri. The church quickly expanded until 1937 when Japan invaded Shanghai. A missionary couple, Sidney Anderson (1889–1978) and Olive Watkins Lipscomb (1890–1978), spent thirty years at Moore from 1922 to 1952. Moore Memorial Church also served as an inspiration for Bob Pierce when he visited Anderson and Lipscomb in July 1947. Pierce was so impressed with the social programs at Moore that he founded World Vision.

Built in 1922, *Jinglin Tang* was the second church by the Methodist Episcopal Church (South). Methodist missionary Young Allen founded the church which could seat over one thousand worshippers, the largest church in Shanghai in the 1920s. After the Japanese occupation, some believers formed a new Methodist church, *Jingwen Tang*, in remembrance of American Methodist missionary Alvin Pierson Parker (1850–1924). In 1953, under the guidelines of the city government, *Jingwen Tang* and *Jinglian Tang* merged as *Huxi libai Tang* (the worship hall in west Shanghai).

Seventh Day Adventist

Seventh Day Adventists (SDA) also maintained an active ministry in Shanghai prior to 1950 through evangelism, publications, education, and medical services where the Chinese Mission of the SDA moved from Guangzhou to Shanghai in 1908. They built a church on Ningguo Road and rented a house for evangelistic meetings and outreach ministries among the local people. In the same year, the printing press of the SDA moved from Henan Province to Shanghai and began to publish Adventist literature. Multiple magazines including *Signs of the Times*, *Minister*, *Youth Friend*, *The Last Day Shepherd's Call*, *Sabbath School Lesson Quarterly*, and *Health and Longevity*, attracted readers to take interest in SDA and to sometimes becoming part of the SDA church.

Adventist missionaries Olga Bertina Osnes Oss (1897–1977) and John Oss (1892–1959)[28] began to work in Shanghai in 1925 after five years of mission service in northeastern China. They both traveled widely and spoke to different circles of government officials, businesspeople, and wealthy women to raise funds for medical and educational institutions. After they were expelled from China in 1950, John translated several of the Adventist founder Ellen White's books into Mandarin while pastoring a Chinese church in Berkeley, California. Olga continued to speak to different churches, introducing her mission experience to groups and individuals and raising awareness of Adventist mission to China. Heidi Campbell remarks how Olga Oss contributed to mission through training other women and fundraising "despite not having official leadership positions."[29]

The Adventist press head artist Mr. Wang, his wife, and two children perished during the Japanese bombing of Shanghai in 1937. Adventists cooperated with the Red Cross hospitals and missionaries such as Olga Oss raised funds for the Red Cross. By 1950, the SDA in Shanghai numbered two thousand worshippers in six churches: Hudong Church (1909), Hubei Church (1916), Nanmatou Church (1940), Huzhong Church (1945), Huxi Church (1946), and Tilanqiao Church (1950).

Concurrently to Anglican, Presbyterian, Congregationalist, Episcopal, Methodist, and Adventist missions, the American Southern Baptist Mission also supported missionary activities in Shanghai. E. F. Tatum and wife, R. T. Bryan and wife, Miss W. H. Kelly, Miss L. W. Price, and F. Rawlingson and wife made Shanghai the hub of their ministries[30] and Baptist missionaries formed churches and schools. Frank Joseph Rawlinson (1871–1937) began *Huaien Tang* (Grace Church) in 1910 and the church also opened Minqiang High School, *Yanmo shi* Girls' School (now Beijiao High School). Qi Qingcai (Charles Chi, 1909–90), one of the forty original pastors who began the Three-Self Patriotic Movement (TSPM), ministered the church (1935–66; 1980–9). The British and Foreign Bible Society also sent G. H. Bondfield, W. Leonard Thompson, T. D. Begg and wife, and Hans Döring to Shanghai.[31]

A relatively new American denomination called the Christian Catholic Church in Zion was also active in Shanghai. Among the listed missionaries George L. Mason, C. F. Viking, Rev. Emma Keeler Mason, Edward B. Kennedy, Rev. Sarah Lehn Kennedy, W. H. Cossum, Rev. Celia Stillman Cossum, and Rev. Betty C. L. Viking,[32] the only ordained pastors are four women. The denomination itself embraced biblical conservative views such as theocracy and church members generally held the beliefs of millennialism and practiced faith healing. It is interesting that a conservative church had endorsed women as ordained ministers in church leadership. Overall, these mission churches from Protestant denominations reached beyond their cultural boundaries and modeled the new churches in Shanghai after their denominational theologies and polities. Attentive to their Shanghai context, they also structured the new churches to meet the needs of education and charitable works.

Volunteer Missionary Organizations

Volunteer missionary organizations in the nineteenth century produced vital consequences for Christian movements worldwide. Such organizations recruited college students who became noteworthy cross-cultural missionaries in Shanghai. CIM's activities in Shanghai marked a new Protestant chapter on the religious landscape. Prior to the founding of CIM, the founder of the Chinese Evangelical Society (CES, 1844–65), Karl Friedrich August Gützlaff (1803–51),[33] acted as a translator for the British and helped with the port opening of Shanghai. In 1854, CES sent James Hudson Taylor (1832–1905) who briefly preached in Shanghai,[34] Shantou,[35] and Ningbo. The missional investigation led Taylor to launch CIM in 1865 and its missionaries joined his vision for China twenty years later.

The initial CIM mission in China called for international attention. Dubbed as the Cambridge Seven, university students Charles Thomas Studd (1860–1931), Montagu Harry Proctor-Beauchamp (1860–1939), Stanley P. Smith (1861–1931), Arthur T. Polhill-Turner (1862–1935), Arthur's brother Cecil H. Polhill (1860–1938), Dixon Edward Hoste (1861–1946), and William Wharton Cassels (1858–1925) arrived in Shanghai in 1885 as CIM missionaries. All seven missionaries were influenced by Taylor's earlier writing, *China, Its Spiritual Need and Claims*, which presented a ripe mission field and an optimistic appeal to the necessity of missionary work.[36] Another major influence of the time were the revival tours of American evangelist Dwight L. Moody (1837–99) in the British Isles. *The Christian's Secret of a Happy Life* by Hannah Whitall Smith (1832–1911) also contributed to the dissemination of a Wesleyan holiness movement called Higher Life.[37]

A second significance of the Cambridge Seven is that their brief stay in Shanghai prepared them as missionaries among different peoples in the western part of China including the Tibetans in Sichuan. Their reputation as pioneer missionaries generated great zeal for evangelism in world missionary movements, especially the Student Volunteer Movement founded by Arthur Tappan Pierson. The Cambridge Seven later exerted more global and transnational influence in their later missionary trajectories as Studd founded the Heart of Africa Mission (WEC International).

CIM strategically moved their headquarters from Hangzhou to Shanghai in 1890 so missionaries could build connections further inland. CIM listed D. E. Hoste and wife, J. W. Stevenson, James Stark and wife, F. H. Neale and wife, J. F. Broumton and wife, J. N. Hayward and wife, Miss M. M. Melville, M. Hardman and wife, Miss E. C. Johnson, Miss M. E. Cox, F. A. Steven and wife, and Miss Mary Allen in Shanghai.[38] CIM built *Shanghai gonggong libai tang* (Public Worship Hall, renamed as *Xin'en Tang* in 1962) in the Jing'an District in December 1939. CIM missionaries were the only ones who used the church until 1951. When CIM missionaries were forced out of Shanghai, CIM assigned Yang Shaotang (1898–1969), a Chinese evangelist from Shanxi, to pastor Xin'en church in 1951.

Other major missionary societies also devoted missionary energy to evangelization. The *Directory of Protestant Missionaries in China, Japan, and Corea* in 1903 listed John R. Hykes and Mrs. Hykes,[39] Charles Hykes, and J. Fritz as missionaries from the American Bible Society in Shanghai.[40] CMS's proceedings showed a record of missionaries in Shanghai including Arthur Elwin and Mary Jacob Elwin, Arthur John Henry Moule, William Augustus Handley Moule, Edith Onyon, and Mary Jane Godson.[41] The foreign Christian

Missionary Society recruited W. P. Bentley and wife, James Ware and wife, Miss Edna P. Dale, and Miss Rose L. Tonkin.[42]

The China Missionary Alliance sent ordained pastors including J. W. Stevenson, A. P. Parker, G. F. Fitch, W. N. Britton, W. P. Bentley, R. T. Bryan, C. J. F. Symons, D. MacGillivray, and D. Willard Lyon.[43] Another spiritual child of the Higher Life movement, Christian and Missionary Alliance (CMA), began sending missionaries to China in 1888. After the Boxer Rebellion in 1900, surviving missionaries such as John Woodberry and his wife moved from their Tianjin post to Shanghai. They began *Shouzhen Tang* (Beulah Chapel, built in 1916–17), an elementary school, and a Bible school in 1909 and 1921.

Missionary endeavors exhibited generational continuity as missionary children continued to be missionaries. The Woodberry children Ethel, Ora, and Earl all later joined the Shanghai mission where Ethel and Ora oversaw the Shouzhen Church and organized revivals and prayer meetings. Protestant missionaries from different mission organizations intersected with one another and interacted with local Christian workers. Their multiform roles in education and medicine also guaranteed their encounters.

Independent and Pentecostal Missions

Independent churches also played a role in the making of Protestant Shanghai. Some American Christians first began to worship at home in 1917. American commercial involvement in Shanghai contributed to a population of four thousand Americans in Shanghai by 1925.[44] When the number of Christian attendants expanded to two hundred, Community Church (*Shanghai guoji libai tang*) was founded and built in 1925. Some missionaries acted as independent entities such as Paul Kranz and wife, Edward Evans and wife, and Miss M. W. Jewell.[45] Petra Tunheim was a Norwegian missionary to West Java at first. While recuperating her health in Shanghai, Tunheim learned Chinese and evangelized in Shanghai. Emma B. Lawler pastored a church (Aimee Semple McPherson's International Church of the Foursquare Gospel) in Shanghai in 1936.[46]

The Pentecostal movement was also active in Shanghai. Church of God Mission (CGM) sent W. A. Hunnex to Shanghai as soon as they began their organization in 1909. After ten years, CGM had two mission stations in Shanghai and neighboring Zhenjiang with six American missionaries and fifty Chinese adherents.[47] By 1937, only one CGM still remained on Changbin Road in Shanghai. The Assemblies of God also had an active mission station in Shanghai beginning in 1934. Another branch of Pentecostal missionaries came from Australia who worked fervently against infanticide and oppression of women in arranged marriage and concubinage in Shanghai in the early 1900s.[48]

FIGURE 2.2 *Community Church (*Shanghai guoji libai tang, *1925) began with independent missionaries and now serves the international community in Shanghai. Photo courtesy of Susangeline Patrick, 2007.*

Pentecostal Christians viewed mainline Protestants as in need of sanctification. The Pentecostal emphasis of the manifestation of the gifts of the Holy Spirit, primarily through speaking in tongues and exorcism, raised suspicion among Protestant missionaries. In 1907, Pentecostal missionary Bernt Berntsen attended the centennial conference in Shanghai. Berntsen's earlier Azusa Street revival experience[49] compelled him to ask other Protestant missionaries if they had received the gifts of the Holy Spirit. They heavily criticized his experience as demonic work.[50] However, the Pentecostal movement developed in Shanghai quickly. In the 1920s, Pentecostal missionaries numbered more in China than in any other country.[51] The Pentecostal movement in Shanghai would also mediate the birth of Indigenous Chinese Pentecostal churches such as the True Jesus Church.[52]

Overall, four types of churches functioned out of their self-perceptions, their theology, and eschatological vision. Building visible churches was not always a priority for some Protestants in Shanghai, but the physical space of a church and its symbolic meanings provided a connecting point for Christians to gather and for non-Christians to see the Christian faith in action. Physical churches also provided a dispensary of charities and a connecting point for missionaries.

Protestant Education (1842–1950s)

Protestant missions heavily invested in education from early childhood education to university level and most schools were directedly tied to Protestant denominations and fellowships. Prior to 1950, three theological schools—Shanghai Baptist Theological Seminary, Shanghai College School of Theology, and St. John's University School of Theology—provided theological education for clergy. Protestant missionary educators also contributed to music education with the understanding of education as a handmaiden to serve evangelization. Women's education also became a significant theme as Protestants redefined gender roles in the 1920s and 1930s.

Primary and Secondary Education

Protestant mission-founded schools in the late Qing Dynasty co-existed alongside local schools[53] and religious schools. The most significant Protestant contribution were their remarkable efforts in providing educations for girls as the first boys-only middle school did not open until eleven years after the first girls' school. I will highlight education for girls and women in a later section. American Presbyterian missionaries including John Marshall Willoughby Farnham and his wife Mary Jane opened Qingxin (Pure Heart) Middle School in 1861. A Chinese chemist Xu Shou and British missionary John Fryer co-founded Gezhi Academy in 1876. In 1889, American Seventh Day Baptists operated Huizhong Middle School. LMS missionaries organized *Yinghua shuyuan* (Mailun Middle School) in 1898. After the turn of the twentieth century, YMCA Middle School opened its door to pupils in 1901. The American Episcopal Mission ran St. John's Middle School and offered classes in both Chinese and English.[54] SDA's China Mission Training School provided training for men. The Southern Baptist Convention (SBC) also saw the importance of training young boys and girls through academies of high schools and middle schools and Ming Jang Boys' School and Eliza Yates Girls' School in Shanghai were among a number of such schools.[55] By 1924, SBC also operated 630 elementary schools with 20,721 students.[56]

Some Protestant mission organizations dedicated themselves to the field of education. CMS sent C. J. F. Symons and wife, W. G. Walshe, W. A. H. Moule and wife (Anglo-Chinese School), G. F. C. Dobson (Anglo-Chinese School), A. J. H. Moule and wife, Miss J. M. Godson, Miss Elwin, Miss E. Onyon, and Miss H. Wood[57] to work at schools in Shanghai. The Educational

Association of China sent missionaries W. H. Hayes, O. F. Wisner, G. A. Stuart, J. A. Silsby, A. P. Parker, and W. N. Bitton as educators.[58] Additionally, YMCA and YWCA also became more involved in education in the 1920s and 1930s. Schools generally hired missionary teachers and Chinese educators, but male staff and teachers usually administrated and taught at boys' schools until co-education was introduced in the 1920s and 1930s.

The works of UCMS were lesser known although UCMS also joined waves of foreign missionaries in Shanghai in the late nineteenth century and early twentieth century. James Ware (?–1913), a British sailor, and his wife (?–1922) worked as missionaries in 1890s Shanghai where James began a mission in the mills district in 1890. UCMS accepted a gift of a school building from the manager of the mills.[59]

Missionaries also formed a network so they could support one another in the varied tasks. Ware conducted classes for the Japanese in Shanghai and opened the Door of Hope Mission to rescue young girls from human trafficking.[60] Early-twentieth-century Protestant missionary biographies sometimes omitted the first names of married female missionaries, but we know that Mrs. Ware taught Bible classes and worked with women and girls.[61] Orvile F. Barcus went to Shanghai in 1912 and lived with the Wares at first. Barcus then worked at the boys' school at the Christian institute.[62] American missionaries W. P. Bentley and his wife worked with the Wares. The Bentleys served in Shanghai for thirteen years before returning to the United States. Bentley established the Shanghai Institute which included classrooms and a chapel.[63]

Education of young children diversified as more missionaries from Australia taught at school, and the student body included children from surrounding countries. In 1901, Australian missionary Rosa L. Tonkin began to work in Shanghai under the Advisory Committee of the China Mission. She mainly worked with other missionary women and Chinese Bible women. In 1916, the Foreign Christian Missionary Society in Shanghai closed, but their two schools and two churches applied the self-supporting principle. Tonkin continued her mission work with the school[64] associated with the Wares. The American Adventist training school in 1912[65] emphasized the wholistic connections of the spiritual, the intellectual, and the physical, and students from seventeen provinces, Korea, and Singapore attended the Adventist school in Shanghai.

Education for Girls and Women

Protestant Christians opened girls' schools and broke the traditional prohibition of girls having access to education under Confucian social philosophy. American Episcopal missionary Eliza Jane Gillet Bridgeman (1805–71) opened *Biwen Nüshu* (Biwen Girls' School) in 1850, the first girls' school in Shanghai. The Bridgemans' two adopted Chinese daughters Ah-yee and Ah-lan from

Guangzhou, and another Chinese girl Jin-mei, became the first pupils of the school.[66] As the school expanded, the famed Song Sisters' mother, Ni Guizhen, graduated from the school.[67] The Women's Union Missionary Society of America (WU) operated two middle schools and one hospital named *Ximen Furu* (West Gate Women and Children) Hospital. WU took over Biwen Girls' School in the 1880s.

Multiple denominations took girls' education seriously. The American Episcopal Church and missionary Emma Jones operated St. Mary's Hall as a training school for girls beginning in 1851.[68] From St. Mary's Hall, although some students came from Christian homes and remained Christians for a long time, social circumstances had pushed people to multiple religious convictions. In the case of Gong Peng (1914–70), a Christian who participated in the anti-Japanese movements and worked for the YMCA, Gong joined the CCP in 1936. She became Chairman Mao's translator, a major spokesperson, and the first woman to head the Ministry of Foreign Affairs of the PRC.

The Methodist Church ran McTyeire School beginning in 1855. Methodist missionary Mary Houston Allen graduated from Wesleyan College in Macon, Georgia, in 1858. Wesleyan College, then Wesleyan Female College, was the world's first college to grant degrees to women.[69] The American Protestant suffrage movement attempted to provide equal educational opportunities for women, and it made an impact on Shanghai through the link with Mary Houston Allen. Allen and her husband Young John Allen (1836–1907) became instrumental in the establishment of the Anglo-Chinese College (1881–1911) and the McTyeire School for Girls. The Allens also built the connections for women graduates from McTyeire in Shanghai to attend Wesleyan College in Georgia. American teachers at McTyeire also taught young girls etiquette and trained them to be educated wives and mothers.[70]

Universities and Theological Education

The American Episcopal Mission founded Shanghai's prestigious St. John's University (SJU) in 1879, the oldest university in China. Missionaries William Jones Boone and Joseph Schereschewsky merged two Anglican colleges, Peiya School and Du'en School, to form St. John's College in 1879 and Chinese priests such as Yan Yongjing (1838–98) contributed to the opening and the operation of the college. Yan studied at a mission school operated by Boone and then the Anglican church sent Yan to study at Keyens College in the United States. In Wuchang, Yan and Scottish missionary Alexander Williamson (1829–90) evangelized. Yan was one of the key founders of the Boone Memorial School (later Huazhong Normal University) in Wuchang. In 1881, Yan became the first president of St. John's College which eventually gained a reputation as the "Harvard of the Far East" and "the Cradle of diplomats in China."[71]

St. John's University began with five American teachers five Chinese teachers, and sixty-two students. The topics covered theology, Western studies, and Chinese studies and all teachers taught in Chinese and the Shanghai dialect. Only after twelve years, at the request of students, did the university begin to teach subjects in both Chinese and English, which afforded the students the opportunity to study further abroad or acquire more social mobility in multicultural Shanghai. In 1907, Zhu Youyu (Y. Y. Tsu, 1885–1986) earned a bachelor's degree as one of the first four graduates at St. John's University. Zhu later became an important church leader and educator in China and the United States.[72] Some pupils later became the Chinese elites such as the prominent Liu business family,[73] and Song Ziwen (known as T. V. Soong), the brother of the Song Sisters, also attended the school. Being bilingual and multilingual for the Shanghai elites became second nature and empowered them to be capable diplomats and businesspeople across continents.

A second Christian university in Shanghai was Medhurst College founded in 1898. Medhurst initially transferred students from the former Anglo-Chinese boarding school and moved to Hongkou District in 1903 with seventy enrolled students.[74] As a Christian school for boys, Medhurst hired teachers interdenominationally. A British congregationalist, Ernest Ralph Lapwood (1910–84), taught there in the 1930s, and the surrounding social conditions of workers at sweatshops spurred his later activism.[75] Australian Congregationalist Rev. Willett Bevan taught at Medhurst in the early twentieth century.[76]

The third major higher education institution was the Shanghai Baptist Seminary, co-founded by the American Baptist Foreign Mission Society and the Foreign Mission Board of the SBC in 1906 providing education as a mission endeavor in Shanghai. Subsequently, the seminary added the Shanghai Baptist College in 1909. In 1911, the two institutions formed the Shanghai Baptist College and Theological Seminary with the support of both Northern and Southern Baptists,[77] later registered as Hujiang University (Shanghai College) in 1929. Bao Zheqing (1893–1957), a later well-known Baptist pastor, graduated from Hujiang University in 1914.

Hujiang University was the first higher educational institution to start co-education in China, starting in 1920.[78] The first female lawyer and judge Tcheng Yu-hsiu (1891–1959) served as president of SBCS (Shanghai University) from 1931 to 1937.[79] Fan Zhangkang (?–1972) attempted to keep Shanghai Baptist College open after the Japanese invasion. Fan took on the role of president in 1939, and organized Zhijiang College, Dongwu College, and St. John's College to form a Christian University Shanghai Association so they could negotiate how to get their campuses back.

T. B. Ray reported that Shanghai and Shanghai College and Seminary (SCS) were two of the twenty-seven mission stations the SBC operated in the 1920s in China.[80] Ray also recorded a Bible woman named Tsung Ta Ta who converted to Christianity under a Chinese rice merchant known as Deacon Wong who built a chapel. Tsung was associated with Miss Willie Kelly, a missionary who later went to Shanghai.[81] The pioneering co-educational style attracted 35 female students and 639 male students in 1923.[82]

The motivation and goal of the SCS were to train Chinese Christian leaders for evangelism in the early twentieth century. Herman Liu Zhan'en (1886–1938) served as the first Chinese president of Shanghai University for ten years from 1928 until his assassination by the Japanese in 1938. Henry Hsien-yang Lin briefly held the position as the president of the university until his imprisonment in 1951. The university was then merged with East China Normal University and ceased to exist. These universities admitted both Christian and non-Christian students and reported statistics on students' profession of the Christian faith upon graduation.[83] Higher education in Shanghai bridged China and its global connections and helped propagate faith, knowledge, and the modernity that Republic Era China in the 1920s and 1930s desired.

Protestant Music Education

Music education was an important part of Protestant mission-founded schools in nineteenth- and early-twentieth-century Shanghai. American Presbyterian missionary Julia B. Mateer (1837–98) delivered an important speech on music in Christian mission "at the Second Triennial Meeting of the Educational Association of China in Shanghai in 1896."[84] Mateer viewed music as instrumental in advancing Christian mission and remained apathetic toward Chinese music traditions.[85] The American Presbyterian Mission Press in Shanghai also published *Xiguo yuefa qimeng* (Rudiments to Western Music) in 1872[86] which assisted Chinese students' learning of Christian music from Mateer's 1892 *Shengshi pu* (Sacred Hymns).[87]

It is significant to note that Protestant missionaries recognized the effectiveness of Christian music as an instrument of evangelism because music addressed the heart. Mateer's advocacy for music education is shared by Chauncey Goodrich (1836–1925), an American Board of Commissioners for Foreign Missions (ABCFM) missionary to China, who equated the importance of a hymnal to that of the Bible.[88] William Soothill (1861–1935) from the United Methodist Mission, an Oxford professor of Chinese, differentiated music from sermons: "[G]ood music takes the shortest cut to the heart, it goes straight there; a sermon has to take a by-way through the mind first."[89] These concrete examples demonstrated that Protestant missionaries practiced a holistic way of understanding mission and humanities. They spent time learning about their contexts and produced works which addressed multiple aspects of Shanghai society.

Protestant Hospitals and Medical Works (1842–1950s)

Christian missionaries and Chinese Christians established 254 hospitals all over China prior to the Japanese bombing in 1937. As one of the major Protestant institutions, trained medical doctors supplied the missionary field and worked to train local doctors and nurses and to care for patients. British medical missionary William Lockhart from the LMS opened Lester Chinese Hospital (also known as Renji Hospital) in 1844 as the first hospital to practice Western medicine in Shanghai. Lockhart pleaded "the cause of medical missions, believing that great good may be done in heathen lands by combining the work of the surgeon with that of the preacher and teacher"[90] and he strongly argued for the separation of being a preacher and a physician.[91] Lockhart recommended qualifications for medical operations and suggested that medical missionaries should be laity.[92] Patients receiving treatment from the early hospitals were from the poor and lower class. Chieko Nakajima speculates that Shandong Hospital by LMS presumably also treated patients from the similar socioeconomic background beginning in 1844.[93] As these earlier clinics and hospitals became equipped with more medical staff, they engaged in treating opium addiction, opening hospitals for women, and training Chinese doctors and nurses to guarantee long-term sustainability.

Treating Opium Addiction

A major type of medical work Protestant missionaries undertook was to help patients addicted to opium. In 1860, the Taiping army attacked Shanghai and then a major battle took place in 1861 and 1862. The British and French troops allied with the Qing army and the United States in the Shanghai Battle. Social instability associated with wars was also coupled with the ongoing opium trade. The extensive British opium trade presented obstacles and ironic and unexpected opportunities to Protestant mission.

As Chinese grew more addicted to opium, Protestant medical missionaries viewed the issue as a moral demise, and they also treated the patients who were seeking help. The CMS Periodicals in 1896 described the prevalent problem with the addiction of opium: "Opium dens abound now, not merely in the back alleys, but oftentimes in the great thoroughfares; and they are crowded with the victims of the drug."[94] Unable to deal with the systematic British colonial system and the Shanghai gangs who profited from the opium trade, Protestant medical missionaries applied a method of gradual reduction in helping patients be weaned from the addiction[95] and resorted to treat the symptoms which generated from the root causes.

Faith and Medicine

Some Protestant hospitals interpreted their medical work as inseparable from the Christian faith. The Women's Union Missionary Society (WMU, *Nügonghui*) established Margaret Williamson Hospital in Shanghai in 1884. The hospital eventually incorporated Bible reading and prayers for the patients. The Women's Medical School of Soochow (Suzhou) united with the hospital as the nucleus of "The Shanghai Union Medical Work for Women" in 1921.[96] The school's training school for nurses and medical school for women also had a medical faculty member teaching and discussing faith-related medical issues.[97]

Mission hospitals also incorporated the Christian faith with patients who were receiving treatment. St. Luke's Hospital reported: "The hospital is visited daily by one of the native clergy and the Bible-readers and catechists, and religious literature is supplied to the patients; so that the hospital is a means by which the truths of Christianity find entrance to thousands of Christian homes."[98] In-patients at the Lester Chinese Hospital read the Bible in the mornings and outpatients uttered prayers at the Tian'an Church prior to seeing the doctors. The hospital also set up funds for patients who could not afford medical expenses in the 1930s. Lester Hospital continued to serve patients until Shanghai Second Medical College's takeover in 1952.

Missionaries also established medical colleges to train doctors and nurses in Shanghai. PEC ran St. Luke's Hospital (1844, 1866–*c.* 1930s), St. John's University (the College of Medicine) in 1880, and Saint Elizabeth's Hospital (1900). PEC and the Methodist Episcopal Church (South) also partnered in operating the Union Medical School–Shanghai in 1922. The American Methodist Church and Women's Foreign Missionary Society (WFMS) collaborated with some other American missionaries in building the Women's Christian Medical College in 1924.

The medical field in Shanghai reflected an integral Chinese and American collaboration. Shi Meiyu (Mary Stone), Phoebe Stone, and Jennie Hughes established Bethel Hospital in 1920. The hospital was part of the larger Bethel Mission which also ran schools and an orphanage. The Shanghai Bethel Band members modeled themselves after evangelistic bands in Japan and conducted revival meetings through their musical talents. Original members of the Bethel Band came from prominent Shanghai families, such as Beatrice Chung. SDA also utilized medical services to treat patients and to generate religious interest among local people. Dr. Harry W. Miller combined natural healing and vegetarianism with other medical treatments. They operated two sanitariums and one hospital beginning in 1928 in Shanghai. The Christian faith was incorporated into the motivation of the commencement of Protestant medical mission in Shanghai until the 1950s.

Protestant Publishing Efforts (1842–1950s)

Protestant missionaries saw the need of publishing Christian literature and newspapers as a ministry aiding evangelism. Some mission organizations specifically focused on publishing Christian literature. The Chinese Track Society included Joseph Edkins, R. T. Bryan, A. P. Parker, J. M. W. Farnham, Ven. Archdeacon Thomson, W. N. Britton, W. P. Bentley, and J. E. Cardwell.[99] Farnham served as the editor of *Chinese Illustrated News* and Cardwell as the editor of *Child's Paper.*[100] Another mission organization, the Christian Vernacular Society of Shanghai, featured D. H. Davis, G. F. Fitch, J. A. Silsby, Miss Emma Silver, and J. W. Crofoot[101] who focused on making Christian texts more accessible. The CMA operated the China Alliance Press and SDA ran the *China Division Reporter.*

Newspapers and Magazines

Protestant missionaries published newspapers and magazines in Chinese and English in Shanghai. Missionaries such as Young John Allen (1836–1907) printed newspapers in the Chinese language. Beginning in May 1868, Allen edited *Shanghai xinbao* (Shanghai Daily) and *Jiaohui xinbao* (Church Daily, later as *Wanguo Gongbao*, Global Magazine, in 1874). Protestant missionaries were involved in *Zilin xibao* (North China Daily News, previously North China Herald), a newspaper published in English. Walter Henry Medhurst from the British Congregation Church and Elijah Coleman Bridgman (1801–61) from ABCFM edited the newspaper.

British missionary Alexander Wylie (1815–87) from LMS began the first Shanghai-based monthly Chinese magazine titled *Liuhe congtan* in 1857. Although the publication only lasted a year, it encouraged other magazines. Wylie, Elijah Coleman Bridgman from ABCFM, and Joseph Edkins (1823–1905) also established the Shanghai Literary and Scientific Society in 1857.

Additionally, the Baptist magazine *Jiaowu zazhi* (Church Affairs) became one of the most important and popular Christian magazines in the early twentieth century. Hungarian-Slovak architect László Hudec (1893–1958) designed the Christian Literature Society (CLS) building and the China Baptist Publication building in the 1930s and 1940s. Donald MacGillivray prepared literature at CLS.[102] The Shanghai Branch of the China Baptist Publication was an offshoot of the original China Baptist Publication Society organized by Dr. R. E. Chambers in Canton (Guangzhou) in 1899.[103] J. T. Williams oversaw the Shanghai Branch[104] circulating Christian literature, Bibles, and tracts.

Promotion of Knowledge

Protestant publishing served to promote cultural, religious, and scientific knowledge. First, some missionaries made intentional efforts to document and share their critical observations of cultural customs. LMS missionary William Muirhead also published widely in history, geography, geology, theology, and religions. The Methodist organization known as the Society for the Diffusion of Christian and General Knowledge among the Chinese operated in Shanghai. W. Gilbert Walshe, a member of the society, published a book on Chinese customs so that newly arrived Methodist missionaries could better serve without unnecessary mistakes. In other words, Methodist missionaries were expected to cultivate intercultural intelligence. Walshe stated: "[A]t the request of the Mid-China Church Missionary Conference for the guidance of missionaries newly arrived in China . . . a better acquaintance with Chinese social methods might prevent many unfortunate blunders and much mutual misunderstanding."[105] Publication about Chinese customs circulated among people who showed interest in mission and equipped them with practical tools to navigate general cultural differences.

Second, Protestant publishing also acted as agency of promoting Christian knowledge. The American Presbyterian Mission Press in Shanghai became the largest publishing house in Asia and George Fitch headed the printing house for many years. Another Presbyterian-supported printing house was the Christian Literature Society for China (*Guangxue hui*) which printed the *Chinese Christian Intelligencer* weekly from 1901 to 1948.[106] Melissa Inouye ascertains that the regular miracle and healing accounts served the goal of revivalism from the editors Samuel Isett Woodbridge and Cheng Chunsheng.[107] The American Baptist Mission owned the Baptist Publishing Company and published a monthly journal *Zhenguang* (True Light). The United Christian Missionary Society (1927) and London Missionary Society Press also generated literature out of Shanghai.

Third, Protestant publications featured specialty knowledge in the scientific fields. A unique journal published in Shanghai was the *China Medical Missionary Journal* that operated for twenty years (1887–1907) and later continued as the *China Medical Journal*.[108] When the Medical Missionary Association of China was founded in Shanghai in 1907, medical missionaries aimed to reflect on issues they encountered while working in China. The journal served as a platform of information, reflection, and support for medical missionaries, and Chinese doctors and nurses.

Publication in the Shanghai Dialect

Protestant missionaries recognized the importance of the Shanghai dialect in their publication and ministry. Bishop Boone's *The Covert's Catechism* (after

1847), *Religious Juvenile Instruction* (1855), *Morning Prayers* (unknown date), and translations of several New Testament books, were in the Shanghai dialect.[109] The Missionary Society of the Methodist Episcopal Church of the United States' missionary couple William G. E. Cunningham and Mrs. Cunningham were in Shanghai from 1852 until 1861. William published *Fuyin zhenlin wenda* (Catechism of Gospel Truth) in 1855 and Mrs. Cunningham published *Mengyang qiming* (Revelation of the Day) in 1860, both in the Shanghai dialect.[110] American Southern Baptist missionary A. B. Cabaniss translated *Aesop's Fables* as moral lessons in 1856, the Gospel of Luke and a hymn book in 1859, and fellow missionary Mrs. Cabaniss published *Sources of Good and Evil* in 1856, all in the Shanghai dialect.[111]

Protestant Social and Charitable Works (1842–1950s)

Protestant missionaries viewed social works of justice and charity as integral parts of their mission in Shanghai, and they actively fought against poverty, social injustice issues, and relief. Natural disasters and periodic wars generated great needs for relief work. LMS missionary William Muirhead founded the China Disaster Relief Committee in Shanghai, mobilizing missionaries, business owners, and diplomats to provide for people who were impacted by a severe drought in the Huabei region between 1876 and 1879. Talitha Gerlach (1896–1995) was an American missionary who worked as a social worker at the Shanghai YWCA from 1926 to 1940. It was in the Shanghai YWCA headquarters that Gerlach and some Christians later started a Marxist study group which included Maud Muriel Russell (1893–1989), Alec Camplin, Agnes Smedley, George Hatem (1910–88), Ruth Weiss, Trude Rosenberg, Heinz Schippe, Irene Wiedemeyer, Lily Haass, Cora Deng, and Cao Liang. The social conditions of Shanghai and the world compelled several Christian missionaries and social workers to adopt a more radically progressive and liberal view.

Rescue Missions

Both Protestant missionary women and Chinese Christian women worked together in rescue missions. The most notable is the Door of Hope (*Jiliang Suo*). The founder of the Door of Hope was Cornelia Bonnell, a Vassar College graduate and human trafficking was a profitable business in Shanghai[112] human traffickers, both men and women, in the 1920s and 1930s tricked or forced girls from rural areas inflicted with famine or other natural disasters. Bonnell and other Christian women addressed the human trafficking problem from the early twentieth century. Gladys Dieterle and Winifred Burlinson were both missionaries who also worked to provide respite homes for children.

The Door of Hope provided three main tangible and intangible means for the women and girls. First, the home became a shelter and a new path for the women and girls who were marginalized and ostracized in Shanghai. As most girls came from rural areas, they experienced culture shock as they were abruptly transported and sold into the urban and industrialized Shanghai. In Bonnell's 1914 article published in the Alumnae Department of the Miscellany, she discussed the social expectations of Chinese women and attributed poverty, social injustice, and fatalism to the trafficking of young girls into prostitution.[113] She reported receiving over a thousand girls within the first year of the opening of the mission.[114]

Second, the home provided education and practical skills so the women would foster financial independence. In the early twentieth century, professional skills for women were not easily available to girls and women, especially to rural dwellers. Education and skills became assets for the women to escape from returning to brothels. Residents at the Door of Hope in Shanghai self-supported the expense of the mission through making mission dolls carved from pear wood with five layers of hand-weaved and sewn clothes. Christian Henriot elucidates the social context made it difficult for Chinese women with professional trainings from the Door of Hope to find employment and marriage was still a priority.[115]

Third, the rescued girls and women received Christian instruction. Missionaries viewed the teaching of the Bible, a prayer life, and instilling Christian values as essential to the rescue mission. Bonnell further commented that the new social transitions had opened doors for new freedom for young people in China and she emphasized the importance of Christian education to guard against licentiousness: "[W]ith little appreciation of the fact that without the inherent standards of Christian manhood and womanhood, upon which such intercourse [conversation about freedom] is based in Western countries, freedom easily degenerates into license."[116] Similarly, Chinese Christian writers in the early twentieth century blamed economic difficulties and moral weakness as the root causes of prostitution in Shanghai.[117] Rescue mission at the Door of Hope functioned as part of a moral reform of Protestant missionaries.

Sue Gronewold interviewed eleven women and a few male alumni from Shanghai's Door of Hope. She argues that both Western and Chinese Christian women constructed a hybrid and complex kinship as "[m]others and daughters, love and gratitude, control and devotion, but also imperialist and colonised, dominated and subordinated, sternness and sentiment."[118] Door of Hope in Shanghai also raised future women leaders who carried on their own mission. Wu Li-tsu (Eleanor Wu) felt called to open a refuge for homeless women in 1937 war-torn Shanghai.[119] Wu became instrumental in sheltering women but also equipping them with skills so they could be self-reliant.

The leadership at the Door of Hope in Shanghai had a consistent continuity of foreign Christian missionaries who took charge of the overall organization of the mission with Chinese women who fulfilled the daily tasks. CMA missionaries Anthony and Evelyn Bollback were in Shanghai from 1947 to 1949. Bollback refers to Edna Johnson and Pastor Wong and their association with the Door of Hope Mission.[120] Another leader was Miss Peacock who suffered internment in a Japanese camp. After a brief stay in Canada, she returned to Shanghai and worked at the Door of Hope until 1951.[121] The mission was connected and relied on the generosity of a network of both international and domestic philanthropists.

The Door of Hope was not the only rescue home in Shanghai. Many Christian missionary women handled social work with girls and women. American Presbyterian missionary Mary Fitch also founded a shelter for young girls who had been sold into brothels. Churches of Christ in Australia (CCA) missionary Rosa L. Tonkin first worked in Shanghai in 1901. After the American Disciples withdrew in 1915, Tonkin became independent and primarily worked with marginalized women and orphaned children.[122]

The existence of Western prostitutes in Shanghai further complicated the issue of rescue mission. Eileen Scully's article "Prostitution as Privilege" points out the ubiquitous problem of European, American, and Russian prostitutes in Shanghai from 1860 until the League of Nations campaigned against the abolishment of "white slavery" in the late 1930s.[123] Missionaries generally treated the problem of prostitution as a vice to overcome and as an individual responsibility.

Furthermore, the plague of white prostitution in Shanghai was systematically integrated to maintain a racialized superiority. Robert Bickers points out the gendered taboo of British women marrying Chinese men. In doing so, the women would lose their British nationality. The taboo was much stronger versus British men marrying Chinese women. European brothels and even the Shanghai Rowing Club excluded Chinese men due to underlined but distorted racial purity.[124] Missionaries criticized the depiction of scantily dressed European women in photographs and films in China and viewed them as more dangerous.[125] Missionaries themselves could not see that even their criticism of white prostitution reflected their self-understanding of race and gender. It is more than individualistic attitude or behavior, but the British imperial and systematic structure has created a mechanism that guided or forced the lives of some people to be exploited and further marginalized.

Other Issues in the Shanghai Protestant Mission (1842–1950s)

The political instability of the late nineteenth century made it necessary for some missionaries in other areas to briefly move to Shanghai. Some of them continued to minister and to serve in ways that stretched them beyond their regular ministry. Effie D. Kellar, a UCMS missionary based in Kuling, moved to Shanghai when the Boxer Rebellion broke out in 1900. Kellar then ministered to American and British sailors for two years.[126] Although her work among the sailors was brief, it was unusual for a single woman to have accomplished such ministry in the early twentieth century. A small number of missionaries served in less conventional ways. For example, Earl Otto of Kentucky directed a dry-battery manufacturing facility and was active in a community church in Shanghai from 1937 until 1941.[127] I will highlight two significant themes concerning the self-identity of Protestant missionaries in Shanghai.

Japanese Internment

Between 1943 and 1945, the Japanese army interned a great number of missionaries who spent varied terms in these camps in Shanghai. Japanese internment camps in Shanghai detained about six thousand expatriates and settlers from ten countries.[128] In Ralph Ansel Ward's case, Ward, originally from Ohio, became a missionary in the Methodist Episcopal Church in Fuzhou from 1909 to 1916. He held various secretarial positions on the Board of Foreign Missions, and he was the president of the Anglo-Chinese College in Fuzhou from 1925 to 1927. Elected bishop in the Methodist Church, Ward had spent time in Nanjing (1933–7), Chengdu (1937–41), and in Suzhou University from 1941. In 1941, Ward was arrested by the Japanese in Shanghai and was interned in the Japanese camp from 1941 to 1945. His wife Mildred May Worley died in 1947. In 1946, when civil war broke out, Ward joined Chen Wenyuan to renew Methodism and emphasize inner spiritual rebirth. In 1950, Ward left China. Later he ministered to the Mandarin-speaking immigrants from the mainland to Hong Kong and Taiwan until he passed away in Hong Kong in 1958.

During the Second World War, the Japanese interned some American missionaries. Edwin Marx, an American UCMS missionary spent a year as a prisoner of war in the Internment Camp on Haiphong Road from November 1942.[129] In 1943, another American missionary Lois Anna Ely was interned at the Chapei Civil Assembly Center for less than a year.[130] As part of the US and Japan prisoner swap, the *MS Gripsholm* repatriated some missionaries including Sidney Anderson whom the Japanese interned in Pudong. None of the Methodist missionaries died in the Japanese internment camps or in the later Chinese liberation in 1949.[131]

Missionaries' internment experiences shaped their theology of suffering. In what ways did survived missionaries interpret their detainment? Most missionary biographies and writings of their family members reveal the events and the tremendous pain missionary detainees endured,[132] but they paid little attention to theologizing their experience. When American missionary internees were repatriated, the public depicted their heroism which could have jeopardized missionaries' reflections. For instance, after Sophie Stevens Lanneau (1881–1963), an educational missionary who spent seven months in a Japanese internment camp in Shanghai, had returned to the United States, the Signal Corps approached her for intelligence work.[133] She declined and returned to China for more educational work in 1946.[134] The added international politics further prevented disclosures of expressing negative emotions. Sonya Grypma sheds light on the little publicized Canadian missionary nurses in China and argues that their internment reshaped the Canadian missionary community.[135]

Protestants Post-1950s

From the first stage of Protestant exploration of Shanghai as a mission field (1817–42) to over a hundred years of missionary endeavors from 1842 until the 1950s, Protestant missionaries created a massive network of mission churches, educational systems, medical infrastructure, publishing, and charitable works during the course of dramatic social and political change. Once again, Protestant churches in Shanghai experienced a systematic uprooting due to the new Chinese government-imposed changes in the 1950s. Almost all Protestant missionaries were exiled out of Shanghai. Most Protestant churches previously connected with foreign missions were shut down or used as various nonreligious facilities. By 1958, the First Presbyterian Church was the only Protestant church preserved in Nanshi District. It was only closed in 1966, almost fifteen years late in comparison to other churches. The new state gradually took over all mission or church-related schools, hospitals, medical colleges, publishing houses, and disbanded mission organizations. Furthermore, over the next twenty years, the state and city authorities reformulated these entities and secularized education, medicine, publishing, and charities. The events that took place in 1950s and 1960s Shanghai may signal the death of both Catholic and Protestant lives detailed in Chapters 1 and 2. However, Rodney Stark and Xiuhua Wang argue that the Cultural Revolution transformed Christianity into a Chinese movement and made religious faith more valuable during the 1960s and 1970s.[136] When state policies on religion relaxed in the late 1970s, the hidden Christians gradually surfaced. Daniel Bays reports the unexpected numerical growth of Protestants from one million in the 1950s to five million in 1979.[137] Christian faith in Shanghai began to reveal a visible restoration and resurrection in the 1970s and 1980s.

3

The Shanghai Orthodox: Russian, Armenian, and Chinese

The history of Orthodox communities in Shanghai presents a lesser known yet surprising and remarkable part of Christianity. In this chapter I will focus on the Russian, Armenian, and Chinese Orthodox believers in Shanghai. The rediscovering section will explore Russian and Armenian Orthodox Christians and their struggles as refugees in the late nineteenth and early twentieth centuries and the simultaneous formation of the Chinese Russian Orthodox Church. The remaking section of the chapter will focus on the Orthodox community in multicultural Shanghai and how they interacted with society and the wider Orthodox community in the late twentieth and twenty-first centuries.

Historical Background of Shanghai Orthodoxy

A brief history of the Orthodox Church in China provides the background and helps locate the Shanghai Orthodox communities in their larger context. It is important to note that Russian Orthodoxy in China first began among the descendants of Russian Cossacks (known as Albazinians *Албази́нцы*) from Albazin, Siberia. After forty-one years of the Manchu conquest of China, the Imperial Qing army took Albazinians as captives to Beijing in 1683.[1] At the height of the Great Qing social and military power, the Kangxi Emperor (r. 1622–1722) fostered religious tolerance and permitted Albazinian Orthodox prisoners to convert a local Daoist Guanyu temple into the Sophia Church and allowed Orthodox believers to celebrate mass under the priest Maksim Leont'ev.[2] Paradoxically, the Kangxi Emperor systematically orchestrated the cultural assimilation of the Albazinians by forbidding them to speak the Russian language and promoting intermarriages with Manchu and Han Chinese people. The European Jesuit missionaries helped to negotiate the Treaty of Nerchinsk in 1685, which resulted in a second Eastern Orthodox church known as the Convent of Candlemas (later the Church of the Purification of the Virgin).[3] The first Russian priest in China, Leont'ev organized the Orthodox Church Beijing Mission in 1715.

The Treaty of 1728 between St. Petersburg and Beijing established legal protection and the tradition of Russian priests and students being sent from Russia to China.[4] Eventually, the Orthodox Albazinians adopted the Chinese family names of Luó, Dù, Yáo, Hè, and Hé. Despite these intentional efforts, some Albazinians maintained their religious identity as Orthodox Christians and the initial Orthodox community remained small and self-concerned without actively proselytizing among the Han and Manchu populations in Beijing.[5] Over the next two hundred years, the Beijing Mission did not expand to Shanghai until the eighteenth mission (1896–1931).

The Beijing Mission to Shanghai did not bear much fruit in the late nineteenth century as its mission effort was disrupted by the Boxer Rebellion (1899–1901) and more than two hundred Orthodox Christians in Beijing died as martyrs in 1900.[6] Although the Orthodox Beijing Mission expanded substantially with nineteen churches and thirty-two missions[7] in other parts of China, the diocese of Shanghai was only established after the Bolshevik Revolution (1917–23), resulting in increased numbers of Russian refugees in China after 1917.

Russian Orthodox in Shanghai (1902–64)

Russian Orthodoxy in Shanghai was first practiced among the Russian tea merchants in the late nineteenth century. As trade grew between Russia and Qing-China, the Russian imperial government requested to establish an Orthodox Church in Shanghai, but the Qing imperial government rejected the request due to suspicions of Russian expansion. In 1896, the Russian consulate in Shanghai began to oversee the affairs of Russian merchants and sailors. At the height of European and American imperialism, Shanghai's status as a free port without visa requirements and its proximity to eastern regions of Russia attracted traders to reside in Shanghai's International Settlement. Russians living in the northeastern Chinese city of Harbin also saw the advantageous move to the thriving trade city of Shanghai. Consequently, Russian Orthodox services were loosely organized at the end of the nineteenth century.

Russian Orthodox Churches

The Russian Orthodox community in Shanghai first had Bishop Innokenty and two Chinese assistants visiting Shanghai with a subsequent Russian school opening in 1901.[8] The Russo-Japanese War (1904–5) demobilized thousands of Russians to move to China, including 354 Russians in Shanghai.[9] From 1905 to 1962, ten Russian Orthodox churches had been active in Shanghai. The Qing government and eleven countries signed the Boxer Protocol (1901), an unequal treaty which forced China to financially compensate the eleven nations and grant more permission for colonial privileges. As a result, the Beijing Mission of the Russian Orthodox Church acquired sufficient funds to purchase land in the American Settlement in Shanghai in 1902 and founded the first Russian Orthodox church in Shanghai called *Zhuxian Tang* (Epiphany Church, also known as the Holy Theophany Church) in 1905.

Surprisingly, the Russian Orthodox mission in Seoul (now South Korea) also maintained a connection with the Orthodox mission in Shanghai. Russian emperor Nicholas II personally ordered 25,000 roubles for the mission in Seoul to purchase furniture, which in turn came from Shanghai.[10] Furthermore, Russia's loss of the Russo-Japanese War reduced the Russian Orthodox mission in Seoul as Japan invaded Korea and deported all Russian citizens. As a result, the personnel of the mission moved from Seoul to Shanghai under the Chinese Orthodox mission.[11] It was unclear if any of the employees of the mission were *Koryo-saram* (Korean Russians) Orthodox from South Ussuriisk.

The Epiphany Church in Shanghai acted as a natural extension of the Russian community. By 1915, four hundred Russians resided in the Tilanqiao area in Hongkou District and the Epiphany Church exclusively served the Russian tea merchants and initiated no evangelistic efforts beyond this tight-knit community. The liturgical celebrations strictly followed the Russian model, reinforcing the religious and social identity of the Russian Orthodox community in Shanghai.

The Russian Revolution in 1917, however, marked a significant cultural shift for the Epiphany Church in Shanghai. The large number of Russian refugees who fled to Shanghai from Russia and Harbin forced the Epiphany Church to make accommodations for refugees who were made up of merchants, the Tsarist royal families, intellectuals, and soldiers whom the Russian Communist Party oppressed. Zhicheng Wang documents approximately 8,000 Russians in Shanghai by the end of the 1920s.[12] Simo Mikkonen estimates the statistics from the Russian Bureau may be higher than the official report of 13,000 refugees from the Russian Empire in 1930.[13]

Mother Russia and Father Tsar

Approximately 25,000 Russians settled in Shanghai between 1917 and 1937.[14] Known as the Shanghai White Russians (Русский Шанхай), they had a strong attachment to Nicholas II (1868–1918). After the emperor and his family were killed during the Russian Revolution, the Shanghai White Russians memorialized the Russian imperial family in a vigil at Epiphany Church and venerated Nicholas II as an Orthodox martyr,[15] sixty-three years prior to the Russian Orthodox Church Outside of Russia officially recognizing the martyr-saints of Nicholas II and his family.

The designation of Emperor Nicholas II signaled a strong religious and national identification with *Матушка Россия* (Mother Russia), an imagery the White Russians used against the Bolshevik revolutionaries, deploring the anguish of exile. The feminine metaphor suggests an emotional bond with both the Orthodox Church and the Russian state and designating the Tsar to be a saint martyr effectively united the church and state with an anticipated hope for unification. The notion of "Mother Russia and Father Tsar"[16] derives from Russia's long-established cultural history and stresses devotion and communion both religiously and sociopolitically.

The presence of the White Russian refugees also shifted the structure of the Russian clerics in Shanghai. Prior to the 1920s, the leadership of the Russian Orthodox Church in Shanghai had been consistently Russian priests directly from Russia. The Beijing headquarters appointed Russian priest Simon Vinogradov (1876–1933) to be consecrated as the Shanghai Orthodox bishop in 1919. He bore the title but primarily cared for a monastery in Harbin and assisted the Spiritual Mission in Beijing before he finally arrived in Shanghai in 1926. Vinogradov was the first Russian priest to have arrived in Shanghai from inside of China. For five years, Vinogradov helped the Orthodox Shanghai mission to expand and added Orthodox schools and a hospital.

The Russian Orthodox community existed in a tumultuous time under the rule of the Chinese Nationalist government's rule in Shanghai. In 1924, the Epiphany Church was promoted to the status of a cathedral, acting as a center for the Orthodox Church in China. Between 1926 and 1927, when Chinese factory workers voluntarily armed themselves and rebelled against the Chinese Nationalists (KMT), the Nationalist army looted and occupied Epiphany Church. However, the Shanghai Municipal Police (SMP, 1854–1943) protected and guided the clergy to safely leave the premises. Epiphany Church was closed in 1932.

Russian House Churches

The second Russian Orthodox church in Shanghai was Saint Nicholas Military Chapel (1922–34). Different from other Shanghai Russian churches, the chapel opened temporarily as a house church. The beginning of the church traces to 1922 when a lieutenant general led ten boatloads of displaced Russians from Vladivostok to find shelter in Shanghai. The Nationalist Party and the elite

Shanghailanders (people who resided in Shanghai who had foreign heritage) declined to grant entry for the Russian refugees. Only after the urgent plea of the general did the government allow three thousand people with no military background to land, and others went on to Manila in the Philippines. The White Russian refugees gathered at the residence of a Russian General Glebov for thirteen years.

Although most of the White Russian refugees resided near Epiphany Church, they gathered at the three house churches which evolved as the number of worshippers increased. One was on Jessfield Road (until 1924), the second one at 876 Avenue Joffre (1927–31), and the third at 929 Avenue Joffre (1931–?). The third house church held an icon of Nicholas II and venerated him as a martyr. Archpriest Alexander Pinyaev pastored the temporary house churches. Church members joined Saint Nicholas Church in 1934 when its construction was completed.

FIGURE 3.1 *Saint Nicholas Russian Orthodox church in Shanghai. Photo courtesy of Susangeline Patrick, 2008.*

Other Russian Orthodox Churches

The Russian Orthodox communities built eight more permanent churches in Shanghai, including *Tihuan Tang* (Tihuan Church, 1924–48), which was built due to the large number of refugees and their need for a spiritual home. Tihuan Church acted as a chapel for the Shanghai Russian Commercial School. The fourth Russian Orthodox church in Shanghai was *Jiuzhu Tang* (Savior's Church, 1926–56), which lasted the longest among the ten Russian parishes. Soon after Savior's Church, the Shanghai bishop Simon Vinogradov rented a small upper room in Fuxing Road (No. 1233) as the temporary *Shengmu Tang* (Notre Dame Church), the fifth church which was active from 1927 until 1936. In 1930, wealthy Russian widow Litvinova donated a large sum of money to cover the cost of the Russian Girls' School's new Notre Dame Chapel (1930–48), counted as the sixth Orthodox church in Shanghai.

Harbin Russians in Shanghai

The Japanese occupation of Manchuria (northeastern provinces of China) in 1931 forced the Russians in Harbin to relocate to Shanghai, which became the second largest Russian settlement in China. Shanghai eventually replaced the northeastern city of Harbin as the most popular center for Russian immigrants[17] and Russian Orthodoxy influenced Shanghai further. The addition of Harbin Russians caused another Russian Orthodox church to be built in Shanghai as *Andelie Tang* (Church of the Archangel Gabriel, 1931–48). Bishop Vinogradov raised funds among the overseas Russians to build a wooden-structured church.

In 1932, the Japanese army attacked Shanghai and bombed Epiphany Church, and the Orthodox Community had to recover from the damage. Therefore, the creation of Saint Nicholas Church (1934–55) became symbolic of uplifting the spirit of the Orthodox community, as well as continuing as an extension of the previous house churches. The Russian community consecrated the church building in 1937. Church members also chose the name to honor Emperor Nicholas II. The church functioned as a cultural and religious center for the stateless Russians. Under the headquarters of Beijing, Shanghai's Orthodox Church became one of the four major dioceses, along with Harbin, Tianjin, and Xinjiang.

The Church of Our Lady Monastery conducted services from 1934 to 1948 as the ninth church. Later in 1936, Shanghai Orthodox Christians built the tenth and the last Orthodox church called *Shengmu datang* (Cathedral of Our Lady, 1936–62) after the Russian Communists bombed the Cathedral of Christ the Savior in Moscow. Bishop Simon Vinogradov participated in designing the cathedral in 1936. Alexander Reyer, a Shanghai Russian who built Cavendish Court and multiple factories, donated to the construction of the cathedral.[18]

The cathedral was active in charity-related works among the Russian refugees whose social status was low.

The Russian Orthodox community held a public and elaborate dedication of the cathedral in 1937. The Metropolitan Anthony appointed a newly consecrated Serbian-Ukrainian Orthodox bishop, later known as Saint John of Shanghai and San Francisco (Mikhail Borisovich Maximovitch, 1896–1966), to care for the diocese of Shanghai in 1934. Bishop John arrived in Shanghai from Serbia and acted as the bishop of Shanghai for the following twelve years. The cathedral was the last Orthodox church to close its doors prior to the Cultural Revolution.

All ten Russian Orthodox churches in Shanghai and the three house churches reveal a short life span as their functions were periodically disturbed. However, they also showed a pattern of resistance in the Russian Orthodox communities, especially in the accommodation of Russian Orthodox refugees. The Orthodox community displayed adaptability as they utilized house churches to deal with unstable sociopolitical situations. The churches carried symbolic meanings for their social and religious belongings. As the Russian Orthodox communities consisted of diverse socioeconomic backgrounds, the commonality of their Orthodox faith formed a communal bond that the wealthy donated money to support community members who struggled with poverty.

Russian Orthodox Women in Shanghai

Russian women played a significant role in the life of the Russian diaspora in Shanghai. Zhiganov's seminal album included Russian professional women in business, the arts, writing, medicine, and charitable activities.[19] Knyazeva points out that Zhivago's utopian depiction of the Shanghai Russians omitted "the widespread poverty, the rampant rates of prostitution, high rates of alcoholism, crime, and suicide among the Russians."[20] Among the Russian women in Shanghai, Orthodox nuns actively involved themselves with charity works to improve the living conditions of Shanghai Russians. In addition to the Orthodox women who worshipped at the ten Russian Orthodox parishes in the French Concession in Shanghai, the Orthodox women's monastic community actively served the Russians and Chinese in Shanghai. Mark Gamsa describes a nun named Rufina Kokoreva[21] (or Ruphina) who relocated her entire convent from Harbin to Shanghai in the 1930s.[22]

The Orthodox nuns gathered resources and subsequently prepared for both a convent and an orphanage. In 1935, the Shanghai Convent of the Vladimir Icon of the Most Holy Theotokos and Saint Olga's Orphanage were founded at the French Concession in Shanghai. The convent was built in memory of the Grand Duchess Olga Nikolaevna, daughter of Tsar Nicholas II.

Saint Olga's Orphanage only admitted orphaned Russian, Chinese, and Eurasian girls. After Prioress Rufina had become ill in 1937, Prioress Ariadna (1900–96)[23] took on the responsibilities of the Mother Superior, working with thirty-three sisters and lay women. The Russian and Chinese girls at the orphanage numbered between forty and fifty and the convent and orphanage relied on the generosity of philanthropists. Both the convent and orphanage functioned for fourteen years until they relocated to San Francisco in 1948.

Additionally, Prioress Matrona headed a second Orthodox Nunnery in Shanghai with fifteen Sisters, a different branch which originated from the Beijing Pokrov monastery.[24] Known as the Shanghai *dongzhengjiao xiunü de jiuji hui* (Shanghai Orthodox Nuns), the Sisters primarily organized charity works to assist the lives of Russian refugees and their adaptations to Shanghai life.

Ordinary Orthodox women's lives are usually less well-documented, but they have contributed to shaping the social and religious lives of Shanghai Orthodox. Piotr Adamek documents an Albazinian woman from Tianjin whose name is Luo Qin (Russian name: Anna Romanova, 1929–?) who went to Shanghai in 1935 and attended the Andreevskaâ Orphanage School with her brother. Luo was baptized at the school and moved to Beijing after the Cultural Revolution in 1966.[25] Adamek recognizes the contributions Orthodox women often made in family, church, and education without public acknowledgment and describes them as "nameless heroes."[26]

The lack of ecclesiastical recognition was in the context of the exclusion of women in the Orthodox priesthood attributed to the Orthodox interpretation that the Holy Tradition did not have women priests. The irony of the time was that the public celebrated professional Russian women who were a visible part of the Shanghai scene, but Russian Orthodox women's works were restrained. Despite the challenges, Shanghai Orthodox women navigated the restrictions and exercised leadership in convent life, education, and charity work.

Orthodox Ministries in Shanghai

Shanghai Orthodox education, charities, and medical work often complemented one another. Russian Orthodox private schools generally provided education for Russian children in Shanghai and as part of the Orthodox Church's educational ministry, the Russian Girls' School enrolled students between 1930 and 1948. The Russian Orthodox Confraternity supported all educational efforts in Shanghai. Kirill Chashchin documents twenty-one Shanghai Russians who served as the Shanghai Volunteer Corp in the 1930s and 1940s. The police were comprised of Russians from Siberia and Harbin who attended the Commercial School of the Russian Orthodox Confraternity.[27]

Orthodox orphanages in Shanghai provided literacy classes for children. Besides the orphanages organized by the Orthodox convent and nuns in Shanghai, Bishop John of Shanghai also founded Saint Tichon's orphanage, which took in boys. The initial small number of Russian orphans quickly grew to a hundred children with a new location on Pushi Road (now Changle, No. 770). A chapel and a clinic were attached to Saint Tichon's so the boys could have access to a religious life and medical care. By the time the orphanage closed, it had sheltered about 3,500 children.

For the poorest members of the Russian communities, medical treatment was a luxury. When Zhiganov fell sick and stayed at a Russian charity hospital in Shanghai, he described the "garbage-like soup and frozen in the unheated room, I felt deeply the poor emigrants' plight."[28] Zhiganov's civic duty obliged him to begin the Mutual Medical Assistance Society in 1928 so that "none of us would have to pawn his or her golden crucifix to pay the doctor anymore."[29] Despite a large member list on paper, the society was unable to sustain itself and dissolved in 1931.[30]

The Russian Orthodox Church sponsored a hospital of the Russian Orthodox Confraternity in Shanghai. Katya Knyazeva reports that the prosperous Russians donated to humanitarian work: "Endorsed by the Orthodox Church, military unions, and merchant associations, they offered shelter, meals, medical treatment, and education to disadvantaged compatriots."[31] In comparison to their Catholic and Protestant counterparts, the Orthodox in Shanghai did not develop into a comparable size of educational, charitable, and medical services, but nevertheless, they organized systems and correlating mechanisms that contributed to the survival of the diverse communities.

The Russian Orthodox did not create any religious publications in Shanghai. Two Russian daily newspapers circulated in Shanghai in the 1930s, one was *Shanghai Zaria* and the other *Slovo*.[32] As the first newspapers published in the Russian language in Shanghai, the third branch in China (after Harbin and Tianjin), *Shanghai Zaria* (Шанхайская заря) was inaugurated in 1925. Olga V. Lembich was both the owner and the publisher of *Shanghai Zaria* which became the largest Russian daily newspaper in the world. The Russian journalist Lev Valentinovich Arnoldov (1894–1957) was *Shanghai Zaria*'s first and main editor who was also a trustee of the foreign branch of YMCA in Shanghai. The Nationalist government forced *Shanghai Zaria* to close in 1945 because of its suspicion of the newspaper's potential collaboration with the Japanese government. Another major newspaper, *Слово* (*Slovo*, literally the Word), was published as a daily newspaper from 1929 to 1943.[33] The newspapers in Russian met the needs of the nostalgia of Shanghai Russians.[34] The papers mainly illustrated local and global events and stories of Russian life in Shanghai and acted as a platform for contacts among the Russian diaspora communities. They also revealed editors' and journalists' construed worldviews and values and did not particularly promote Russian Orthodoxy.

Russian Orthodox Paradoxical Identity

The Russian Orthodox identity is paradoxical in Shanghai. Several factors contributed to their struggles and internal conflicts. The Shanghai Russian Orthodox were part of the large "Russian" settlement in Shanghai. Vladimir Zhiganov (1896–1978) published the first ethnographical study of the Shanghai Russians in 1936. As an insider of the community, his *Russians in Shanghai*[35] richly illustrates the comprehensive aspect of life of "Little Russia" in Shanghai. The pan-Russian identity was formulated in the 1930s and 1940s in Shanghai. Katya Knyazeva shows that the Russian Empire included populations of "the Polish, Czech, Jewish, Greek, Latvian, Estonian, Lithuanian, German, Armenian, Georgian, Ukrainian, Tartar, Hungarian, and other ethnicities. When they converged in Shanghai, they considered themselves Russian, while simultaneously engaging in associations which varied along the lines of faith, ethnicity, and politics."[36] Many people from the Russian Empire were not necessarily Russian Orthodox and they identified with their Catholic, Protestant, or other faith in Shanghai.

Second, prejudice and bias ravaged the Russian Orthodox communities. Serbians, Greeks, and Ukrainians made up the Orthodox Church's demographic and they were often divided by ethnic boundaries. White Russians took an anti-semitic stance toward the Russian Jews and later other European Jews. and the Russian Orthodox religious faith became intricately linked with their political identity. The Orthodox religiosity amalgamated the diverse Orthodox communities and Saint John of Shanghai attempted to unite the Orthodox communities. During the Japanese occupation, he continued his visitations and pastoral care of members and in 1946, the Holy Synod of the Russian Orthodox Church outside of Russia appointed Saint John as the Archbishop of China. The second Shanghai bishop, Victor Sivyajin (1893–1966), also sought to lead the Orthodox adherents during chaotic circumstances.

Third, the ubiquitous status of Russians in Shanghai plays a key in understanding the complexities of the Russian Orthodox communities. They were both marginalized and privileged. White Russians, unlike the British, French, Americans, or other Europeans, did not have extraterritorial protection in Shanghai. The elite Europeans and Americans established a racial hierarchy where many Russians were placed at the bottom with some exceptions, such as the famed Russian writer Natalia Ilynia (1914–94). Stateless Russians in Shanghai struggled to obtain permanent status and to make a decent living as Shanghai Russians as a collective group did not have government backing or "represent international enterprises or national interests."[37] The refugee status did not exclude some occasional European privileges in semi-colonial Shanghai.

Shifting alliance to international politics for survival was also a feature of Russian life in Shanghai. When the Japanese gained control of Shanghai in 1937, they effectively arrested nationals of eight European and North American countries, but the former citizens of the Union of Soviet Socialist Republics (USSR, 1922–91) were not interned or stripped of their properties. Stateless Russians now allied themselves with Japan until 1945.[38] International events impacted the Shanghai Russians during wartime in the 1930s and 1940s and in 1941, when war between Germany and the USSR broke out, Russians in Shanghai held divided political opinions between the defeatist and the monarchist. The monarchist Russians in Shanghai viewed the Nazi invasion of Russia as a liberation of Bolshevik Russia.[39] Interestingly, after the USSR defeated Germany in May 1945, Shanghai Russians rejoiced and celebrated.[40] The White Russian Orthodox communities' paradoxical identity reflected their external and internal struggles for survival and how marginalization and privilege could co-exist.

Armenian Christians in Shanghai

Although smaller than the Russian Orthodox, Armenian Christians played a role in shaping the religious landscape of the city of Shanghai in the first half of the twentieth century. The National Archive of Armenia preserves a document titled *Resolution of the Echmiadzin Catholicosate regarding the Election of the Chairman of the Armenian Community in Harbin* for 1933–4 showing ninety Armenians in Shanghai.[41] Beginning in the late nineteenth century, the construction of the Chinese Eastern Railway under imperial Russia attracted Armenian workers from Syunick Province, Republic of Artsakh, and Russia to settle in Harbin, Shanghai, and Macau.[42] Although Armenian Christians were already present in Shanghai prior to 1900, their presence was only highlighted after the Armenian Genocide in modern-day Turkey.

During the First World War, the Republic of China officially welcomed Armenian refugees, who were fleeing from the Ottoman Empire's genocide of the Armenians, including building churches to accommodate the spiritual needs of the Armenian people. The most intensive persecution and massacres of the Armenians in the Ottoman Empire occurred between 1895 and 1914.[43] Armenians fled to the United States and the former USSR.

In 1910, the Armenian Relief Society in Shanghai organized the Armenian Club of Shanghai, which served as a social hub of humanitarian services for refugees escaping from the Ottoman Empire. The Shanghai-based newspaper *The North China Herald* (1850–1940s) published articles on the Turkish genocide of the Armenians and the community center which was opened in Shanghai. Most Armenians in Shanghai belonged to the Armenian Apostolic Church, which traces its ancient origin to 301 CE when Gregory the Illuminator converted King Tiridates III who declared Christianity to be the state religion of ancient Armenia.

Beginning in the 1910s, Armenians in Shanghai began to settle down and some built thriving businesses, such as the Tchakalian Brothers pastry shop. In E. G. Sergoyan's autobiography, he describes the context of the Armenian Club of Shanghai as "the most open and least regulated metropolis in the world"[44] in the early twentieth century. The later Bolshevik Revolution further generated another wave of forced Armenian migration. The Armenian Club also evolved to assist Armenians from Russian-occupied Armenia.

Armenian Apostolic Churches in Shanghai

Although Armenians in 1920s Shanghai did not establish an official church as did the Armenian community in the northeastern city of Harbin, Armenian scholar Khatchig Mouradian documents that the Shanghai Armenians used a two-story apartment building as a gathering place and a worship hall on Sundays.[45] The rented temporary setting allowed the Armenian Apostolic Church members to process the traumatic pain they endured from escaping the genocide. The gathering place in Shanghai also assisted survivors to recover and restore in exile.

Armenian pastors from Harbin and Vladivostok occasionally visited the Armenians in Shanghai. Sergoyan states that Rev. Assoghig Ghazarian arrived from Jerusalem to minister to the Armenian Church in Harbin beginning in 1937. Rev. Ghazarian made regular visits to preside over services with the Armenian congregation in Shanghai. The Armenian congregation occasionally used a corner of Saint Nicholas Orthodox Church because Father Ghazarian collaborated with the Russian Orthodox bishop Victor.[46] However, the infrequent visits of the priest were also supplemented and most of the services took place at the Armenian Social Club in Shanghai. Ghazarian became the archbishop of the Armenian Apostolic Church in Los Angeles thirty years later. Interestingly, some Armenian refugees in Los Angeles in the 1970s came from Harbin and Shanghai, including some people Ghazarian had pastored prior to the Second World War.[47]

A China-born Armenian daughter of a survivor, Virginia Meltickian, provided a wedding photo of Yervand and Nunia Markarian in 1942 in Shanghai.[48] Although Meltickian does not identify the name or precise location of the wedding, the photo appears to have been taken at the altar with two boys holding icons in an Armenian Apostolic church setting. It shows that the

Armenians in Shanghai transformed a public space into a religious one, linking their identity with their faith especially when they were living away from their homeland. Icons and other religious symbols accompanied their liturgical celebrations in knitting the socioreligious dimensions of their identity, binding the community together with hope through post-traumatic events.

Wars and Migration

During the Second World War, Armenians in China joined the resistance movement against the Japanese invasion, either with the Nationalist Party or the Communist Party, including fighting against the Japanese military in Shanghai. During the Japanese occupation of Shanghai (1931–45), some Shanghai-born Armenians relocated to the United States due to Japanese-instigated persecution and harassment. Shanghai Armenians mainly migrated to the Los Angeles area. Sheila Eileen Henry's dissertation states that the American Immigration Department recorded Armenians as "Asiatics."[49] Armenians settled or born in Shanghai and other parts of Asia could explain such identification. It was not a racial term in the 1930s but rather a categorization of the location in which migrants originated. The Armenian Immigration Project's primary material has identified Joseph Gabriel Azadian (1916) as a "student for priesthood" who moved to Mount Saint Michael, a Jesuit scholasticate (1915–68) in Spokane, Washington, in 1945.[50] Later in the 1960s, most Armenians in Shanghai fled to Central Asia, India, or San Francisco because of the systematic destruction of religious buildings, including the few Armenian gathering places in Shanghai.

Chinese Orthodox in Shanghai

Chinese leadership emerged in the Shanghai Orthodox Church in the 1930s. Daniel Bays reported that, by 1916, the Orthodox Church with the leadership of Bishop Innokentij Figurovskil counted six thousand Chinese Orthodox believers in China, mainly in Harbin, Shanghai, Henan, Hubei, and Xinjiang.[51] From 1916 to 1935, the Shanghai Russian Orthodox churches only had Russian priests but two major Orthodox organizations played a role in installing Chinese Orthodox leadership in Shanghai beginning in 1935. The Chinese Orthodox Brotherhood of Shanghai (COBS) was founded in 1935 and functioned as a religious organization.

Additionally, Archpriest Nikolai Li Xunyi sponsored the Chinese Orthodox Association (COA) of Shanghai in 1935. As a second-generation Orthodox believer from Beijing, Li was elected as secretary and advisor of the COA and he compiled the Chinese Orthodox Catechetical Prayer Book in 1948. After the closure of the Diocese of Shanghai in 1956, Li was transferred to Beijing.

Bishop John of Shanghai encouraged the establishment of the COA. Andrew Yu Hede (1867–1945) became the first president of the association and Elias Wen Zizheng (1896–2007) became the first vice president. Wen came from Beijing and attended the Russian Orthodox seminary in Beijing. After being a priest for twenty-one years in Beijing, he served as the rector at the Surety of Sinners, Russian Orthodox Cathedral in Shanghai.

Another major founding member and contributor was Yu Qiaqing (Anlilie Pavlovich Yu, 1867–1945), a renowned Ningbo-born businessperson in Shanghai and a rare example of an Orthodox believer. Apart from his successful banking career, Yu also presided over the COA for two years. The COA also founded a Russian-language school for Chinese children, which dissolved when the Japanese army fully took over Shanghai in 1937.

Conflict, Exile, Destruction, and Survival (1945–1970s)

The political leanings of the Shanghai Russian Orthodox Church caused an internal conflict in the 1940s. After the Second World War, the CCP began to rise to power during the Civil War. The official anti-Communist and anti-USSR stand of the Chinese Russian Orthodox Church began to concern the future of the church. The first Shanghai Russian exodus occurred when the Civil War broke out in China. Many Russian Orthodox left Shanghai and four of the seven churches were closed in 1948.

In 1946, Archbishop Victor (1893–1966) in Beijing acknowledged the leadership of the Russian Orthodox Church in Moscow. Orthodox communities in Shanghai were mainly anti-Communist due to their identity as White Russians who were exiled from the Bolshevik Revolution. Archbishop Victor's declaration caused a bitter split among the Orthodox in China. Victor Annsimof (1884–1962) in Harbin allied with the archbishop, but Bishop John in Shanghai and Bishop Philip Osopov in Tianjin still pledged loyalty to the Russian Orthodox Church outside of Russia. Unfortunately, the archbishop's pledge to the authorities of Moscow did not ultimately save the Russian Orthodox Church in China.

Conflict

Self-governance became the most divisive issue within the Russian Orthodox Church in China. After 1946, St. Nicholas and another church obeyed Beijing's

Archbishop Victor in Moscow. Bishop John of Shanghai led five churches, including the Shanghai Cathedral, to pledge allegiance to the Russian Orthodox Church outside of Russia. External international political actions also intensified the internal conflict. In 1947, the Russian government baited the overseas Russians in China with Russian citizenship under the condition of returning to Russia, but many Russian returnees were sent to Siberia. The Moscow Orthodox leaders popularized the concept of self-governance of the Chinese Russian Orthodox Church.

Conflicts culminated to the final mutual excommunication of the two sides of the Orthodox Church. In 1946, Archbishop Victor arrived in Shanghai from Beijing and tried to persuade Bishop John of Shanghai to follow the leadership of Moscow. Bishop John then accused Archbishop Victor of being part of the Communist Party and turned Victor over to the Nationalist government. As a result, Archbishop Victor was imprisoned in the Gulag in 1948. After the release of Victor, the archbishop excommunicated Bishop John of Shanghai and President Elias Wen Zizheng. Bishop John of Shanghai then excommunicated Archbishop Victor out of the Russian Orthodox Church.

Exile

The second wave of the Orthodox moving out of Shanghai took place right before the PRC declared the founding of a new China in 1949, with five thousand moving to Tubabao Island in the Philippines, but still four hundred Russians remained in Shanghai.[52] Bishop John in Shanghai and other Orthodox joined the refugee camp in Manila, the Philippines. Later, some of the Shanghai Orthodox, such as Bishop John of Shanghai and Father Wen Zizheng, moved to San Francisco, and others, including Bishop Philip, went to Australia. After 1949, the Moscow patriarchate took charge of all Orthodox believers in China.[53] Overseas Russians gradually left China in the 1950s and some Shanghai Russians who were former members of the KMT moved to Taiwan.[54]

Between 1949 and 1964, four hundred Shanghai Russians witnessed the dramatic changes in Shanghai. Zhivago reported that the portrait of Chairman Mao Zedong had replaced the icon of Saint Nicholas at the altar, and he interpreted the construction of a public bathroom across from the cathedral as a malicious act.[55] In 1953, only a few hundred Russian Orthodox were still in Shanghai. In 1954, two hundred Russians and seventy Chinese Orthodox believers were still active in Shanghai. On October 29, 1955, the Chinese government officially expelled all Russian Orthodox priests. The next year, the Patriarch in Moscow also ordered all Russian clergy to leave China.

Creation of the Chinese Autonomous Orthodox Church

The year 1957 marked a paradigm shift for the Orthodox Church not only in Shanghai but also in China, because the Chinese Autonomous Orthodox Church (CAOC) was created by gaining independence from the Russian Orthodox Church without breaking the communion.[56] With the permission of Chinese and Russian governments, Vasily Yao Fu'an (1888–1962) was appointed as the new Chinese bishop of the CAOC. The ceremony took place in Moscow on May 30, 1957.

In the Shanghai Cathedral, Li Fengci (1925–2016), Wang Quansheng (1924–2015), and Lu Yafu (1927–2017) took responsibility for church affairs from 1949 until the 1960s. In 1963, only eighty-six Orthodox believers were in Shanghai with forty-four Chinese Orthodox. The anti-religious zeal forced the last Orthodox church to close its doors after the death of Bishop Du Runchen in 1965.

Destruction

Epiphany Church had been bombed by the Japanese in 1932, Saint Nicholas Military Chapel closed in 1934, and Notre Dame Church was shut down by the Nationalist Party, four orthodox churches (Tihuan Church, Notre Dame Chapel at the Russian Girls' School, Andelie Church, and Our Lady at the Monastery) had already stopped worship by 1948, and three others (Saint Nicholas, Savior Church, and the cathedral) closed their doors in 1955, 1956, and 1962, respectively. During the Cultural Revolution (1966–76), young teenage students formed the Red Guards and labeled Russian Orthodoxy as *heijiao* (black religion), one of the old things which must be destroyed. By 1966, out of the seven orthodox churches, five of them did not survive the destruction of churches during the Cultural Revolution. Only Saint Nicholas and the Orthodox Cathedral survived.

Survival

Some Shanghai Orthodox priests and adherents chose to stay in Shanghai. Bishop Symeon Du Runchen (1886–1965) was the last Eastern Orthodox bishop in China. Prior to his appointment as the bishop of Shanghai in 1950, Bishop Du took on active missionary work in Chinese cities, including Shanghai. He led the Chinese Orthodox Church, an autonomous branch of the

Russian Orthodox Church, for fifteen years until his death in Shanghai. The Du family had Albazinian and Chinese heritage.

In 1950, Bishop Victor celebrated the consecration of five Chinese priests, which was an unprecedented event. Johann Du Likun (?–1965), Mihail Li Fengci (1925–2016), Anikitavah Wang Yunlin (?–1967), Nikita Li, and Ioann Luo received their official ordination as recognized by the Russian Orthodox Church. Four Chinese assistant priests, Fataled Mao Delu, Nicola Zhang Jumin, Fina Du Ensheng (1919–70), and Anthony Yao Anshun, also were ordained. Du Ensheng and Yao Anshun later became Orthodox priests. Such a consecration made a bold statement about the Orthodox ties between Russia and China.

The Chinese Orthodox priest Michael Wang Quansheng (1924–2015) also played a role in Orthodox history in Shanghai. Wang served as a priest in Shanghai, and he stayed in China as the only Chinese Orthodox priest when all others left Shanghai in the 1950s. At Pentecost in 2008, the Russian consulate in Shanghai hosted Divine Services and Father Wang attended a service for the first time after 1962 when the Chinese government stopped all Orthodox services. Patriarch Alexius II of Moscow awarded Father Wang the Venerable Sergius of Radonezh I degree in 2008. Evangelos Lu Yafu, a protodeacon in the Chinese Orthodox Church, also stayed in Shanghai. Deprived from communion, Lu attended the Holy Communion when another priest, Father Vladimir Boikov, visited Shanghai. In 2008, Lu received an award of the Venerable Sergius of Radonezh along with Father Wang.

Complicated Restoration (Post-1976)

The restoration and revival of Orthodoxy in Shanghai demonstrated complications. After sixty-one years of multiple uses as a warehouse, a laundry, a French restaurant and a Spanish tapas bar, a casino, and later a coffee house, Saint Nicholas Church briefly resurrected the building's sacred function by reconsecrating it during the Shanghai Expo in 2010. The church has then again been used as a bookstore called Sinan Books since 2019. Realizing the historical value of the church building, the bookstore built another interior structure to support and to preserve the integrity of the original church. The Shanghai city government also renovated the Orthodox Cathedral in 1988 and reopened it in 2013, but only to Russian passport holders. Since the definition of Russian is different from the historical "Russian," the access to the cathedral still poses a restriction to Chinese Orthodox believers and others who had religious connections to the Orthodox Church.

From 2002 to recent years, the Shanghai city government has adopted a tolerant attitude and practice toward Orthodoxy in China. The city government restored two Orthodox churches in Shanghai and made them into conference halls and an art gallery. In 2007, when some scholars discovered the fresco of the Trinity covered in heavy paint, the city government financially sponsored a project to restore the Orthodox icon.

The restoration of Orthodox churches also presents a hopeful picture. As a result of government policies moving toward openness and tolerance of religious practices, Chinese Orthodox priests obtained opportunities to move to other parishes in different regions in China. In 1984, the Harbin City government allowed the Orthodox Church in Harbin to reopen under Zhu Shipiao. The Shanghai priest Li Fengde went to assist Zhu from 1986 until 2000. However, the city government did not allow Li to be the succeeding priest after Zhu passed away in 2000. Several more recent official visits also contribute to the hopefulness of the Orthodox community in Shanghai. Archbishop Hilarion of Sydney (1948–2022) was the First Hierarch of the Russian Orthodox Church Outside of Russia to visit China. Metropolitan Hilarion maintained close contact with the Chinese Orthodox priests in China. In 2013, the Orthodox Cathedral in Shanghai celebrated its first Orthodox mass when Gilier visited from Moscow.

In the twenty-first century, a new group of Armenians in China reorganized themselves with a renewed interest in the history of Armenians in China. They named themselves as ChinaHay, a social network, beginning in 2013 with Vache Petrossian as the representative of Shanghai. On November 9, 2013, the Armenians in China officially opened the Jack and Julie Maxian Hong Kong Armenian Center, serving as a hub for Armenian cultural learning. The honored guests included Karekin II, the Supreme Patriarch and Catholicos of All Armenians, who blessed the altar in the center for future religious ceremonies. In 2017, ChinaHay met with Ambassador Manassarian in Shanghai. All these recent events illustrate a recovery of historical memories of the Shanghai Orthodox, and a realistic envisioning of the future.

Exiled Chinese Priests

Chinese Orthodox priest Elias Wen Zizheng served at the Holy Virgin Cathedral in San Francisco from 1957 until his death in 2007 and a small number of Chinese Orthodox priests relocated internationally to Australia. In 1999, Orthodox priest Li Fengci (1925–2016) moved to Cabramatta in Australia and pastored at the Holy Protection Church for seventeen years with the former Russian Orthodox believers from China. There is relatively little information about the details of their service as exiled Chinese Orthodox priests, but it does intrigue conversations about transnationalism and religion.

Shanghai Orthodox in the Twenty-First Century

Three major issues occupy the center stage of Orthodoxy in Shanghai in the context of China and global relations. Currently, the Chinese government recognizes the legitimacy of Catholicism, Protestantism, Islam, Buddhism, and Daoism as five major religions, which excludes Orthodoxy of any kind (Russian, Oriental, or Chinese branch). Although Catholicism and Protestantism are treated as separate religions, the legal status of the two denominations dispenses a public legitimacy which is not readily available for the Orthodox Christians in China.

The second major issue is the question of Chinese Orthodox priesthood for the future of Orthodoxy in China in the twenty-first century. In 2004, *Forum 18 News* expressed the uncertainty of whether Father Mikhail Wang Quansheng and Protodeacon Evangelos Lu Yafu in Shanghai, the only Chinese Orthodox clergy left in China, would be allowed to perform Orthodox services in the City of Shanghai.[57] The most historical Orthodox event post-1976 took place in the Russian embassy in Shanghai in 2008 when the Chinese government permitted Chinese Orthodox priests Wang Quansheng and Lu Yafu to participate in the Orthodox mass. Wang later attended the new dedication service in Hulunbeier City in Inner Mongolia in 2009 and the Easter service in Harbin in 2010. In Shanghai, Wang and Lu also participated in the St. Nicholas ceremonies in 2010 and 2012. In many ways, the Shanghai Orthodox faith almost circled back to its original state as there are currently no Chinese Orthodox priests after the passing of the former ones. A couple of dozen Chinese Orthodox believers reside in Shanghai with no official place to worship.

The Russian consulate in Shanghai has served as a place for the international Orthodox worshippers. For instance, Metropolitan Anthony of Chersonesus and Western Europe visited Shanghai in 2019 and held a divine liturgical service at the consulate.[58] Father Ioan Schelkov, the rector of the community, and deacon Sergiy Kalashnikov currently serve the congregation, so the visit was important to the congregation as an illustration of how to offer pastoral care for Orthodox believers in Shanghai, which remains an essential question. Some congregation members play a significant role in the legitimacy of Orthodox Christianity in Shanghai, such as M. Drozdov, chair of the World Coordinating Council of Russian Compatriots, and A. Semenov, vice chair of the Interregional Council of the Russian-Chinese Committee for Friendship.[59]

The third major challenge the Shanghai Orthodox face today is theological training in the twenty-first century. The global Orthodox community has some innovative ideas about utilizing the digital space to equip believers and Chinese American Orthodox Mitrophan Chin launched a virtual hub on the internet in the spring of 2014.[60] Based in the Boston area, Chin serves as the president of the Orthodox Fellowship of All Saints of China (OFASC) which provides rich liturgical resources in Chinese, English, and Russian. OFASC has also revived a historical journal titled the *Chinese Good News*, published in Chinese and English to reach a wider global audience. An online seminary in the Chinese language is forthcoming which would equip clergy and laity with seminary education.[61] The formation of the Center for Study of Orthodox Culture at the University of Shanghai in 2014 may provide some academic opportunities for students in China and Russia.

In sum, the Russian, Armenian, and Chinese Orthodox in Shanghai and beyond embody the complexity of diaspora, identity, conflict, and allegiance. The diverse memoirs and Orthodox activities reveal the varied interpretations of the Orthodox faith, and so the Orthodox presence in Shanghai merits further scholarly attention.

4

Indigenous Christians and Globalization

This chapter encapsulates the lives, events, and meanings of Indigenous cosmopolitan Christians in Shanghai. Chapter 1 has shown that the founding and organizing of Shanghai Catholicism depended on Indigenous leadership and participation from 1608 to the mid-nineteenth century and wrestled with French leadership until the 1950s. Chapter 2 has underscored the works and influence of Protestant missions in Shanghai. Chapter 3 has revealed that Russian and Chinese struggled with an autonomous Indigenous church with Indigenous priests. Therefore, the following section will highlight the Indigenizing efforts and lives of Catholics and Protestants from the nineteenth century to the 1950s.

I divide the exploration through four sections. Indigenous-initiated mission and churches reveal dynamic and interactive patterns of cultural exchange, sinicization, and globalization. The initial phase of the Indigenous Protestantism in Shanghai took root as the Indigenous consciousness emerged in the historical context of semi-colonialism from 1842 to 1912. The second section features elite cosmopolitan Shanghai Christians in their multidirectional participation in the Republic of China. The third section features Indigenous Christians in their rejection of Christian denominations and institutions from 1912 to the 1950s. The fourth phase features a transformation of the Shanghai churches from multifaceted to a bifurcation of Christians in the 1950s. Local Shanghai Christians connected with the foreign missions and independent Christians undertook an external and internal process of diverging into two streams. In the intensified spirit of anti-imperialism of the new China, some Christians further severed their ties with foreign Christian connections and formed the Three-Self Patriotic Movement (TSPM). Other Christians formed house churches where Christians secretively gathered and broke bread in homes. The bifurcation ended the ecclesiastical form of multiple denominations and further developed in the late decades to the two churches of the

Three-Self Church and House Church in Shanghai with significant theological incongruities and political divergences.

Stage One: Chinese Missionaries to Shanghai (1842–1912)

I must clarify the meaning of the term "Indigenous" in context. Indigeneity indicates sociocultural, political, and theological aspects. Indigenization of Christianity adopts and adapts local cultures and customs, and the political aspect of Indigenization concerns the administrative structure, power, and leadership. Theological Indigenization primarily focuses on sourcing theological meanings from native texts, philosophy, and ideology. Different Indigenous-initiated churches and organizations in China have used Indigenization in different ways.

Studies on the history of Christianity in nineteenth-century Shanghai primarily feature the Jesuit mission in Xujiahui. The Protestant missionary activities sometimes eclipse the vibrancy of Chinese Christians in Shanghai. Surprisingly, many European and North American Protestant missionaries and Chinese Christians attempted to initiate churches with Chinese leadership starting in the late nineteenth century. The first stage was training Chinese Christians to be missionaries to Shanghai. The theory and practice were two-directional. While European and North American missionaries in Shanghai worked to empower Chinese Christians in Shanghai, another fascinating experimentation was forming in the United States.

Cao, Song, and Wang as Missionaries

American Protestants attempted to send American-educated Chinese Christians to Shanghai as missionaries in the late nineteenth century. In Shanghai, Methodist missionaries Dr. J. Walter Lambuth and his wife initiated the idea of educating Chinese young boys in the United States and then sending them back to China as missionaries. Pioneer female medical doctor Dr. Li Yuin Tsao's minister father Tse Zeh Tsao (Cao Zishi, 1847–1902)[1] was one of the Lambuths' adopted children.[2] In 1859, Mrs. Lambuth took Cao to study at Macon, Georgia. Following Cao's baptism in 1861, he even enlisted and fought as C. K. Marshall in the Confederate Army throughout the American Civil War (1861–5).[3] During a Foreign Mission Conference, Tsao kindled a call to do mission work in his native China.[4] Tsao went to Shanghai in 1869 as a missionary. There he met Episcopal pastor Y. K. Yen's sister who was unusually educated. The couple moved from Shanghai to Suzhou, pastored a church, treated patients, and raised four sons and two daughters.[5] One son was later the secretary of the Shanghai YMCA.[6] All of the Tsao children later contributed to the Christian developments in China with their medical and educational skills.

The second such case of a Chinese missionary to Shanghai was Song Jiashu (Charlie Soong, 1861–1918), father of the famous Soong Sisters. Song was among one of the first Chinese-born missionaries to Shanghai who later turned into a revolutionist and a publisher. A Hainan native, Song had spent most of his life in Boston, Massachusetts, and later as a cabin boy on the *US Revenue Marine*. He became a Christian at Fifth Street Methodist Church in Wilmington, North Carolina and his pastor, Thomas Ricaud, conceived the idea of training Song to become a missionary to China. A tobacco tycoon and Methodist philanthropist, Julian Carr, sponsored Song's theological education at Trinity College (later Duke University) and then Vanderbilt University.

In 1886, Song went to Shanghai as a missionary. What was ironic was that Carr supported white supremacy and the Ku Klux Klan, but sponsored a Chinese Methodist. Carr advocated for women's suffrage movement, but openly celebrated violence against African Americans. Carr not only became the benefactor of Song's theological education, but he also further financed Song's Bible publishing business in Shanghai, and later even invested in Song's son-in-law, the father of modern China, Sun Yat-Sen's revolutions in 1911. As for Song, he quickly abandoned his missionary career and founded a thriving business. The dream of sending American-trained Chinese Christian missionaries to Shanghai dissolved.

Concurrently, some Protestant missionaries in Shanghai actively worked with Chinese people. Wang Tao (1828–97), the nineteenth-century publisher and reformer, presents a case of agency. His story traces to the LMS which operated a printing press in Shanghai from 1843 to 1863. The LMS had taken Shanghai as their headquarters. *Mohai Shuguan* (Mohai publishing house, literally the ocean of ink bookstore) was the earliest modern publishing house in Shanghai. It was the first to engage the Western type of movable printing structure and in adapting how to print Chinese characters stereotype. The stereotype equipment was powered by an ox cart on the outside of the printing room, utilizing a conveyor belt which came through gaps in the walls. Mohai also contributed to the first group of Chinese scholars of European studies such as Wang Tao and Li Shanlan. These "Occidentalist" scholars, along with missionaries and sinologists Joseph Edkins and Alexander Wylie (1815–87), translated many English books into Chinese, introducing politics, sciences, and religions of the West.

When Wang visited his father in Shanghai, he also visited with Walter Henry Medhurst and a few other LMS missionaries and the printing press they operated. Wang assisted Medhurst in translating the New Testament into Chinese and worked at the press from 1849 to 1863. Wang was baptized around 1854.[7] Steeped in the Chinese *literati* culture, Wang patronized courtesans[8] as his traditional education did not condemn such a lifestyle. He even wrote a detailed account which showed the dividing line between courtesans who sold their arts and prostitutes who sold their bodies.[9] During the Taiping Rebellion in the 1850s, Wang supported the overthrow of the Qing government. Having committed treason in written evidence, Wang sought refuge in Hong Kong. Still connected with the LMS, Wang formed a long-standing friendship with Scottish missionary James Legge (1815–97) and assisted Legge's translation of the Chinese classics. Eventually, Wang lived in Scotland (1867–70) and Hong Kong (1870–84) as a translator and newspaper publisher before he returned to Shanghai in 1884. Wang was a significant historical personality who advocated for Western education and formed part of China's reformist movement in the late nineteenth century. His life and works crossed significant geographical, literary, and religious boundaries.

Comparison with the Chinese College in Italy

The pattern of training native missionaries for China was not a novel idea of the nineteenth century. Pope Clement XII sanctioned *Collegio dei Cinesi* (Chinese College) in Naples, Italy, founded in 1732 and intended to train Chinese priests and then send them back as missionaries.[10] The innovative idea came from Matteo Ripa (1682–1746), a *Propaganda Fide* missionary in the Qing imperial court from 1711 to 1723. When Ripa returned to Italy in 1723, he brought four young Chinese, ranging in age from 10 to 22.[11] The four Chinese seminarians Giovanni Gu (*c.* 1700–63), Giovanni Yi (*c.* 1704–35), Phillipo Huang (*c.* 1711–76), and Lucio Wu (*c.* 1713–63) received their priestly ordinations. Gu, Yi, and Huang eventually returned to China as missionaries, but Wu ran away from the college and Ripa perceived Wu's behavior as a betrayal and severely punished Wu.[12]

The tragic ending did not stop the Chinese College from admitting more pupils from China as the later British Macartney diplomatic mission chose two ordained Chinese priests, Paul Ke Zongxiao and Jacob Li Zibao, as translators for the British embassy. Both Ke and Li were trained to be missionaries to China, and they spent almost two decades in Naples from 1773 to 1792.[13] The lives of Ke and Li fulfilled the original missionary vision of the Chinese College as Ke served in Zhili (Hebei) and Shandong and Li missionized in Gansu and Shaanxi.[14] Studying in Italy prepared the Chinese missionaries through first-hand experience in Europe and their intensive trainings in philosophy, theology,

Chinese, Italian, and Latin would further equip them to become cultural and religious ambassadors.

Ripa's traveling with the four Chinese youths to Italy in 1723 and Mrs. Lambuth's accompanying Cao to the United States in 1859 revealed similar attempts. The former became increasingly institutionalized, and the latter provided more space for individual discernment regarding one's calling in ministry. Protestant missionaries' attempts at training Chinese missionaries for Shanghai in the late nineteenth century worked together with sending foreign missionaries to China. In many cases, the foreign missionaries in China acted as the links for Chinese Christians to be educated in universities in the United States. Friendship between foreign missionaries and Chinese Christians further tied the webs of familial, social, and even political relations together, especially between China and the United States in the nineteenth century and the first half of the twentieth century.

Indigenous Colporteurs, Bible Women, and Educated Women

Indigenous colporteurs, Bible women, and educated women in Shanghai played a significant role in distributing Christian literature to the wider society. They became the feet of the gospel message and missionary photographs and magic lantern slides show visual documentations of Indigenous workers. Robert Grierson, a CIM missionary, documented a colporteur named Bing yie Yieh selling devotional literature in Shanghai in 1901.[15] Bible women received basic theological training and they worked with other girls and women to achieve literacy in reading and writing. Educated Chinese Christian women also contributed to the development of Christianity in Shanghai. At the turn of the twentieth century, universities and theological seminaries admitted Chinese female students with the requirement of them having natural feet because foot-binding was seen as a compromise to feudalism. The abolition of foot-binding afforded women more freedom to travel. Beginning in 1905, more Chinese female students studied in the United States and Japan.[16] When they returned, some of them became medical doctors or educators in Shanghai.

Some foreign Protestant missionaries in China expressed the idea of a Chinese church which would be independent and free of foreign control in the late nineteenth century. The missionary bishop William Jones Boone endeavored to translate the Bible and the Book of Common Prayer to make Christian texts accessible to the Chinese. He ordained the first Chinese Episcopal priests,[17] the first of which was Wong Kong Chai (1851–86) at the Diocese of Shanghai.[18] Scottish Presbyterian missionary

John Campbell (1849–1919) repeatedly urged fellow missionaries to build a united Indigenous church when he reported to the 1910 Edinburgh World Missionary Conference.[19]

Stage Two: Indigenous Christians in Republic Era Shanghai (1912–1950s)

The idea of Indigenous Christian leadership matured in the 1910s. The New Culture Movement (1910s–1920s) heavily criticized traditional values and promoted democracy, science, and egalitarian ideals. After the First World War broke out, Japan declared war on Germany and quickly annexed Manchuria while the German army occupied Shandong Province. In 1915, Japan pressured the first president of the Republic of China, Yuan Shikai (1859–1916) to sign the Twenty-One Demands that triggered a national anti-Japanese campaign which culminated in the May Fourth Movement in 1919.[20] Students from universities openly protested with strong anti-imperialism sentiment. This historical context set the tone for different types of Indigenous Christians and their participations in Shanghai. I argue that both Catholics and Protestants in Shanghai reflected and fostered a multidirectional participation of Indigenous Christian leadership. One type of Chinese Christian leadership took place by force in 1920s Shanghai. The second type of Christians helped to transform the social and political atmosphere of Shanghai.

Forced Chinese Christian Leadership

The forced Chinese Christian leadership in Shanghai was born out of the height of anti-Christian movements. In the 1920s, Shanghai, like many parts of China, went through a surge of Chinese nationalism with anti-Christian sentiments.[21] Social conditions of Japanese and British dominance, incompetent Nationalist governance, and economic disparagement often pressed workers to go on strike. In Shanghai, the largest student demonstration took place on May 30, 1925, known as the May Thirtieth Incident. The International Settlement police shot and killed thirteen demonstrators and wounded others and mission schools expelled students who participated in protests. Consequently, the May Thirtieth Incident triggered waves of anti-Christian movements. Out of the state and church struggles, some Christians sought unity and ecumenism. Diana Junio investigates the relation between the Nationalist government and the Church of Christ in China (CCC) and documents 120,000 members when the First General Council of the CCC was held in Shanghai on October 1, 1927.[22] Within two years, three thousand missionaries exited China, and mission schools, churches, and hospitals transitioned to Chinese staff.

Christians as Reformers

Christians in Shanghai helped with the democratic reform movement and China's struggle to modernize. Dr. Sun Yat Sen (Sun Zhongshan), a Christian, founded *Guomin dang*, the Nationalist Party, and the Republic of China.[23] During the early twentieth century, Christian organizations such as YWCA, YMCA, and leading Shanghai Christian elites such as the Methodist Song family and medical doctor Shi Meiyu (also known as Mary Stone) became instrumental in social reforms amid political turmoil.

Chinese YWCA and YMCA served as a place for Shanghai Christians to participate in social reform and political activism. The YWCA began in Shanghai in 1890 and members organized their first committee meeting in 1899. The Shanghai YWCA under the leadership of Grace Coppock (1882–1921) and Mary Ting (Ding Shujing, 1890–1936) first focused on non-Christian elite female students in Shanghai and then expanded their work to women who worked at factories, including Jews and White Russians.[24] The headquarters building cornerstone was carved with "ye shall know the truth, and the truth shall make you free" in 1932. Yan Huiqing, Song Yaoru, and Huang Zuoting founded the YMCA in Shanghai in 1900. After moving to several locations, they finally had a new building near the Baxian Bridge area in 1931. The YMCA organized students to serve wounded soldiers and refugees and even hosted a national carving exhibition in 1936. A separate YMCA location was built in 1928 for expatriates in Shanghai. The building mainly served as a facility for swimming, basketball playing, and gymnastics.

In April 1927, the KMT leader Chiang Kai-Shek (Jiang Jieshi) broke away from the First United Front, an alliance of the KMT and the CCP in their combined combat against the warlords.[25] Instead, Jiang collaborated with the notorious Du Yuesheng, the head of the Green Gang. Together, Duo and Jiang unleashed violent killings of people who were Communists or under the influence of communism. The KMT feared the CCP and their ideology of equality and the action of land reform. The eradication caused approximately 120,000 deaths in Shanghai alone, later known as the White Terror.[26] The massacre of the communists on the streets of Shanghai generated serious and long-lasting impacts for the trajectories of the city and nation's history. Some Christians felt the need to remedy the situation through social reform.

Shanghai served as a dynamic hub which connected Chinese Christian diplomats and military leaders. The father of acting premier of the Republic of

China Chengting Thomas Wang (1882–1961) shepherded an Anglican church near Shanghai, and Wang attended the mission school prior to his education in Tokyo, and the University of Michigan and Yale University in the United States. Wang briefly led the YMCA in Shanghai in 1911 and founded the Shanghai Brokerage House while serving as minister in various spheres in China's international relations.

Wang's Christian faith also heavily influenced Feng Yuxiang (1882–1948), who received baptism in the Methodist Episcopal Church in 1914. Feng integrated Christian ethics in his military discipline with the prohibition of prostitution, gambling, and opium trafficking. Controversially, Feng's religious intolerance ushered destructions of Buddhist and Daoist temples. Later, Feng and his army played a role in defending Shanghai from the Japanese forces in 1937. Feng even delivered a message at the chapel of the University of Shanghai advocating for compassion based on Matthew 15:32 and Mark 8:2 and called for human empathy and shared suffering.[27] Feng's wife, Li Dequan (1896–1972), who graduated from Beijing's Methodist Women's College, would later become the general secretary of the Beijing YWCA.[28] Although Li never set foot in Shanghai, she organized the Wartime Children Fostering Commission and helped to relieve the suffering of children and women during the Sino-Japanese War.

Additionally, Christians wrestled with the German ideology of communism and the Bolshevik Revolution in Russia. The philosophical ideas of Christianity and communism in Japanese-controlled Shanghai found their mutuality in the 1930s and 1940s. Students who had been influenced and radicalized with nationalism in the 1920s were struggling with the fate of the nation. The influential Liu family's sixth son Nianti (Leonardo, 1916–88) converted through the preaching of American Methodist evangelist E. Stanley Jones in Chongqi in 1937.[29] Liu contemplated on the different means and same goals of Christianity and communism and finally joined the communists in 1938.[30]

Young students in 1930s Shanghai could belong to both the YMCA and CCP-affiliated associations such as the Student Union. The Association of Shanghai Christian Student Fellowships officially sponsored *Lian sheng* (The United Voice) but the CCP Committee directed the publications and placed left-wing university students such as Ding Jingtang as editor of the magazine before Japanese troops took full control of Shanghai in 1941 and after the war ended in 1945.[31]

People who lived in 1920s and 1930s Shanghai struggled to make sense of the suffering and Christians from various denominations have offered different theologies of evil and suffering. The Green Gang under the leadership of Du Yuesheng were secret society members which controlled Shanghai's wealth and politics through the opium trade and other lucrative businesses. They not only ruled with fear, but they also joined the Nationalist army killing communist workers. Christiana Tsao speaks of her American Baptist teachers interpreting her as "blessed to live in the French Concession that year, somewhat distanced from the cruelties within the Chinese City."[32]

Pastors and Chinese Nationalism

Chinese pastors and evangelists wrestled with the changing internalization of Chinese nationalism and acted as important figures in the Republic of China (1912–49). Jiang Changchuan (1884–1958), a Shanghai native, was one of the first Chinese Methodist bishops. In 1912, Jiang graduated from the Dongwu University's seminary in Suzhou and from 1913 to 1917, he pastored at the then Moore Memorial Methodist Church (Mu'en Tang since 1958). From 1918 to 1920, he pastored in Huzhou and pastored Saint John's Church in Suzhou from 1920 to 1923. Then from 1923 to 1931, Jiang was the pastor at *Jinglin Tang* Methodist Church in Shanghai. When the Chinese Christian Council was founded in 1922, Jiang became the vice president. In 1927, Jiang refused to allow Jiang Jieshi and Song Meiling to have their wedding at the Jinglin Methodist Church. Only in 1930 did Jiang baptize Jiang Jieshi in the Song Residence at Ximuo Road and Jiang Jieshi's name was officially added to the Methodist Church. In 1939, a major Methodist conference was held in Kansas City, and Jiang represented China and attended the meeting. When Chinese Methodists held their first unified conference in Shanghai in 1941, Jiang and Chen Wenyuan became the bishops.

The political changes that marked the shift of Christianity in China came after 1950. In 1951, Bishop Jiang participated in an accusation movement that swept the churches. The movement took place in the context of CCP-initiated land reform, the Korean War, and the New China's oppression of the so-called anti-revolutionists. Jiang accused American Methodist missionaries Bishop Ralph A. Ward (Huang Ansu, 1882–1958), An Disheng, and Chinese Bishop Chen Wenyuan. On June 21, Bishop Jiang published an article titled *Kongsu Meijiang Liyong Weiligonghui qinlue zhongguo de zuixing* (accusing American Jiang's sinful use of the Methodist Church to invade China). In the article, Bishop Jiang accused Bishop Chen Wenyuan and listed three specific actions of how Chen had been aiding the Nationalist Party leader Jiang. Bishop Jiang also briefly stated his own oversight and swore to preserve the "purity" of the Methodist Church under the New China's leadership and directions. In 1954, when the Chinese Christianity Three-Self Patriotic Council formed in Shanghai, Bishop Jiang became the vice president. Jiang and other Chinese pastors reconciled their Christian faith with the TSPM.

Mission to Ethnic Minorities

Two Indigenous-founded cross-cultural mission organizations focused on reaching out to ethnic minorities in China. The Chinese Home Mission Society (CHMS) was formed in 1918 as an Indigenous and interdenominational mission. Seven Chinese Christians, Dr. Cheng Jingyi, a Manchu Christian, Dr. Shi Meiyu (Mary Stone), Cai Sujuan (Christina Tsai), Yu Rizhang (David Z. T. Yui), Dora Yu (Yu Cidu), Hu Suzhen, and Ding Limei, established CHMS to reach out to the ethnic minorities in southwestern China. As a result, Chinese Christians became missionaries to ethnic minorities who were identified as people who were yet to be reached by the Christian gospel.

One of the most outstanding Chinese missionaries in the early twentieth century was Chen Yuling (1886–1965), a female evangelist who served among the Miao ethnic minority people in Yunnan for twenty-five years. After the Sino-Japanese War broke out in 1937, one of the CHMS co-founders, Cheng Jingyi, and many of his Japanese Christian friends, worked on Christian unity between China and Japan. Cheng also had traveled to carry out mission work among ethnic minorities in Guizhou. Marina Wang explains both the contribution and complexity of how Chinese Christians viewed denominationalism as a Western product but the ecumenical consciousness of CHMS did not extend to Catholic or Eastern Orthodox churches.[33] Wang also points out the nuance of Han Chinese CHMS missionaries as cultural "insiders" and "outsiders" in their interactions with ethnic minority groups.[34]

The mission from Shanghai to Yunnan sustained longevity. Chinese journalist Liao Yiwu met a Shanghai Christian surgeon, Dr. Sun, in Yunnan in 2004. Dr. Sun gave up his lucrative medical career as the dean of a large medical school in Shanghai and chose to be a modern medical missionary in rural southwest China.[35] Liao observed another pattern of how foreign missionaries' work from a hundred years ago had translated the Christian faith into a local religion in the Yi villages and Miao villages in Yunnan: "Through the efforts of that foreign missionary, who had found a fertile ground in which to plant the seeds of faith, Christianity had taken root earlier than it had in other parts of China. Three or four generations later, Christianity was part of the heritage of each individual family and an integral part of local history."[36] Liao's interviewee Zhang Yingrong, a then 86-year-old church elder in the Yi village of Zehei, recounted how the CIM missionaries from Shanghai had labored among the Yi ethnic people who practiced shamanism 150 years ago.[37]

A second major Indigenous-initiated mission organization was the Shanghai-based Chinese Christian Mission (CCM) from 1945. Most of the missionaries in CCM came from Shandong Province which had spiritual revivals in the early twentieth century. Han Chinese missionaries studied the Uyghur language, and some served as medical missionaries among the Uyghur people in Xinjiang.[38] Although the Chinese government terminated the mission in the 1950s, it was the only significant Han Christian effort from Shanghai to intentionally carry out mission work among Muslims in the 1940s and 1950s.

Indigenous Catholic Struggles (1920s–1950s)

Shanghai Catholics in the early 1920s raised their consciousness of anti-imperialism and began to reject foreign leadership and establish independence. In 1929, the four Catholics He Lizhong, Zhang Xianting, Zhu Kongjia, and Ma Xiangbo (1840–1939) joined the Christian Indigenization movement. Ma Xiangbo founded Fudan University and other schools independent from the French Jesuits. While many Chinese Catholic leaders in Shanghai were also educated in European countries, they raised their awareness in the importance of the independence of Shanghai Catholic churches. For instance, the late bishop Aloysius Jin Luxian (1916–2013) was deeply aware of the issues with the Chinese Catholic Church's leadership not being in the hands of the Chinese people in the 1910s and 1920s.[39] He studied in France, Italy, Germany, Austria, and earned a PhD in the Pontificia Università Gregoriana in Rome in 1950.[40]

Bishop Jin maintained significant international connections, at the same time as he remonstrated with his personal history and insisted that he needed to return to China and care for the Catholic congregations: "I was Chinese, a Chinese believer. I ought to be a good pastor and return to care for them."[41] Bishop Jin later suffered imprisonment and house arrest. He had to wrestle with his own perplexity about the Congregation for the Propagation of the Faith absorbing the Shanghai Jesuit diocese's financial assets while the CCP did not confiscate properties of the diocese.[42]

Christians also confronted their theological understandings and occasionally navigated the cross-denominational spaces. Francis Hsu Cheng-ping (Xu Chengbin, 1920–73), the first ethnic Chinese Catholic bishop of Hong Kong, was born into a Methodist Episcopal family, a descendant of the Ming Catholic Xu Guangqi. His father Xu Kesheng was a Methodist who did business in insurance but also was the director general of the YMCA in Shanghai. Francis Xu studied journalism at Saint John's University in Shanghai from 1936 to 1940. He earned an MA at Oxford University, then became a professor in English at Nanjing Zhongyang University. In 1949, Xu converted to Catholicism and studied in Rome from 1955 to 1959. Xu's brother Xu Zhongyue (Immanuel Chung-Yueh Hsü, 1923–2005) earned his PhD at Harvard in 1954 and then taught at the University of California, Santa Barbara. His most famous book is *The Rise of Modern China*.

Catholic and Protestant Philanthropists

Business was another significant area Christians undertook. When the Protestant Beulah Chapel became influential in the 1920s, Chinese pastor Zhao Shiguang's preaching attracted Shanghai elites such as the business tycoon Bao Guochang. Bao was brother of the famed Bao Zhecai (1833–1895) who pastored the Pure Heart Church in southern Shanghai. As an influential businessman, Bao Guochang pioneered printing the Chinese Bible and Christian pamphlets.

Active Catholic philanthropists in Shanghai also asserted influence in business. Brian Martin assesses the political power rivalries of the notorious Green Gang in the 1920s and traces the extensive network of prominent Roman Catholic Chinese businessmen known as the "Gentry-Councillor Clique" (*Shendong Pai*).[43] All members of the Gentry studied in France because they were educated in the French Jesuit-operated schools in Shanghai. Catholic leaders such as Lu Bohong and Lu Zhiyao organized the Union for Chinese Catholic Action (UCCA, *Zhongguo Gongjiao Jinxing Hui*). Martin also lists Wu Zonglian, Lu Songhou, Zhu Yan, and Wei Tingrong as prominent members who promoted French interests in Shanghai.[44]

Chinese Christian Intellectuals

Chinese Catholics in Republic Era Shanghai contributed to the intellectual development in Shanghai. As a Catholic, Zhang Ruogu (1905–67) wrote extensively in the areas of art, plays, music, opera, guidebooks to the Sheshan Cathedral and the Vatican City, the orphans in China, a book on Ghandi, and the biography of Ma Xiangbo. Having graduated from the Jesuit Aurora University, Zhang taught art as a professor, became a journalist and editor for newspapers, and even interviewed Pope Pius XI (1857–1939) in Rome in 1933. Briefly stationed in Cuba (1930–2), Zhang traveled extensively in Europe and studied at the University of Leuven in Belgium, the oldest Catholic university founded in 1425. Zhang became the editor of the Catholic journal *Yishi bao* in Nanjing (1945–55) until his arrest and subsequent labor reform in the northeast. He persisted in his faith by chanting the rosary with other Catholic prisoners. The Shanghai People's High Court eventually revoked the original case judgment and released him.

Many exemplary Chinese Protestants served the church and academy and contributed to the richness of Shanghai Christianity. Ni Wenshan (1846–89) encountered British and American missionaries and became a Christian in 1859. Ni married Xu Yaomin (1848–1900), a descendant of the Ming Dynasty Catholic Xu Guangqi. Ni pastored Tian'an Church of the LMS for twenty-two years.

Chinese Christians in Shanghai contributed to printing Christian literature beginning at the end of the nineteenth century. In 1897, Xia Ruifang (1871–1914) and his brothers-in-law, Bao Xianchang and Bao Xian'en, and another business partner, Gao Fengchi, founded the first modern printing organization called *Shangwu Yinshu Guan* (The Commercial Press). Chen Qimei, part of the Green Gang, assassinated Xia in 1914. American-educated Chinese Christians contributed to publishing in English newspapers in Shanghai. Hollington Tong Xianguang (1887–1971), the later Chinese ambassador to Japan (1952–6) and the United States (1956–8), managed the largest English newspaper as the chief editor in Shanghai. Tong came from a Christian background.[45] He studied journalism at Park College and the University of Missouri, and later at Columbia University.

Prominent Chinese Christians contributed to theological education in Shanghai. Dong Jing'an (1875–1944) was the first Chinese professor in Hujiang University. Dong attended a Baptist elementary school founded by American missionary Josiah Ripley Goddard (1840–1913) and became a Christian at the age of fourteen. In 1901, Dong encountered another missionary Francis Johnstone White (1870–1959) and stayed at the seminary in Shaoxing from 1904 to 1906. Dong, White, and another American Baptist missionary, Robert Thomas Bryan, founded Shanghai Baptist Theological Seminary in 1906 and Dong began to lecture in 1911. Together with a Manchurian Christian leader Cheng Jingyi (1881–1939), Zhang Tingrong, and two other Chinese Christian leaders, Dong represented China and attended the World Missionary Conference in Edinburgh. After resigning from teaching at Hujiang College, Dong devoted himself to promoting literacy. He also contributed to the Ningbo Baptist presence in Shanghai.[46]

Indigenous Christian Women in Shanghai

Under the cultural movements of liberation, Christians participated in the Chinese women's suffrage movement in Shanghai. Christians in Shanghai were responsible for making the Nationalist Party adopt equal rights in the 1920s and 1930s. Wang Liming (1896–1970), an important leader in the Woman's Christian Temperance Union (WCTU) in China, transformed the Shanghai branch of the Women's Suffrage Association (WSA) into the Chinese Women's Suffrage Association.[47]

Chinese female Christian evangelists boldly stepped out of their restricted roles and traveled to share the gospel with others. Cai Sujuan (Christiana Tsai, 1890–1984) was a Nanjing-born Chinese evangelist and author. Aged sixteen, she attended *Mingde Nuzi Xuexiao* (Mingde School for Girls), founded by American Presbyterian missionary Charles Leaman. Cai became a Christian and later led fifty-five members of her family to Christ. She partnered with Charles Leaman's daughter, Mary Leaman, spreading the gospel. In 1921, Cai and Leaman gave sermons in the United States. Cai was even received by American president Warren G. Harding in an official White House visit. Cai worked as an evangelist in Shanghai and, in 1931, after contracting serious malaria and not getting treatment because of the Japanese invasion of China, Cai lost her eyesight and in 1949, Cai and Leaman moved to Lancaster, Pennsylvania. She wrote articles that attracted large numbers of people to come and visit her, including Billy Graham. Her book was published in 1953 titled *Queen of the Dark Chamber*.

Shanghai women evangelists dedicated themselves to the works of the Christian faith. I will highlight a few individuals in the following section. The first female evangelist Li Yuanru (1894–1969) originally came from Hubei. In 1917, she oversaw students at *Nanjing Nüzi Shifan Xuexiao* (Nanjing Female Normal School). The music teacher Cai Wenjuan led seventy-two out of two hundred students to Christianity, but it caused a stir among parents. Li, being anti-Christian, burned thirty Bibles that belonged to the students. In 1918, Li was influenced by Mary Leaman and accepted Christ, she was baptized in *Yanliao Fang Fuyin Tang* (Yanliao Gospel House). She became a full-time evangelist in 1920 and worked with her students and also taught at Jinling Women's Theological Seminary and edited *Lingguang bao* (Light of the Spirit) newspaper. In 1923, Li was invited by another Chinese evangelist Wang Zai to go to Fuzhou where she met Watchman Nee. Later she went to Nanjing and began to attend meetings, but when the Beifa army attacked Nanjing, Li and others had to move their publishing work to Shanghai. During the Sino-Japanese war, Li went to southeastern China for evangelization. She was responsible for publishing Nee's theological books and in 1956, Li and other Chinese evangelists Wang Peizhen, Zhang Yuzhi, and Lan Zhiyi were arrested in Shanghai. Li was sentenced to fifteen years in prison under the accusation of being a member of the anti-revolutionist group of Watchman Nee. She and another female evangelist Wang Peizhen were imprisoned in Tilan Qiao Prison for women. She died in prison in 1970.

Another significant woman evangelist from the Republic Era was Wang Peizhen (Peace Wang, 1844–1971), who was born to a lieutenant-general father. When she was young, her biological mother passed away and she was raised by her Japanese stepmother. Under the influence of a Chinese medical doctor and evangelist Shi Meiyu (Mary Stone), Wang became a Christian and joined the Baptist Church. In 1918, she was moved by Pentecostal leader Yu Cidu and she decided to dedicate her entire life to mission and evangelism. Her parents firmly objected, but she went against their will and attended Jinling Theological Seminary for Women. In 1921, after Wang graduated from the seminary, she preached in many provinces in China and received the nickname of China's female Spurgeon. In 1925, she preached in Yantan,

Shangdong, and as a result, the later evangelist Li Changshou became a Christian. She was against the TSPM and her attitude dissuaded many local churches from joining the movement because of their trust in Wang. She was arrested in 1956 and was heavily investigated. She lived in prison for fifteen years and was released in 1971, but shortly after that she passed away. Wang's extensive traveling, endurance, and influence continued to impact Christians in the following decades.

Chinese Christian women also occupied leadership roles in education and Christian organizations. Wu Yifang (1893–1985) was originally from Hubei province. In 1916, she entered *Jinling Nüzi Daxue* (Jinling University for Women) in Nanjing, Jiasu province. She was baptized in *Huai'en Tang* (Grace Church), a historical Baptist church in Shanghai in the same year. After graduating from Jinling, she taught at Beijing Female Normal University, then in 1921 she went to study abroad where she earned her PhD in biology at the University of Michigan. After returning to China, she became the first female president of Jinling University for Women. Not only did she make contributions to the educational world, but she also played a significant role in Chinese Christianity and was the president of *Zhonghua quanguo jidujiao xiejinhui* (National Christian Council of China) from 1935 to 1947.

Chinese women evangelists also suffered greatly. Zhang Pinhui (1902–71) was from Fuzhou. Zhang's father Zhang Ruzhou and two uncles became Christians when her father was studying in *Yike Daxue* (Medical University) in Tianjin. CMA missionary John Woodberry preached among students in 1895. In 1932, Zhang graduated with a master's degree in biology and she also became an active Christian. In 1934, she married Watchman Nee and worked as an evangelist. Zhang was arrested in 1956 but released the next year. During the Cultural Revolution from 1966 to 1976, she was frequently abused, paraded, and persecuted by the Red Guards. In 1971, she fell at home and was sent to the hospital, but no one would treat her. She died in the hallway of Zhongshan Hospital in Shanghai. Only in 1986 was her name restored by the police bureau in Shanghai. Chinese women's fervent faith also led them to persevere through their suffering for the sake of Christ.

Stage Three: Independent Indigenous Churches

Gaining financial independence without funds from overseas was a significant goal of many Protestant mission churches in the early twentieth century. For instance, the SBC in Shanghai supported Chinese-initiated churches on the self-support principles and by 1924, among the 172 SBC churches of 30,096 Christians in China, twenty-four were self-supporting with an overall 61 ordained Chinese pastors, 438 lay male native workers, and 186 lay women workers.[48] T. B. Ray also reported one Shanghai dialect-speaking church and another Mandarin-speaking church in the Central China field.[49] Their support for the vernacular aligned with their idea of more Indigenous autonomy.

At the beginning of the twentieth century, foreign missionaries continued to encourage churches in China to apply the three-self principles: self-sufficient, self-preaching, and self-pastoring. The initiation of Shanghai churches was born in the context of social and political chaos and a searching for a new direction. After the imperial system's stepping down, the new Republic of China experienced a yearning for democracy in the 1920s. Four significant movements emerged and spread in Shanghai: Bethel Mission (1920–30s), *Difang zhaohui yundong* (Local assemblies movement, 1926–present), True Jesus Church (1926–present), and *Lingliang Tang* (Bread of Life). Hundreds of Chinese Christian-founded churches formed a federation independent from mainline Protestant denominations. Edmond Tang summarizes these movements as "generally conservative . . . strongly proselytizing and often anti-ecumenical and anti-foreign."[50]

Bethel Mission

In 1920, a medical doctor Shi Meiyu (Mary Stone, 1873–1951) and American missionary Jennie V. Hughes (1874–1951) resigned from the Methodist Episcopal Church and began Bethel Mission in Shanghai. Bethel Mission first included Bethel Church and Bethel Hospital (1920–52) and later added Bethel High School (1922–50), Bethel Bible College (1925), and Bethel Orphanage in Shanghai. Bethel Church began in 1920 and had a second location in the French Concession. Bethel Church also expanded from Shanghai to Daming County in Hebei Province in 1930. Also in 1930, Bethel Bible College was renamed Bethel Bible Seminary where students would study for three years.[51] By 1934, Bethel Church in Shanghai had two foreign missionaries, five Chinese evangelists, and six hundred followers.

Chinese Christians in Shanghai between the 1920s and 1940s employed diverse methods in their evangelistic efforts. The Bethel Mission School produced some excellent alumni who carried out mission work. Ji Zhiwen (Andrew Gih, 1901–85) first joined the "Worldwide Evangelistic Band in 1928, led by George Rideout of Asbury College, Wilmore, Kentucky."[52] Ji, Nie Zhiying (Lincoln Nieh), Li Daorong, Lin Jingkang, and John Sung (Song Shangjie) organized the Bethel Worldwide Evangelistic Band in 1931. In the 1930s, both John Sung and Andrew Gih participated in Bethel Mission's evangelistic tours around the country. Gih went on to establish the Evangelize China Fellowship in 1947 and eventually developed the organization into a worldwide movement to bring the gospel to the Chinese diaspora.

Chinese Leaders in Mission Churches

Shen Zaichen (Tsae-seng Sing, 1861–1940) was the first Chinese assistant bishop in the Anglican Communion in Shanghai. His consecration in 1918, fifty-two years after the initial Anglicanism in Shanghai, marked a new beginning of Anglican leadership in the region. However, the Church of England usually appointed retired or suffragan bishops as assistant bishops who were subordinate to diocesan bishops and they did not hold jurisdictional roles or have cathedrals assigned to them.

Multiple new Indigenous churches began to spread all over China, including Shanghai, and Yu Zongzhou founded a Gospel of Grace Church (*Fuyin Tang*) in 1906. Female evangelists in Shanghai played a significant role in local churches and they generously opened their homes as gathering places. A medical doctor and evangelist Dr. Dora Yu (Yu Cidu, 1873–1933) also played a significant role in Pentecostalism in Shanghai. After being a missionary in Korea from 1897 until 1903, Yu returned to Shanghai. She gave up her medical career, rented a place in Hongkou as an independent church, and became an evangelist in 1904. Yu heavily influenced the birth of the local church movement.

Founded in Shanghai in 1924, the World Wide Revival Prayer Movement further nurtured local churches. Many church leaders across denominational lines gathered for the prayer meetings. Dr. Walter Lowrie from the American Northern Presbyterian Church, Dr. and Mrs. Robert Bryan from the American Southern Baptist, Dr. and Mrs. S. Woodbridge (American Southern Presbyterian Church), Ethel Woodberry and Ora Woodberry from CMA, Ruth Paxon, Edith Davis, Dora Yu, and Mary Stone, all were involved in the meetings, praying for revival around the world.

The Local Church Movement

Local assemblies related to Watchman Nee evolved into a movement in Shanghai after Nee first began local churches in Fuzhou in 1922. From 1927 to 1952, Nee and his two hundred colleagues centered in Shanghai and planted about seven hundred churches or gathering places across China. Jennifer Lin describes the Shanghai Christian Assembly: "[They] had no ties to missions, no affiliation with Protestant groups. They did not attend a church in the traditional sense but shared fellowship in a 'local church'."[53] The Shanghai Gospel Bookroom (1927–58) primarily published Nee's books circulating the concepts of the local church movement and the main editor, Yu Chenghua, also translated Brother Lawrence's *The Practice of the Presence of God* in 1937. In 1928, Wang's church rented a *Shikumen* (Jiangnan and British style) house on Hatong (Hardoon) Road in Wendeli.[54] Gradually, the number of attendees grew to a hundred. They rented three more adjacent buildings as the numbers swelled to four hundred people and the church gathered there for twenty years.

Financial Independence

Indigenous churches sought partnership with churches overseas but rejected financial assistance. Part of the reason was that the self-support principle had made an impression on the Indigenous churches and their leaderships. To be able to raise money on the local church's own terms would indicate the long-term health of the church. A second reason was that receiving financial assistance from overseas sometimes meant strings attached. For the Indigenous leadership to be independent from interference, local churches in Shanghai often relied on members from the congregation. For example, in 1933, Nee visited England and spoke to the Brethren Movement, known as the Plymouth Brethren.[55] The Plymouth Brethren suggested if Nee's church chose to follow beliefs and practices of the Plymouth Brethren, then they would provide funds for Nee's church in Shanghai. Nee rejected the idea.

The assemblies in Shanghai also followed a strict principle of tithing without public recognition. Another opportunity arose when an elderly woman believer in the congregation suggested her willingness to sell a parcel of land to the church at half price. The woman's daughter brought up that the condition for the church receiving the land was to erect a stele indicating her mother's contribution. However, the local Shanghai churches' elders insisted that tithing without recognition was a biblical principle. As a result, they did not build a new church.

The church persisted through war, including the Japanese invasion of Shanghai in 1937, and internal conflicts within the church. Indigenous churches made a clear distinction between the spiritual and the worldly almost resembling dualism. In 1942, the Shanghai church elders terminated Nee's leadership: Nee was involved with his brother's biomedical factory but the elders insisted that it was not "spiritual" for a church leader to be involved with what they perceived as worldly affairs. Shortly afterward, the Japanese shut down the church. After the defeat of the Japanese in the Second World War, Wang Peizhen and another leader, Yu Chenghua, invited prominent Chinese evangelist Li Changshou to revive the church. In 1947, the church numbered more than a thousand worshipers. They even installed more than ten loudspeakers. Christians from the local church donated 2,100 taels and the church purchased a residential house and converted to a church later known as Nanyang Church.

Nanyang Church

Nanyang Church (1948) is in Jing'an District with the capacity to host three thousand people. *Shanghai Fuyin Shufang* (The Gospel House of Shanghai, a publishing house) was also located here. In April 1948, the church restored Watchman Nee's leadership. The church experienced a revival and believers would parade on the streets of Shanghai to evangelize others. Another significant phenomenon was how the believers followed the model in the Book of Acts and donated their own properties to the church. Church members' generous actions created a shock in Shanghai and became well-known. Within a year, Christians numbered several thousands in this local church. According to the statistical record of the Chinese government, one-third of the Christians were intellectuals, mostly university students from Jiaotong University and Guofang Medical School. Contrary to the traditional interior styles of churches, Nanyang Church focused on simplicity and pragmatism. Like other Watchman Nee churches in Qingdao, Fuzhou, Nanjing, Beijing, and other cities, the church had no art or decoration, not even Christian symbols such as the cross.

Indigenous Leaders

Indigenous church leaders Watchman Nee, Zhang Yuzhi, Lan Zhiyi, Wang Peizhen, Li Yuanru (1894–1969), and Catholic bishop Gong Pinmei all had endured imprisonment in Tilan Qiao. Nee's wife Zhang Pinhui (1902–71) also contributed to the local church movement and her linguistic abilities helped her to publish Christian literature. During the Cultural Revolution, she refused to divorce Nee and as a result suffered significantly.

Lan Yizhi (1908–88) was one of the most prominent Indigenous church leaders. Originally from Jiangsu Province, Lan became a devout Christian at an early age. Known as a praying Christian on his knees, Lan opened an orphanage in Hankou and founded a church there. He served the Indigenous church with Zhang Yuzhi in Shanghai for about five years until his arrest. He spent more than ten years in a labor camp in Qinghai but never gave up his Christian faith and continued to be a fervent and generous evangelist.

The local churches movement also gained some converts from missionaries such as Thornton Stearns (1886–1967). Influenced by John Song and Watchman Nee, Stearns left the American Northern Presbyterian Church in 1932 and later became a significant leader in the local church movement in Ji'nan, Shandong. In the 1940s, Stearns worked as a physician at the Shanghai Red Cross, and Nee ordained him as an elder in the Shanghai local churches. After his imprisonment in a Japanese internment camp, Stearns returned to the

United States and continued to be involved with Chinese local church leaders such as Jiang Shoudao.

True Jesus Church

The True Jesus Church (*Zhen Yesu Jiaohui*) moved its general coordination board from Nanjing to Shanghai in 1926. The Apostolic Faith Mission in Shanghai also actively influenced other Pentecostal churches and leaders such as Zhang Lingsheng (1863–1935) who played a role in the True Jesus Church.[56] After biblical studies at the Shanghai Apostolic Faith Mission in 1909, Zhang received baptism there in 1910, and Norwegian-American missionary Bernt Berntsen (1863–1933) ordained Zhang in 1916. Founded in Beijing in 1917 by Wei Baoluo (1877–1919), the True Jesus Church joined the early Pentecostal movement in the 1900s, encouraging followers to receive the gift of the Holy Spirit, especially speaking in tongues. Ironically, these Indigenous and charismatic churches went against cultural indigenization because they viewed church as a drastic discontinuity from culture. When the Nationalist government under Jiang Jieshi ruled China from 1928 to 1949, the True Jesus Church maintained a constructive cooperation with the government.[57]

Bread of Life

The Bread of Life Church (*Lingliang Tang*) traces its origin to Shanghai in 1942. The founder, Timothy Dzao (Zhao Shiguang, 1908–73), came from a CMA background. Zhao was born in Shanghai and learned about Christianity from school. In 1924, while still a high schooler, he was baptized at Moore Church (now Mu'en Tang). English missionary Paget Wilkes' Shanghai revival meeting in 1925 influenced Zhao. Zhao's wife Tang Ling'an also participated in evangelistic works. After his ordination 1932, Zhao received training at the Bible College of the Mission Alliance Society and then attended revival tours with the *Zhonghua guowai budao tuan* (Chinese Overseas Evangelistic Circle) in Southeast Asia in 1936.

When Zhao returned to Shanghai, he founded the Spiritual Bread Movement. The Bread of Life Church followed the three-self principle and emphasized the gifts of the Holy Spirit. It first started in the auditoriums of schools, and then as a house church at the Yan residence on Difeng Road. In 1947, 1,085 attendees began a charismatic movement in other parts of China, East Asia, and Southeast Asia. Zhao even conducted a revival with the famed Billy Graham in Germany.

Stage Four: Bifurcation of Shanghai Christians (1950s–present)

The issue of the self-supporting principle became a contesting point among Shanghai Christians in the 1950s. The TPSM accused the Catholic and Protestant churches of being imperialistic despite the diverse positions among the churches. Religious changes in Shanghai occurred both in institutions such as churches and Christian universities and in individual lives. Assistant editor of *China Weekly Review*, Mary Barret, and Chun-chang Kiang sketched the curriculum alternation in Christian universities in Shanghai which added New Democracy and history of social development, historical materialism, and the Chinese Revolution.[58] The Shanghai Bureau of Higher Education recommended faculty to teach the newly added courses.[59] Both national and city authorities utilized the political ideologies of Marxism-Leninism to reform the faculty, personnel, and students in Christian universities.

Three-Self Patriotic Movement

In Shanghai, like the rest of China, the 1950s and 1960s became a turning point for Christian churches. From 1949 to 1951, the church experienced a limited or reduced religious freedom. They quickly adjusted to the new government's rules and participated in some of the anti-American parades, attended political classes, and even engaged with the accusation movement. They were still permitted to evangelize the public, so they experienced numerical growth.

The social-political situation changed as most churches had been incorporated into the three-self system. The only independent branches of the Chinese church were the *Yesu Jiating* (Jesus Family), *Zhen Yesu Jiaohui* (True Jesus Church), *Difang Jiaohui* (local churches), and Wang Mingdao's the Shi Family Alley Christian church in Beijing. The new Chinese government oppressed the Jesus Family church first. In April 1952, local authorities secretly arrested Watchman Nee in the northeast of China. Nee went missing for four years. Then in 1956, all church members in Shanghai were arrested. One elder Yu Chenghua died during investigation, and Wang Peizhen, Li Yuanru, Zhang Yuzhi, and Lan Yizhi were imprisoned in the Tilan Qiao Prison. Other Christian leaders such as Tang Shoulin, Ren Zhongxiang, and Zuo Furu joined the government-sanctioned Three-Self Church. In 1958, Nanyang Church was confiscated by the government to "assist the construction of socialism." It was first converted to a conference hall then, in 1976, it became Jing'an Gymnasium. Two other church buildings were converted back to residential buildings, beauty salons, and restaurants.

Many mission churches went through the transformation of pledging alliance to the state. Xin'en Tang, the British Inland Mission Church, also had a change of leadership after the *Kongsu* (Accusation) Movement which coerced Christians to accuse one another and surrender the names of the accused. In 1951, when CIM missionaries left, Yang Shaotang (1898–1969), the famous Chinese evangelist from Shanxi Province, took charge of it. In 1962, it was renamed as *Xin'en Tang* (New Grace Church). In 1966, the Red Guards labeled Yang as an anti-revolutionist (*fan geming*) and he was sent to a labor camp and monitored. Another mission church, Shanghai Community Church, was originally built by Americans in the 1920s. The vibrant interdenominational church had received many dignitaries and political figures such as Jimmy Carter, Archbishop of Canterbury George Carey, and Desmond Tutu. It also became a TSPM church which was widespread throughout Shanghai. Female pastors in the Three-Self Church usually received their theological training at the Jinlin Theological Seminary in Nanjing. Out of forty-four pastors, twelve are women. Lin Weici currently pastors at Mu'en Church. CCC and TSPM reported 2,500 believers at Hongde Church (Fitch Memorial Church) as of 2019.[60]

Ding Guangxun (1915–2012) played a significant role in the Three-Self Church movement in the 1950s.[61] Ding's maternal grandfather was an Episcopal priest and Ding earned a master's degree in theology from St. John's College in 1942 and was active in the YMCA. After five years of Christian service and studies in Canada, the US, and Switzerland, Ding joined the Three-Self movement in 1951. He also became the president of the Jinling Union

FIGURE 4.1 *A Sunday worship service at Mu'en Church, Shanghai. Photo courtesy of Susangeline Patrick, 2019.*

Theological Seminary in 1953. Ding actively promoted that Christianity in China should align with socialist ideologies.

The process of socializing and domesticating Christianity in Shanghai took effort from many Christian leaders and supporters. Wu Yaozong (1893–1979) was another prominent Three-Self leader. Originally from Guangzhou, Wu was educated at Union Theological Seminary and Columbia University in New York in the 1920s. He first went to Shanghai for a role at the YMCA and later, in 1950, Wu first drafted a document that recommended cutting off Chinese churches' contacts with oversea churches. In 1952, he organized the accusation movement forcing former mission churches to join the Three-Self movement. Ironically, Wu was sent to labor reform during the Cultural Revolution. He was regarded as a controversial figure, praised by the Chinese government but criticized by some Christians as a traitor. The mutual enmity between the TSPM and the House Church in Shanghai, like many parts of China, features the almost impossible-to-reconcile theological and political disparities from the 1950s until the present time.

House Church

The Cultural Revolution (1966–76) were strenuous years for Shanghai Christians who refused to join the TSPM. Some Chinese Christians have chosen to stay in China despite their suffering during the Cultural Revolution. Qu Xixian (1919–2008), a significant composer and a 1944 graduate of St. John's College in Shanghai, endured the traumatic events. While some Christians died, some other Christians suffered long terms of imprisonment or house arrest and survived.

Jie Li engages a palimpsest approach, a method similar to microhistory, in historical writing about the private life in Shanghai homes.[62] Li shows how Mrs. Zhang, the wife of the principal of the East City Middle School her mother attended, was a devout Christian. The survival story is stunning because Mrs. Zhang was a pastor's daughter who married a CCP member in the 1940s and was forbidden to teach her children anything related to Christianity during the Cultural Revolution. She did not attend church on Sundays but played hymns on her harmonica and prayed silently before meals.[63] Mrs. Zhang's adaptation represents how some Christians in Shanghai could ambiguously preserve their Christian faith. Ultimately, Christians as part of the House Church movement regard allegiance to Christ as more superior than commitment to state power, especially when the state or society marginalizes the church.

One interesting case study demonstrates the complexity of how the TSPM and House Church relate to each other. The political change compelled the SDA churches in Shanghai to join the TSPM. However, between 1951 and

1980, Chinese Adventist pastors and laity went through the trials of accusations of imperialism, loss of church properties, and restrictions of preaching. Some left the Adventist Church and others endured imprisonment. From the early 1980s, the religious tolerance of the government permitted the SDA churches to gradually recover. From 1989, the Shanghai SDA church began to hold services in Mu'en Church and called themselves Mu'en Adventist Church which is part of the Shanghai Christian Council and the TSPM. Although about five thousand Adventists were official members of Mu'en Adventist Church, other Shanghai Adventists prefer to worship in private homes. The biggest challenge modern Shanghai SDA churches face is not the government, but the lack of theological training among church leaders and laity. As a result, many misinterpretations of the Bible and SDA literature have resulted in disunity with non-SDA Christians and SDA's theological implications in the social and political spheres.

Both Christian theologians and the Chinese government use the same term, "sinicization" of Christianity. The meanings, actuality, and means of realization are different. The means of sinicization for the Three-Self churches are to reflect more Chinese characteristics and context via music, the arts, and other aspects of church life. In August 2022, a committee held a three-day meeting in making efforts to further revise and indigenize the styles, tunes, lyrics, and names of the Christian hymns.[64] On the other hand, Shanghai House Church's sinicization is to maintain freedom of inquiry without state interference. A major need for house churches in Shanghai is theological training and resources for church leaders and *tonggong* (co-workers).[65] The issue is two-fold because the lack of legal recognition prevents a widely distributed opportunity for theological studies. Paradoxically, many House Church leaders perceive theological education as superfluous.

The Shanghai city government has restored most Catholic and Protestant churches as TSPM churches. Mu'en Church reopened in 1979; Xin'en Church was restored on September 24, 1989, and they host a special Cantonese service; Qingxin Church was reopened in 1979. TSPM organized Christians from Hubei Church to worship at Jinglin Church and TSPM also rebuilt some church buildings such as *Jiayin Tang* (Good News Church) in Minhang District in October 2020. They also maintained other churches for non-religious purposes. For instance, although the Waitanyuan Project and architecture professor Qing Chang had restored and rebuilt the church building of Fitch Memorial Church, the church has become a place for social events. TSPM also owns the Hubei Church property and rents it out as a hotel and restaurant.

Christians in Shanghai aim to recover their Christian identities in the free-market economy after Shanghai was made the most important economic zone of China in 1979. In the twenty-first century, migration, traveling, and the internet have afforded and intensified the cultural and religious exchange between Shanghai and the world. Some Indigenous Chinese churches have morphed into cosmopolitan churches facing the pressure of sinicization and globalization. Paradoxically, the bifurcation of the Chinese church from the 1950s still follows us in the twenty-first century.

5

The Multicultural Church and Cosmopolitan Shanghai

From the beginning of the seventeenth century, a sense of cosmopolitan disposition was already forming and maturing. Chinese Catholics and European Jesuit missionaries in Shanghai mutually embodied a cross-cultural openness. Some Christians in the Shanghai of later centuries had also embodied multicultural and cosmopolitan attitudes. They exhibited capabilities and skills in languages and cultures. As shown in the first four chapters, historical Christians in Shanghai were not monolithic or homogenous. The recovering section of this chapter discusses the memories of under-discussed Japanese Christians, Korean Catholics and Protestants, and multicultural churches in twentieth-century Shanghai. The remaking section of this chapter shows how Protestant churches have refashioned themselves in the context of systematic and rapid urbanization in the twenty-first century. Japanese, American, Korean, and African Christians and others have made their temporary or long-term homes in Shanghai and young and educated Catholic and Protestant Christians in Shanghai have exercised upper mobility in many aspects of social reality.

I will offer an investigation of under-studied multicultural and multiethnic Christians in Shanghai. This chapter aims to reveal how the micro-communities and the larger social, cultural, and religious environment influence each other. Multiethnic churches do not always transform into multicultural churches and I will examine how prejudice and bias and common Christian endeavors play roles in including and excluding members from these multicultural churches in Shanghai.

Shanghai's cosmopolitan outlook as a global city is not a new product of the twenty-first century. As early as 1936, Shanghai was already established as one of the world's largest cities with a population of three million.[1] Its cosmopolitan nature is not only reflected by its residents from more than one hundred nations, but also by its churches collectively and individually. In 1937,

Peter Lefebvre used the term "cosmopolitan congregation" to describe the Sacred Heart Church and Parish. A Catholic priest, F. X. Farmer, was a former Methodist missionary who ministered to a large multicultural church of Chinese, Japanese, Portuguese from Macau, and other nationalities.[2] Helen Gilbert and Jacqueline Lo's definition of cosmopolitanism uses three categories: moral/ethical, legal/political, and cultural. I adapt and emphasize the cultural aspect of cosmopolitanism as "an attitude or disposition characterized by openness to divergent cultural influences, as well as a practice of navigating across cultural boundaries."[3]

Japanese Christians in Shanghai

The history of Japanese Christians in Shanghai is often under-played and neglected. As early as the late nineteenth century, some intellectual and religious exchange gradually took place in Shanghai. Interestingly, James Curtis Hepburn (1815–1911), an American missionary to Japan, and Ginkō Kishida (1833–1905), a Japanese co-founder of the first Japanese newspaper in China (1865), traveled to Shanghai and published the first Japanese–English dictionary at the American Presbyterian Mission Press.[4] Both China and Japan were actively dialoguing with social and political reform and negotiating with modernity. Shanghai's port city status induced further Sino-Japan exchange and conversations.

Early Sino-Japanese Exchange in Shanghai

Some Japanese who resided in Shanghai in the late nineteenth century viewed Christianity in a negative light. Kaijiro Nōtomi (pseudonym: Kaido, 1844–1918), a pioneer Japanese industrial artist who studied painting in Shanghai, recounted his confrontation with intellectual Chinese proselytizers who presented a heterodox work of Jesus to Nōtomi's colleague.[5] The encounter only deepened the Japanese diaspora's mistrust of Christianity. In the context of the Opium War and the pseudo-Christian Taiping Rebellion, Nōtomi and another shogunate delegate Hibino Teruhiro (1838–1912) both linked opium and Christianity as harmful to the stability of the state.[6]

In the early twentieth century, Japanese Christians affiliated themselves with the Shanghai YMCA and held a presence in Shanghai. According to Christian Henriot, Lu Shi, and Charlotte Aubrun, the Japanese population in Shanghai numbered 15,000 in 1920 and 19,500 in 1925.[7] A contemporary Japanese visitor Akutagawa observed that Japanese in Shanghai retained a distinct Japanese identity and refused to integrate with Shanghai. Lianying

Shan compares the Japanese accounts of Shanghai in the late nineteenth and early twentieth centuries. Shan interprets Akutagawa's travelogue as an "Orientalist depiction of Shanghai thus functions as a reaffirmation of the dominant values of modern Japan."[8] Another Japanese writer Muramatsu Shōfu's *Mato* published in 1924 had resulted in the nickname of Shanghai as the demonic city, filled with contradictions and excitements.

Resistance and Peacemaking

Japanese Christians played a significant role in peacemaking and political activism in war-torn Shanghai (1912–49). Kenzō Uchiyama (1885–1959) and his wife Miki Inoue, both Japanese Christians, moved to Shanghai in 1913. In 1917, Inoue founded the Uchiyama Bookstore (Neishan Bookstore, 1917–45) and Uchiyama joined her later, co-hosting as an intellectual salon for Chinese and Japanese writers, philosophers, and activists. Naoto Kato describes these intellectuals as "cosmopolitan individuals who continued to form ties with each other, even as their respective nation-states were wither at war, or did not have normalized diplomatic relations."[9] In light of the Japanese victory in the Russo-Japanese War and the Japanese control of Manchuria, Uchiyama viewed the Chinese as compatriots[10] and formulated his own sense of duty and responsibility in his early years in Shanghai.

The Uchiyama Bookstore specialized in Japanese-language books and Chinese intellectuals who studied in Japan and Japanese Christians frequented the store. Uchiyama arranged meetings for Japanese writer Tanizaki Jun'ichirō (1886–1965)[11] to meet with Tian Han, Guo Muoruo, and Ouyang Yuqian, who were well-versed in Japanese literature and spoke Japanese with a Tokyo accent.[12] *Keiseisha*, a publishing company in Japan, primarily published Christian literature and supplied all the books for the Uchiyama Bookstore in Shanghai.[13] Ibukiyama Tokuji was a member of the Japanese church in Shanghai and a regular customer at the Uchiyama Bookstore.[14] The Uchiyamas protected their Chinese friends such as Lu Xun and Kaiming Bookstore's owner Zhang Xichen from the Japanese authorities, they chose friendship over loyalty over government.

Like the Uchiyamas, many Japanese Christians in Shanghai responded to the Japanese government's expansionism with defiance and a pacifist stand. Part of the influence came from the Quakers in Japan. For Japanese Christians, the rise of Japanese nationalism conflicted with the universal *agape* (love) of Christ. With the rise of Chinese nationalism in Shanghai in the 1920s, Japanese Christians also faced the challenge of living in the liminal space as anti-Japanese protests followed Japanese expansions to Shandong, Manchuria, Shanghai, Nanjing, and other Chinese regions. After Miki Inoue's death and the closing of the Uchiyama Bookstore in 1945, the Nationalist government sent Uchiyama back to Japan. He went on to establish the Japan-China Friendship Association, undeterred with his commitment to promote peace and friendship between the two countries.

What is most extraordinary is that after more than a century of the original opening of the Uchiyama Bookstore, the Tianjin Publishing and Media Group acquired the Uchiyama family's permission and reopened the bookstore in Tianjin in 2021. The grandson of the renowned writer Lu Xun and daughter of another celebrated intellectual Guo Moruo, close friends of the Uchiyamas, attended the opening ceremony.[15] It is unclear if the Tianjin publishing company has any religious interest besides honoring the memory of the Uchiyamas who remained faithful friends and risked their own safety for their Chinese friends in Japanese-occupied Shanghai.

Korean Christians in Shanghai

Shanghai is historically and politically significant to both Korean Catholics and Protestants. Korean Catholics regard Shanghai as one of the most important pilgrimage sites because the first Korean martyr, Saint Andrew Kim Taegon (1821–46), received his ordination as a deacon from French bishop Jean-Joseph Jean Baptiste Ferréol (1808–53) on August 17, 1845, in Shanghai. Kim led French missionaries from Korea to Shanghai and then became a priest. In 1846, Ferréol wrote a letter to the Superior of the Foreign Missions in Paris and translated Kim's prison letter from Latin, recounting Kim's martyrdom, and last words: "It is for Him that I die. My immortal life is on the point of beginning. Become Christians if you wish to be happy after death, because God has eternal chastisements in store for those who have refused to know him."[16]

After Kim and 102 other Korean Christians' canonization in 1984,[17] Kim became a significant symbol linking Korean and Shanghai Catholics. Saint Andrew Kim's relic was installed and venerated in the old Jinjiaxiang Church (Immaculate Conception Church) in Pudong District, Shanghai. As of 2004, the church had attracted thirty pilgrimage tour groups of South Korean Catholics.[18] As of 2022, six hundred Korean Catholics worship at Jinjiaxiang Church where most of the members are businesspeople in Shanghai. They celebrate mass in the Korean language and a priest from Korea pastors the Korean Catholic congregation.

Korean Protestants and the Independence Movement

Shanghai holds a special place for the Korean independence movement (1895–1945). The Korean Provisional Government (KPG) in exile was founded in Shanghai in April 1919 when Korea was under Japanese colonial rule. Joong-Seok Seo analyzes the surge of Korea's national consciousness and states: "Political oppression and the policies of racial assimilation and *kominka* [to transform the Korean into Japanese] involving the suppression and denial of Korean history, Korean language, Korean tradition and the consciousness of the Korean people."[19] The Korean identity formation also took place among Korean diasporic communities in Siberia, Manchuria, Hawaii, and mainland United States.[20]

The KPG in Shanghai was a product of Japanese oppression and Korean nationalism. The awakened Korean consciousness manifested itself through social movements such as women's movements and the liberation of the *baekjeong* (outcasts)[21] in Korean society. These ongoing struggles culminated in the March 1st Movement in 1919 when Japanese police reacted with violence toward the unarmed and peaceful Korean demonstrators, "accounting for some 47,000 arrests, 7,500 deaths, and 16,000 injuries"[22] in Korea. The magnitude of the event triggered other revolutions and quickly inspired the formation of the KPG in Shanghai. It is important to note that sixteen of the thirty-three signatories of the Korean Declaration of Independence (1919) were Protestant Christians[23] and some came from what would later be known as North Korea.

Freedom Fighters and Transnationalism

The common cause for Korean independence united unlikely partners and transnational and interreligious collaborations. Korean Protestant leaders in the independence movement drew inspiration from a synthesis of Protestant ethics and modernity. Syngman Rhee, the first president of the KPG in 1919 and later the first president of the Republic of Korea in 1948, spent six years in Shanghai from 1919 until 1925, endeavoring to restore Korean independence. Educated in an American Methodist school in Seoul, Rhee's participation in the Korean independence movement was closely tied to not only Christianity, but a version of American Christianity that supported modernization. David Fields argues: "Rhee and the Korean independence movement used the ideology of the American mission, in its many forms, as an entrée into American foreign policy debates and as a means to shift American perceptions and policy toward Korea."[24] Therefore, the Korean Christians in Shanghai successfully delivered an American Protestant ideology of modernity. Korean Protestant Christians collaborated with fifteen leaders who came from Cheondoism (the Heavenly Way, an indigenous Korean religion), and two signers were Buddhists.[25]

A few American Jewish rabbis joined the transcontinental Korean cause and Rhee's Christianness can be seen through both his public speeches and private conversations. He advised the immigrant Jewish rabbi George

Benedict by affirming the active work of Christ in the rabbi and compelling Benedict to see the humanity of Christ in Christianity.[26] The Korean cause for independence from Japan also appealed to the unlikely supporters such as Jewish rabbis Benedict and Henry Berkowitz in Philadelphia.[27] Both rabbis advocated for the Korean cause and even spoke at Christian churches despite the short-term support.[28]

Faith and Political Actions

The Christian faith motivated Korean Christians' political actions in the early twentieth century. Korean Christian leaders in the independence movement interpreted the annexation of Korea to Japan as God's divine punishment for Korea's non-Christian religions and superstitions.[29] Their theological reasoning claimed that Christianity would turn around the fate of Korea, free from Japanese colonization and control. The KPG leaders also had to navigate through the opposition from some US-educated Christian leaders who supported Japanese aggression toward Korea and China in the 1920s and 1930s.[30]

From 1927 to 1945, Kim Ku (Kim Gu, 1876–1949) acted as the president of the KPG. Kim escaped after being imprisoned for killing a Japanese man. After his father passed away in 1900, Kim became a Christian convert and was baptized in 1903.[31] In Shanghai, Kim worked with hundreds of Koreans from Korea, Japan, Russia, the United States, and Europe, countering Japanese intelligence from the Japanese consulate in Shanghai.[32] French authorities in Shanghai provided some assistance and the American Presbyterian missionary couple George and Geraldine Fitch briefly sheltered Kim in their house in the French Concession.[33]

Ahn Changho (1878–1938), a Korean American Christian, became another key figure in the Korean independence movement. Born in present-day North Korea, Ahn converted to Protestantism through attending a Presbyterian mission school in Seoul named *Gusae Hakdang* (Save the World School). Ahn was arrested in Shanghai in 1932. Hong Jin (also known as Mano or Andre, 1877–1946) was the fourth president of the KPG and a practicing Christian. Kim Kyu-sik (1881–1950) studied with American Presbyterian missionary Horace Underwood at a young age and Kim was baptized as Johann and later earned academic degrees from Roanoke College in 1903 and Princeton University in 1904. After the Japanese annexation of Korea (1910), Kim was exiled to China where, in Shanghai, Kim Kyu-sik, Kim Won-bong, and Cho Soang organized the Korean National Revolutionary Party. Then from 1940 to 1947, Kim contributed to the Korean independence efforts as vice president of the KPG in Shanghai. Kim Kyu-sik and his wife Kim Sun-ae (aunt of Maria Kim) both raised national and international consciousness of Korean independence.

Several Korean Christian women such as Maria Kim (1891–1944) led Korean independence activism in Shanghai and beyond. Kim participated in an anti-Japanese protest and the March 1st Movement in Korea. After the Japanese government's detaining and torturing of her, Kim escaped to Shanghai with the help of American missionaries and continued to fight for Korean independence with other Christian activists in Shanghai. She even enrolled at Jinling College in Nanjing. In 1923, Kim studied at Park College in Missouri and the University of Chicago. Later, she studied theology in New York and continued to mobilize Korean women in the United States and then taught at Martha Wilson Seminary in Korea.[34] Korean Protestant Christians who were the key leaders of the Korea independence movement connected their Christian beliefs with the political goals of gaining independence from invasion and colonial rule and building a democratic society.

Cantonese Australian Christians in Shanghai

Rapid economic developments in early-twentieth-century Shanghai attracted Cantonese Australian Christians to carry out Christian ministries. Mei-fen Kuo highlights the previously little publicized remembrance of Chinese Australian women's pioneering work in cultivating "a new style of philanthropic sociability"[35] in Australia and China in the first half of the twentieth century. Some prominent Chinese Australian Christian women such as Mrs. Rose Quay supported Fujitang (Fujit Hall, Cantonese Union Church)[36] and schools, nurseries, and medical facilities in Shanghai.[37] The Cantonese Union Church also published the *Weekly Journal of Fujit Hall* (*Fuji tang hui we zhoukan*).

Another Chinese Australian pastor, Rev. Cheok Hong Cheong, spoke against race-based immigration to Australia and inspired the charitable works of Chinese Christian businesspeople known as Shanghai's Four Great Companies. Chinese Australian Christians formed the Cantonese Christian Church of Shanghai,[38] focusing on hometown-related networks. Denise Austin affirms the Chinese business Christians in early-twentieth-century Australia and links their Christian identity to their desire to impact society in both Australia and China.[39]

Under the influence of women's liberation, the Cantonese Australian Christians contributed to creating new employment for women through their businesses. Shanghai's Four Great Companies, Sincere (Xianshi, 1917), Wing On (Yong'an, 1918), Sun Sun (1926), and Da Sun (1936), and these businesses' profits, supported Shanghai Christian charities. Known as the father of Chinese department stores, Chinese Australian Christian Ma Ying-piu (Ma Yingbiao, 1860–1944) opened the Sincere Department Store, the first Chinese-owned department store in Hong Kong in 1900, and then a branch in Shanghai in 1917.

FIGURE 5.1 *The Wing On (Yong'an) department store (1918), opened by Cantonese Australian Christians, still stands on Nanjing Road in Shanghai. Photo courtesy of Susangeline Patrick, 2020.*

The five-storied store was the first to hire women as shop assistants to work in public which broke the convention of women as housewives.

Ma and his wife Fok Hing-tong (Huo Qingtang, 1872–1957) were also social reformers who attempted to abolish the *mui-tsai* system that exploited the young daughters of the poor in southern China. The purchasing of young girls as house servants, prostitutes, or concubines also existed in Shanghai.[40] Organizations such as the Anti-Mui Tsai Society in Hong Kong argued that the status and treatment of servant girls were like slaves.[41] Lady Fok directed the Chinese YWCA of Hong Kong (1920–8; 1948–57) and chaired the organization from 1920 to 1923.

Cantonese migration to Shanghai also generated an increase of Cantonese prostitutes[42] due to how prostitution in Shanghai functioned in a structure of class, wealth, and regionalism. Christian Henriot reports that the Cantonese population mostly resided in the Hongkou District and Cantonese courtesans and prostitutes moved to the area in the 1930s and 1940s.[43] Cantonese Christians continued to advocate for the dignity of young girls and women and fought against prostitution in Republic Era Shanghai.

Portuguese and Russian Catholics in Shanghai

Portuguese and Russian Catholics resided in Shanghai as part of the Catholic community in the early twentieth century and Christ the King Parish Church originally catered to Shanghai-born Portuguese business people. Wang Zhicheng conducted research on the Portuguese population in Shanghai[44] and found Portuguese students numbered 194 out of the 471 pupils from twenty-four foreign countries attending St. Francis Xavier's College in 1922.[45] By 1949, the Portuguese in Shanghai had blended with the local cultures due to their distance from Portugal for several generations. Most Portuguese of Shanghai spoke English, Shanghainese, and/or Mandarin. After the regime change, the Portuguese in Shanghai migrated to Macau, and were known as *Shanghai Puqiao* (Macanese from Shanghai).

Russian Catholic priest Archimandrite[46] Alexéjeff Nicola first arrived in Shanghai to establish a church. Peter Lefebvre reported the Russian Orthodox Church's "adverse propaganda" as the Russian Catholics attempted to celebrate mass in the Slav-Byzantine rite under Nicola and another Jesuit priest, V. Javorka.[47] Lefebvre also described the difficulties of the social conditions as "[v]ery involved marital cases, dire poverty and the extreme moral depression of the Russian youth,"[48] but maintained an optimistic tone in the progress of the 260 Russian Catholics and the possibility of a Russian school.

Prominent Chinese Catholics in Shanghai (1912–54)

Three main themes feature the Chinese Catholics in Shanghai. The first prominent characteristic of Shanghai Catholics is their cosmopolitanism and their ability to function in the multilingual world. Many of the old Shanghai Catholic families formed alliances through marriages. The Zhu family from Qingpu County and Ma and Lu families from Dantu County had clustered near the St. Francis Xavier Church after the Taiping Rebellion in the mid-nineteenth century. Other Catholic families are Zhou, Pan, Qin, Yao, and Shen in Zhuxiang near Dingshan Lake in Songjiang. These Chinese Catholic families intermarried with one another and maintained close relations to France as most of their children acquired the French language from priests and Catholic schools. Many of them were able to travel to Europe for education which in turn strengthened Sino-French exchange.

Second, Shanghai Catholic philanthropists formed the social elites but empowered the marginalized communities with their finances and charitable works. The two leaders, Zhu Zhiyao (1863–1955) and Lu Bohong (Joseph Lo Pa Hong, 1873–1937), traced their family heritage to the Shanghai Catholic families.[49] As a successful businessperson, Lu also became increasingly religious. He sponsored many churches, clinics, and schools such as the *Xin*

Puyu Tang, *Puci Liaoyang yuan*, Sacred Heart Hospital, China Public Hospital, and Jinke Middle School. He became the president of Catholic Action and contributed to charity works until his assassination in 1937. Baptized as Nicolas, Zhu received a Catholic education from the Jesuits. After making a fortune in shipping and other businesses, he donated land and funds to schools and hospitals. Zhu also partnered with Lu in prison ministry in the French Concession and even baptized prisoners who faced the death penalty. Lu and Zhu were two of the nineteen Chinese Catholic philanthropists who formed an alliance among themselves. They utilized their power and prestige to serve the most marginalized in Shanghai society.

Third, in addition to priesthood, Chinese Catholics in this era slowly took on higher-level ecclesiastical leadership. Zhu's brother Bishop Simon Zhu Kai-min (1868–1960) became one of the first six Chinese bishops in the Republic Era. Having joined the Jesuits in 1888, Zhu Kai-min received his title as a bishop in 1926. Bishop Zhu met with the important religious figures in Europe and Canada and during the Japanese invasion, he refused to collaborate with the Japanese government. In the 1950s, Zhu endured house arrest but his name and reputation were cleared in 1984. Throughout Bishop Zhu's life, he devoted himself to founding schools, hospitals, nurseries, and churches. From 1839 until 1998, Shanghai Catholics witnessed sixteen bishops. Prior to the nationalization of churches in the 1950s, the first three bishops came from Italy, and nine bishops were from France. Four Chinese bishops took on the leadership after 1950.

Chinese Protestant Women

As one of the most prestigious schools, McTyeire School graduated many notable alumni such as the Soong Sisters and Grace Zia Chu (1899–1999) who later taught at her alma mater after receiving an education from Wellesley College. Chu advocated for women's education as the vice president of the YWCA from 1942 to 1947 and later contributed to culinary skills in the United States. Some students became Christians while attending the school, such as Ding Maoying (Me-lung Ting, 1891–1969), who later received her medical training at the University of Michigan. From 1922 to 1950, Dr. Ding worked with orphans and unwanted Korean refugees who fled from Japan, and did vaccination and other relief work in Tianjin. She later continued to contribute to the field of medicine in various areas of the United States.[50]

The education of girls prepared a group of young women and enabled them to pursue incredible opportunities and accomplishments in the field of medicine in the early twentieth century. Li Yuin Tsao (1886–1922) was another extraordinary medical doctor who attained her early education at McTyeire in

Shanghai. Tsao came from a Methodist home and later received her training at the Woman's Medical College of Pennsylvania. After her successful internships in Chicago and St. Louis, Tsao actively worked as a physician and educator in Nanjing and Tianjin.[51]

The numerous girls' schools in Shanghai became a cradle for young women who later played significant roles in their fields in the United States post-1949. Pauline Woo Tsui (1920–2018) was another McTyeire and St. John's University graduate who later became a fervent advocate for Chinese American women in the United States. Another former student, Cecilia Sieu Ling Zung (Cheng Xiuling, 1903–78), made contributions to law, education, and writing in Shanghai and the United States.

Some of the graduates stepped into leadership roles in Shanghai and the United States. Another McTyeire graduate, Cheng Wanzhen (Zung Wei-tsung) attained her music education at North Carolina College for Women in Greensboro and a history degree from Smith College in 1919. From the early 1920s, Cheng, as the secretary of the YWCA[52] and the National Christian Council of China, worked tirelessly to abolish child labor in factories.[53] She also organized the Shanghai Suffrage Association in 1922 aiming to improve women's social status and working conditions. Cheng's capabilities led her to speak at the Second International Congress of Working Women and the International Labor Conference in Geneva in 1921 and even to tour factories in England so she could further the cause of stopping child labor exploitation. When she married W. Y. Chiu in 1926, she left the YWCA.

Young women's theological education was deemed an important task in Shanghai as well. To meet the need for Chinese women evangelists and their works in Shanghai, Newberry Bible School for Women and WU's Down Foundation Women's Bible School were the two theological schools for non-Christian women. The minutes from the General Assemblies in 1925 reported that Newberry's initial seventeen out of forty students became Christians and three became evangelists.[54] Protestant missionaries who were motivated by the women's suffrage movement contributed to endeavors in gender equality through education for girls and women. Bible women in Shanghai worked alongside missionaries in evangelistic works, conducting Bible classes, introducing literacy, and organizing mission societies and day schools. These activities are well-documented in church newspapers such as the *Christian Advocate* by the Methodist Episcopal Church.[55]

Transnationalism of Missionary Children

Although many Protestant missionaries in Shanghai were single female missionaries, Protestant missionary families presented the need to educate their children from the late nineteenth century until the 1950s. Some of the children became the first pupils of some of the nineteenth-century schools for children in Shanghai. At the end of the nineteenth century, a new model of missionary children's schools emerged as the Miss Jewell's Day School began in 1896. Missionary children's schools originally accommodated the children of foreign Protestant missionaries in Shanghai.

After the Qing Empire collapsed in 1911, more missionaries arrived in the area with more missionary children enrolled in the schools. Therefore, the Southern Presbyterian Church in the United States funded the Shanghai American School (SAS) in 1912. The school had kindergarten through high school. Student enrollment quickly grew from the initial thirty-eight to five hundred within eight years so the SAS added a second campus in 1923. The conditions at the school must have been comparably more comfortable than the missionary school in Pyongyang, Korea (now North Korea), in the 1930s. American medical missionaries Virginia and L. Nelson Bell (1894–1973) assessed the Pyeng Yang Foreign School to be more academically rigorous and Bible-based, so they sent their children to Pyongyang instead of the closer Shanghai.[56]

Schools for missionary children retained a connection between the missionaries' host society and their home country. Most missionary children would return to their parents' home country for university education, and some would later serve in Shanghai or other parts of China as missionaries. These schools provided a shared framework for missionary children to relate to one another as they formulated their own identity and transnationalism.

Adopted Children of Missionaries

A much-neglected study of Chinese Protestant mission history is the adopted children of missionaries. Regardless of the unofficial or official status of their adoption, the Chinese children lived with their foreign missionary parents and sometimes their foreign siblings. For example, James Ware and his wife had one adopted daughter. Although her name and her British siblings' names were not documented, the UCMS documented that the daughter studied in Nanjing Christian School for Girls and later became a gifted teacher.[57] Elijah and Eliza Bridgman adopted two young Chinese girls when they were in Guangzhou in 1845 and the Bridgmans took their daughters to Shanghai in 1847.[58] Adventist missionaries Olga and John Oss adopted three Chinese orphans,[59] but little research has surveyed and analyzed these early Protestant transnational adoptions.

Cross-cultural adoption in late-nineteenth and early-twentieth-century Shanghai was an authentic Christian response to care for the widows and orphans, but we have little qualitative or quantitative statistics to examine.

However, tracing missionary writings and the journeys adoptees made between 1890 and 1950s clarifies a much-neglected act of love and justice. Cross-cultural adoption also opened ways for the adoptees to acquire education.

Protestant Transnationalism

Protestant history in Shanghai exhibits transnationalism because of the extensive intercontinental traveling and networks of both missionaries and Chinese Christians. The 1907 China Centenary Missionary Conference in Shanghai commemorated the centennial Protestant mission in China and further revealed optimism in Christian mission and evangelism. More than one thousand Protestant missionaries attended the conference. Protestant missionaries in Shanghai may have differed in their theology from the Catholic missionaries in Shanghai, but some Protestant missionaries have become sinologists like their Catholic predecessors and contributed to scholarship in Europe and North America.

American missionaries to China in the early twentieth century served as an important link between Asia and North America. Most missionaries upon retirement or return to the United States continued to have important roles teaching courses about Asia or pastoring congregations. Missionaries have brought back knowledge and experience that has enriched the understanding of Americans.

Shanghai Christians of All Nations

Christian expatriates in Shanghai come from many places around the world in the twenty-first century, a trend showing similarity to a hundred years ago. From 1997 to 2017, Warren Kinne from the St. Columban Mission Society served as missionary in Shanghai for twenty years. As a priest, Kinne founded the You Dao Foundation to assist migrant workers. Kinne also mentored expatriates in their faith. Isabel, born in Hong Kong, testifies about how her faith grew in Shanghai and she subsequently started a grief ministry and a book club.[60] Yumei from Singapore spoke of gaining new perspectives from the Emmaus Retreat during 2012–15.[61]

Steve Sang-cheol Moon identifies the Shanghai Korean Community Church as a good model of a missional church with an emphasis on the kingdom of God and holistic learning and practice among Korean diaspora churches in 2010.[62] Sam Cho further discusses the Shanghai Korean Community Church's Shanghai Korean Business Forum (2007) which convened Korean and Korean

Chinese (*Chaoxian zu*) who were interested in the intersection of business and mission as a holistic way of sharing the kingdom of God through lifestyle, financial management, and other business activities.[63]

Evangelical churches in metropolitan Shanghai reveal cultural diversity, upper mobility, and transnationalism. Out of the official 2010 statistics of 162,481 foreign residents, 35,075 were Japanese, 24,358 Americans, and 21,073 Koreans.[64] Shanghai hosts five international fellowships. All five multicultural churches abide with Chinese law which states that only foreign passport holders including residents from Taiwan, Hong Kong, Macau, and Chinese citizens who hold permanent residency in foreign countries can worship in such international fellowships. Hasegawa Eiko's 2004 and 2005 interviews of Japanese women in Shanghai portray that Shanghai as a global city mediates a positive bilateral relationship between China and Japan and forges economic, social, and cultural ties.[65]

One of the largest churches is the Abundant Grace International Fellowship which meets at HongEn Church. Being English-spoken, the members of the congregations are from many different parts of the world. Senior Pastor John Willison had been a pastor at Kampala International Church in Uganda from 2005 to 2016 and was a 1988 graduate with a Master of Divinity from Trinity Evangelical Divinity School. The Abundant Grace International Fellowship provides Stephen Ministry for people who go through emotional difficulties. Theologically speaking, the church emphasizes the second coming of Christ and the gifts of the Holy Spirit.[66]

Shanghai Christian Fellowship has members from more than a hundred nationalities, and a pastor and staff from diverse cultural backgrounds. The church partners with various organizations locally and globally in community development and humanitarian work. Shanghai West International Fellowship is also a multidenominational church which offers a hospice ministry to Xujing hospital. The community outreach started in 2012 and is known is *Ai tongxing* (Journey with love). International Church Shanghai has six hundred weekly attendants. Thanksgiving English Fellowship also has vibrant programs for adults and youth.

Unexpected Ways

Generations of missionaries to Shanghai often discover unexpected opportunities to serve the church with the permission of the Chinese authorities. Lawrence Flynn, an ordained priest of the Maryknoll Fathers and Brothers from Massachusetts, encountered two such surprises. One was when the president of Fudan University invited Flynn, then an English teacher, to give a lecture on the Bible to students and faculty. A second opportunity was Bishop Jin Luxian opening the door for Flynn to become the first foreign priest to teach at the reopened regional Catholic seminary in Shanghai.[67] Shanghai has attracted and hosted international Christian public speakers: in August 2016, Australian evangelist Nick Vujicic held a large lecture and ten thousand people made up the audience, including people with disabilities.[68]

Sociologist Fenggang Yang reports more than a hundred government-approved Protestant churches in Shanghai and numerous house churches such as Shanghai Wanbang Mission Church.[69] As one of the largest urban churches, Wanbang Church regularly had twelve hundred worshippers. However, the *Gospel Herald* reported that Shanghai police had urged the church to stop gathering in February 2009 and began investigating four pastors, Cui Quan, Cu Longguo, Liu Quanqin, and Huang Yun. The church refused to join the government-approved three-self church and continued outdoor gatherings despite persecution for over a year. Since 2017, the Chinese government has been intentionally promoting Chinese culture and dichotomizing Christianity and labeling the religion as a foreign religion and a commercial activity. Churches and schools in China were forbidden to celebrate Christmas, although some churches still took risks and moved the celebrations to hotels and restaurants.

Christian Work with Children

Like Protestant mission through education in the first half of the twentieth century, foreign Protestant mission supplies education on a much smaller scale. The reason is that the well-equipped Chinese public school system in Shanghai meets the educational needs and still leaves space for children who enroll in international schools. The schools may have Christian teachers but the schools themselves are not attached to a local church. For example, the Lutheran Church–Missouri Synod operates Concordia International School Shanghai.

Many Christian programs such as the Shanghai Healing Home (2011) provides care for children on the margins. As a nonprofit organization, Shanghai Healing Home cares for orphaned children with medical needs. James and Christina Weidner served at Shanghai Healing Home from 2011 until 2016 when they moved to Taiwan. The Baobei Foundation works with children who have disabilities and local churches in Shanghai have partnered in providing social aid. Eleven churches collectively held bazaars to raise surgery funds for children in 2018.[70] Living as a religious minority in Shanghai, Christians have formed a collective identity and a sense of Christian kinship in how they relate to one another as brothers and sisters in Christ.

New Media and Covid-19

The Covid-19 pandemic starting in January 2020 has been pushing churches to adapt to new realities. While gathering in person was difficult, many churches in Shanghai expanded Christian presence on social media. The most recent Shanghai lockdown occurred from March to May 2022 and presented challenges for residents in Shanghai. Christians in Shanghai re-evaluated the importance of community and a "neighborology attitude." Christians from various churches signed up for voluntary services of disinfecting affected areas, distributing supplies, and assisting testing sites. Zhu Lijing, a recent East China Theological Seminary graduate, exemplifies such Christian participation.[71] Eva Chou, a Christian journalist based in Shanghai, also reports churches teaming up in helping their neighbors.[72]

Administrative measures for the Internet Religious Information Service began to re-enforce regulations of religious content online from March 1, 2022. Any Christian books, music, or Bible study is forbidden unless TSPM churches are operating online with a license. For instance, on April 12, 2022, well-known Christian website Jona Home was no longer accessible after being online for twenty-one years. Some other Christian websites have also closed for similar reasons. Additionally, government censorship of religious content also extends to Chinese social media platform Weixin (WeChat) and other group chats. Christians have been adapting to find alternative means such as acquiring a VPN to avoid being blocked.

A major theological theme that emerged from Shanghai Christians during lockdown was faith amid suffering and difficulties. A Christian named Karen reflected her faith from her mobile cabin hospital experience, emphasized a sense of connection with the 300,000 infected Covid patients, and the importance of the grace of God: "Yet when we are in pain and despair, our hearts are open, and we will truly seek God."[73]

Elderly people and migrant workers were the most vulnerable during the Shanghai lockdown. The elderly population in Shanghai encountered challenges because food and medicine delivery required access and skills in technology. Some domestic migrant workers were forced to be homeless because the lockdown prevented them from going back to their hometowns. As a result, Christians have actively found creative ways to provide much-needed help. They organized an online group on WeChat and shared information to care for others.[74]

Nonprofit Christian organizations have also played a role in the social welfare of Shanghai. The Shanghai Agape Foundation has partnered with other organizations such as the Aikang Cancer Rehabilitation Center to care for cancer survivors and offer spiritual guidance. Founded by Christian elder and deputy chairman of the Christian Affairs Council Chen Zhimin in 2015, Shanghai Agape Foundation has launched various projects in battling poverty and disease, such as the "Love Smile" Poverty Relief Fund for children with a cleft palate which began in 2017.

Diverse Languages in TSPM Churches

Given the patriotic standing of the TSPM churches, it is easy to perceive them as monolithic. Surprisingly, diverse languages among the TSPM churches are shaping them to be more multicultural. *Xin'en Tang* (New Grace Church) in Jing'an District hosts Cantonese services every Sunday afternoon. Christianity in Shanghai, like the rest of China, is full of complexities, while some churches are torn down, new churches are being built. While some Christians are being persecuted, some others are allowed to deliver public lectures and exert social influence.

Overall, the three-self church, house church, and international church movements make up the three types of contemporary churches in Shanghai. Three-self churches are open to both Chinese and foreign passport holders. House churches meanwhile often offer a liminal space for both Chinese and non-Chinese Christians who have an issue with the symbiotic relationship between the state and the official church. The Chinese government only permits foreign passport holders including residents from Macau, Hong Kong, and Taiwan to gather at international churches.

The dividing lines of political views and passport status have created some artificial segregation and an expatriate culture. In Marie Sander's ethnographic study of expatriate youth, she sheds light on how international schools often provide a map of foreign-run medical centers, churches, and restaurants which form the major nodes in expatriate life.[75] Sander views Turner's "safe havens"[76] metaphor as problematic, and instead she argues that the expatriate experience unifies the expatriate community and formulates an identity that "transcends the national, cultural and ethnic differences among the various expatriate communities in Shanghai."[77] However, in the case of international churches, the exclusion of Chinese passport holders in Shanghai, creates an "otherness" and separation with the majority of the residents. Returning Chinese Christian students or employees from other countries are still restricted to the international fellowship which may perpetuate the image of Christianity as foreign. Despite these challenges, diverse multiethnic and multicultural churches continue to seek creative ways and provide innovative Christian services in education, business, and charities.

The Central Role of Shanghai in Chinese Christianity

Beyond the multicultural and multiethnic characteristics of Shanghai Christianity, the city of Shanghai played three main central roles in the development of Chinese Christianity. First, Shanghai has been the headquarters of most Christian organizations, both historically and at the current time.[78] After the Edinburgh Missionary Conference, the National Christian Council of China formed in Shanghai in 1922 and promoted the unity of Chinese Protestants and foreign missionaries until its dissolution in 1950. The China Christian Council (*Zhongguo jidu jiao xiehui*, 1980) is also based in Shanghai.

Second, the urban and cosmopolitan nature of Shanghai Christians distinguished them from Christians in other regions in China. Daniel Bays argues that the rural and urban divide in Chinese Christianity is a distinctive characteristic.[79] However, in the highly urban Shanghai, the rural–urban divide of Christians does not describe how Christians interact with one another. The diversity in educational background and financial stability may guide the ways Shanghai Christians connect and gather in fellowships.

Third, Christianity in Shanghai served as a force to modernize the city and China; consequentially, Christianity from the nineteenth century to the 1990s left an impression of the religion as a major symbol of Westernization and modernization. Urban intellectuals are attracted by tenets in Christianity, not necessarily because of its unique theological arguments, but due to cultural comparisons and moral persuasions.

6

Interreligious Encounters

This chapter provides a religious topography and outlines how Shanghai Christians as a religious minority have perceived their social and religious belonging and interacted with other religions and philosophies. I investigate whether Christians have sought ecumenicism and peaceful co-existence with other religions and diverse ideologies. This chapter examines the multiple perspectives of how Christians have approached other religious interlocutors in Shanghai.[1]

The first section of the chapter highlights how Shanghai Christians viewed and related to Daoism, Buddhism, and Chinese folk religions. The second section features Christian encounters with Muslims in Shanghai. The third section underscores Christian interactions with Freemasonry, Judaism, Nazism, Shintoism, and Sikhism in Shanghai. The final section brings attention to the challenges Christians face in dealing with cults and nonreligions in a pluralistic and postmodern society in the twenty-first century.

Christian Encounters with Daoism, Buddhism, and Chinese Folk Religions

The earliest Shanghai Christian encounters with different religions and philosophies began with the theological interpretations of Chinese Catholic converts and European Jesuit missionaries in China. First, the Chinese Catholics in seventeenth-century Shanghai came from the backgrounds of Daoism, Buddhism, Chinese folk religions, or neo-Confucian philosophy. Their own understanding of their previous religions provides the initial interreligious dialogue, thus becoming valuable aids to understanding how the first Chinese Catholics have negotiated the agreements and disagreements of both theoretical comparisons and folk practices.

Christians and Taoism

Some early Catholics encountered Daoist and Buddhist doctrines in superficial ways. As a child, Xu Guangqi encountered Daoism and studied at Longhua Buddhist Monastery for six years in Shanghai which may have provided a secular model of education.[2] However, his later commitment to Confucian philosophy prior to his conversion to Catholicism does not evidence his familiarity with Daoism and Buddhism. Erik Zücher argues that Xu criticized Buddhism and composed a polemical essay titled "A Refutation of Errors" (*Pi wang*) which only dealt with eight Buddhist superstitions from Xu's perspective, and Xu did not touch on the most fundamental doctrinal disagreements of divinity, transcendence, or the Mahâyâna ontology.[3] Many folk practitioners of Indigenous religions or Buddhism would have paid more attention to pragmatic daily concerns instead of doctrines or theologies.

A significant common space for Christians and Taoists, however, was about dreams and exorcism. The late-sixteenth-century Jesuit mission to China firmly believed in spiritual warfare and they produced significant missionary accounts of campaigning against the invisible demons manifested through other religions from the Jesuit perspective. António Vitor Ribeiro draws from the little-studied Portuguese source of the Jesuit missionary accounts in the seventeenth century from the *Biblioteca da Ajuda* (Ajuda Library) in Lisbon and shows how local Taoist frameworks and Christian mysteries have negotiated supernatural manifestations and interpretations. Among the accounts Ribeiro compared, three of them occurred in seventeenth-century Shanghai. One account was of a Christian boy whom the Jesuits reported as seeing a vision of ladders to heaven, conversing with his already dead Christian mother and sister, and then coming back to life after nearing death in 1641.[4]

A second narrative of Chinese Christian dreams and vision describes how a boy raised by a grandson of Xu Guangqi had resplendent light from his (the boy's) face after he received baptism in 1649.[5] A third account from the Jesuit archive in Lisbon came from Shanghai in 1656. The skeptical story depicts hell with thorns and retells how a reluctant Christian was chased by a group of demons and saw a Jesuit priest pointing to a church.[6] Jesuit missionary André Ferrão in Shanghai validated these accounts and defended them in 1656 citing that some cases of dreams and visions resembled similar types of stories approved by the Church and its contemporary Inquisition.[7] All three accounts point to the theme of change and transformation. A dream or vision in these accounts acts as a rite of passage and ultimately transports the participants to a place of the Catholic faith.

Shanghai Catholics in the seventeenth century tried to distinguish themselves from other religious faiths. They often viewed books or objects of other religions as idols and practiced burning ceremonies to demonstrate

FIGURE 6.1 *Affiliated with Taoism, the former folk temple Chenghuang Miao (City God Temple) stands near the Old Catholic Church (Jingyi Tang) in Shanghai. Photo courtesy of Susangeline Patrick, 2019.*

their allegiance to the Catholic faith.[8] Catholics did not share a unified attitude toward other religions and some showed interest in learning specific aspects about Daoism such as the ideas about the supernatural. Candida Xu's son Xu Zuanzeng, a Catholic, read and explicated Daoist concepts.[9] Candida interpreted his actions as weakening to his faith and ordered his other religious books to be burnt.[10] Shanghai Catholics in the seventeenth and later eighteenth centuries generally wrestled with a countercultural strictness of official church guidelines and abstained from what they viewed as superstitious.

Christians and Buddhism

Although Buddhism originated from India and spread to China via multidirectional traveling, people in Shanghai already viewed Buddhism as an Indigenous religion by the sixteenth century. Christians and Buddhists in Shanghai debated on the question concerning the origin of humanity and the world. One of the most important Chinese Catholics in the seventeenth century, Xu Guangqi, refuted the Pure Land branch of Buddhism which stated that human beings originated from lotus flowers:

> Even when the Lord on High [Jesus] was born into this world, he had to be born by the most virtuous and kind human being, the Holy Virgin Ma-li-ya

> [Mary], and not of some propitious clouds or lucky stars, so how much less possible is it (for anyone to be born) of a lotus flower? Besides, what do the Buddhists value more, lotus or human beings? If they hold lotus to be more valuable, why not just let lotus beget lotus? If they think human beings are still more precious, then why not have human beings reborn from immaculate humans, rather than from some lotus which has no senses?[11]

The second question of the afterlife is one of the most significant questions that dominated the Chinese quest. Matteo Ricci documented that Xu Guangqi held extensive conversations with Buddhists and other religious adherents and sought satisfying answers for why and how souls would enter heaven after death.[12] After becoming Christians, former Buddhists practiced a systematic destruction of Buddhist texts and objects. Qiong Zhang details the Jesuit iconoclasm against texts and objects from other religions such as smashing Buddhist idols or divination manuals.[13] Some Chinese Catholic converts displayed ritualistic objects and spontaneously and systematically replaced Buddhist items.[14] All of these actions aimed to institute their religious identity in a pluralistic society.

Buddhism in Shanghai became increasingly institutionalized at the beginning of the twentieth century. In 1918, Buddhist clergy, laity, and supporters founded a large center called Shanghai Buddhism *Jushi lin* located in Jing'an District. The center served as a place of learning for both traveling Buddhist clergy and interested local seekers. In 1930, Buddhist *jushi* (*upāsaka*) Wang Yiting and Li Jingwei founded publishing house Shanghai *Foxue shuju*, the largest for Buddhist literature. In the 1930s, non-Christian Chinese students enrolled in Christian-operated schools naturally blended their religious practice at home and their Christian discipline at school. In Christina Ching Tsao's autobiography, she attended the American Baptist-operated Elizabeth School for Girls in the Chinese area and recalled:

> At home, we followed our Chinese customs, observing ancestor worship and paying respect to the God of Heaven [*Yuhuang dadi*], the Goddess of Mercy [Guanyin], and the Kitchen God [Zao wangye] . . . But at school, we were subject to the discipline and education of our American Baptist teachers. We were taught to kneel down [kneel] in church, say prayers to the Christian God, and read aloud from the Bible.[15]

The operating and the measurement of success of mission schools often come from missionary writings and reports, and Tsao's reflection as an alumna offers insights on the reception and interpretation of the interactions of Christianity and folk Buddhism. In difficult situations, Tsao prayed to the Christian God, Buddha, and her ancestors.[16] Tsao eventually became a Catholic and found great comfort in her Catholic faith in Hong Kong.[17]

The "mix-and-match" approach to different religions in Shanghai was not a strange one in the early twentieth century. The well-known Baghdadi Jewish business tycoon Silas Hardoon married Luo Jialing, a devout Eurasian Buddhist. The blend of marriage also generated an open attitude in generously donating to both Buddhist temples and the Beth Aharon Synagogue.[18] Buddhism in Shanghai also grew out of education with the first Buddhist school Huayan in the 1940s and the second school called *Sheng Cang Mingzhi* University.

Shanghai Christians and Buddhists share some more recent suffering, both between the 1920s and 1940s, and the 1960s and 1970s. The narrative of the Nationalist Party's religious tolerance was rather wishful thinking. In 1930, Shanghai's Municipal Public Security Bureau listed a long survey of improper shrines and heterodox cults including Guanyin temples and Chan (Zen Buddhist) temples.[19] KMT essentially desired religions, clergies, and religious sites to serve the interest of the party-state. The impulse and tension to differentiate heterodoxy from orthodoxy has been in Chinese Christian history since the Jesuit mission in the late Ming Dynasty.

Shanghai Buddhism experienced a similar fate with Christianity during the Cultural Revolution (1966–76). Red Guards destroyed Buddhist literature and book collections at the publishing house and Buddhist clergy were oppressed or imprisoned. The Buddhist center *Jushi lin* resumed religious activities in 1987 and the Buddhist publishing house was restored in 1991. Like Christianity, Buddhism also showed a revival narrative at the end of the twentieth century.

Although Tibetan Buddhism is uncommon in the Shanghai area, Tibetan lamas occasionally visit Shanghai. My interviewee Joanna Gu's house church in Shanghai welcomed a Tibetan child-monk when he escaped from the monastery in Chengdu. The nine-year-old monk previously endured much beating when he could not chant the sutras. After the Christian church cared for him, he eventually went to Chengdu and joined other Tibetan Christians who converted to Christianity.[20] Joanna remarked on her amazement at the baptismal ceremony of Buddhist-backgrounded Christians in Chengdu. She viewed the local language as an important missiological tool in transmitting the Christian message. She remarked how the Han Christians in her church were assisted by British and American missionaries who spoke fluent Tibetan.[21] Some churches in Shanghai and other cities share this vision of taking the gospel to Buddhists in their families, community, and other regions.

Christians and Confucianism

A key issue in both Catholic and Protestant thought and praxis is how they have related to Confucianism. From the beginning of Shanghai Catholicism in

1608 until 2022, the question of how Christians interact with ancestral worship has been a point of debate and discrepancy as Christians have argued from different theological perspectives. Ancestral worship or the veneration of ancestors generally constituted a crucial component in filial piety from Confucian thought while Catholicism generally allows more theological accommodation to attend to ancestral worship.

Most Protestant missionaries in the nineteenth and twentieth centuries regarded Confucian philosophy as inferior and false. Arthur H. Smith (1845–1932), missionary of the ABCFM, wrote numerous books presenting his perceptions of China to English readers both in China and overseas. One of Smith's most influential books, *Chinese Characteristics*, depicted Confucianism as the root cause of all social vice including opium addiction, foot binding, infanticide, and concubinage in late-nineteenth-century China. Smith stated: "The most melancholy [melancholic] characteristic of the Chinese mind [is] its ready acceptance of a body without a soul, of a soul without a spirit, of a spirit without a life, of a cosmos without a cause, a Universe without God."[22] Additionally, Smith viewed Confucian philosophy as atheistic without recognizing the systematic oppression of women not perpetuated by Confucian thoughts or the British colonial strategy of inducing opium addiction to China as a way of imperial control. His book received a wide readership and influenced how foreign missionaries viewed social conditions.

Chinese Protestants in Shanghai overall abstained from participating in ancestral worship while enduring serious consequences of social and familial alienation and even criminal punishments. In 1877, the American Presbyterian Missionary Conference held in Shanghai stated that Chinese Christians should abstain from the annual customary offerings to ancestors.[23] M. T. Yates presented the seriousness and the necessity of ancestral worship in the Chinese system by explaining that for a Christian to repudiate ancestral worship impacts not only one's immediate family but also five generations.[24] Yates then provides an example of a Chinese Christian in Shanghai whose parents threatened to commit suicide so they could deter their only son from becoming a Christian.[25] Furthermore, their self-annihilation would inflict the most severe crime of murder on their son according to Qing imperial law.[26]

While the American Presbyterian mission recognized the tremendous complications and obstacles new Chinese Christians had to overcome in the late nineteenth century, Yates continued by referencing what he saw as five social and political ills attached to ancestral worship: the betrothal of children, polygamy, heavy tax on the veneration rite, the manufacturing of articles in ancestral worship, and the overcrowdings of the country due to one's fear of neglecting one's ancestral tombs.[27] Yates blamed ancestral worship as the root of all evil: "The result, is squalidness, vice, thefts, piracy and insurrection.

Hence they [Chinese who practice ancestral worship] devour each other while chained to the tombs of their ancestors."[28]

Protestant missionaries' exclusivist stance toward ancestral worship led them to expect Chinese Christians to drastically turn away from one's familial, social, political, and spiritual duties. Yates's stern warning called the conference attendees' attention to such postures and practice: "To supplement Christianity, and thereby make it more acceptable to the Chinese, by allowing, or conniving at *any* [Yates's emphasis] of the customs practiced in the worship of the dead, *is to yield everything*."[29]

Paradoxically, a significant number of Protestant missionaries from Europe and North America also contributed knowledge to how Christianity compares with other religions or philosophies in China. Ernst Faber (1839–99), a German Protestant missionary, wrote extensively about comparative religions. Faber first worked with the Rhenish Missionary Society in Guangzhou from 1864 until the early 1880s. Joining in the *Allgemeiner Evangelisch-Protestantischer Missionsverein* (General Evangelical Protestant Missionary Society) in 1885, Faber subsequently moved to Shanghai the next year and produced volumes on comparative religion and theology in German, English, and Chinese.

In his 1897 *Problems of Practical Christianity in China*, Faber exulted in his German Protestant ideals. Although he spoke against missionaries transplanting their denominational particularities to the mission field,[30] he criticized the sixteenth-century Jesuit missionary Matteo Ricci's cultural accommodation of Chinese custom regarding ancestral veneration.[31] Faber further surveyed six areas he viewed as irreconcilable with Protestant Christianity: language and literature, religion, superstition, domestic life, social life, and government.[32] He thoroughly investigated and compared many aspects of Chinese life and custom with his Christian ideas. For example, Faber viewed the keeping of long fingernails as a disgraceful idleness and suggested: "Theological seminaries and normal schools should require the learning of some trade as a fixed condition of graduation . . . to clip the long fingernails at baptism."[33] Faber's assessments revealed his extensive knowledge of everyday life in late-nineteenth-century Guangzhou and Shanghai, and at the same time, he held a stern attitude toward how some of the Chinese customs must be abolished. The legacy of the Christian exclusivist stance continued in most Protestant circles in twentieth-century Shanghai.

Christians and Islam in Shanghai

Although Islam has a long history in the region near Shanghai, its small percentage of adherents has gained little scholarly attention. Different from Buddhism and Christianity, Islam in Shanghai has primarily reserved the religious space for the adherents and occupies the public space with less access to tourists and spectators. Christians in Shanghai share some commonalities with Muslims. Both Christians and Muslims in the Shanghai area could trace a long history, although Islam is 230 years older than Christianity in Shanghai. Songjiang Mosque is the oldest mosque in the area having begun its construction in the 1360s during the Yuan Dynasty. The rulers of the Mongol Empire relocated Muslims further south, resulting in several key establishments of Islamic communities in southern China. Following the convention of the time, the building complex synthesized both traditional Arabic and Chinese architectural styles. Renovations in the following centuries continued to build on and to accommodate the worship, teaching, and ritualistic functions of Islam.

Although both Catholics and Muslims in Shanghai have co-existed since the early seventeenth century, very few historical records detailed how these two communities have related to one another. One historical event suggesting a potential troubled relation is the Chinese Muslim astronomer and official Yang Guangxian and his dispute with the Jesuit missionary Schall von Bell. Yang attacked Christianity in his *Bu deyi* (I Cannot Do Otherwise, 1664), showing Jesus as a criminal.[34] Seventeenth-century Catholics in Shanghai generally had an exclusivist vision of religion, regarding Christian teachings as the ultimate truth and path to salvation. Theological writings by one of the pillars of Chinese Christianity, Yang Tingyun, had evaluated different religions and regarded Christianity as the *Zhenjiao* (True Teaching). Seventeenth-century Chinese society, however, did not differentiate or oppose Christianity, Buddhism, Taoism, or Islam if the religion did not threaten the state orthodoxy.[35] While Christians and Muslims in Shanghai may have theological differences, they have some functional similarities due to the Chinese perceptions of religion and sociopolitical contexts in seventeenth-century Shanghai.

In many ways, Christians and Muslims in Shanghai almost exist as parallel communities with occasional encounters through the workspace. The second mosque, Fuyou Road Mosque, was built in 1870 embracing Arabic and Chinese building styles. Fuyou Mosque acted as the most important Islamic center dispensing political ideologies, Islamic culture, and spiritual formation for Muslims in Shanghai until the 1950s but then resumed religious activities in the 1970s. The third mosque, Shanghai Xiaotaoyuan (Little Peach Garden) Mosque, was built in 1917 in the urban center. The prayer hall has the capacity to host five hundred people for Friday Prayer, a library, and a display room with Islamic relics. The fifth mosque, Pudong Mosque, was built in 1935. Pudong and Jiangwan mosques are the only two mosques with dominant Arabic architectural characteristics. The Huxi Mosque was built after 1949.

A distinguishing feature is a female mosque known as Xiaotaoyuan Female Mosque which was built in 1920. Mosques built exclusively for women are common in China, such as the ones in Xi'an City, He'nan Province, and other cities tracing their history to the seventeenth century. Women's mosques in China also have their own female *imams* (clergy, known as *nü ahong* in Chinese) who are responsible for leading Muslim women in religious teaching and practice.

Most important, as religious minorities in Shanghai, both Christians and Muslims share a common wrestling with the tension between social and religious realities. Ahmad Atif Ahmad's 2007 seminar participation in Shanghai reveals that urbanization and the social pressures of material success are the main struggles for Muslims in Shanghai.[36] External and governmental guidelines expect both Christians and Muslims to *aiguo aijiao* (love the country and love the religion). Muslims and Christians in Shanghai can relate to one another in how they relate to the state. However, due to the Islamic extremists' militant religious movement in Xinjiang and its ties to Iran and other Central Asian countries after 2001,[37] the Chinese government closely monitors any real and potential disturbances among the Muslim communities across China, especially the Islamist nationalists' attempt to revive the nation of Turkestan in Xinjiang and bordering regions.[38] The government's investigation of people movement from Xinjiang to Shanghai has led to a few restrictions such as hotel registration and long-term work permits. As a result, some families of patients could not find lodging in the city. For instance, the Han Christian pastor and his wife at Joanna's house church in Shanghai took in a Muslim family for a month in the summer. When the Muslim family was returning to Xinjiang, they told the pastor's family, "Even though you did not mention anything about Christianity, we see Jesus in you."[39] In facing discrimination, Han Christians in Shanghai can form solidarity with Muslims. At the same time, how to maintain distinctive social and religious identity without alienation is a dilemma Christians and Muslims face in today's Shanghai.

Christians in Shanghai reveal more cultural and ethnic diversity. As a religious minority, Muslims in Shanghai practice what anthropologist Dru Gladney describes as "ethnoreligious"[40] practice in their blending of religion and ethnic identities. To face the challenges presented by a secular state and its socioeconomics, Shanghai Muslims respond with a focus on preserving the community with key symbols, principles, and activities. One's religious identity is closely linked with one's cultural heritage with little distinction. Mark Juergensmeyer analyzes Chinese Muslims' intentional effort to intertwine religious and ethnic identities as embracing religious values with a broader concern for the world, instead of a simple rejection of the secular.[41]

Another factor to consider is that the crossroads of Shanghai has attracted Muslims from Central Asia, West Asia, North America, and other places, which raises a two-directional consciousness. First, the global Muslim community, the *Umma*, is deeply embedded in Islamic theology. Muslims in Shanghai could relate to one another because of shared beliefs and practices. Second, cultural differences are not obliterated but heightened. Muslims in Shanghai thus find themselves in a dynamic dialogue about ethnoreligious allegiance, patriotism, and cultural unity and diversity.

Christians and Freemasonry, Judaism, and Nazism

Shanghai's cosmopolitan characteristic from 1842 until the 1950s is reflected through its diverse religious and ideological thought and movements. Freemasonry, Christian Scientism, Shintoism, Judaism, and even Nazism have actively shaped the intellectual, social, and religious landscape of Shanghai. Beginning soon after Shanghai's opening as a port city in 1842, Freemasons from Britain and the United States established over eleven branches in Shanghai in the next one hundred years. Most masons were white, male Protestants from the British Isles and the United States. The first masonic lodges called the Northern Lodge (1849), the Sussex Lodge (1863), and the Masonic Hall (1865) were being established in Shanghai.[42] The first two lodges and Tuscan Lodge funded the construction of the Bund, a famous tourist attraction on the Huangpu River. In Consul W. D. Medhurst's 1863 letter, he addressed the naming of the masonic hall to give consideration to how the ancient sage Mencius viewed the compass and square as symbols of order and propriety and therefore proposed *Guiju tang* as the appropriate name for masonic halls in China.[43] As a high degree mason himself, Medhurst provided the most comprehensive historical account of the masons in Shanghai.

As a secret society which originated in Scotland and was well-established in the United States, Freemasonry in Shanghai viewed itself as a natural and authentic expression of Protestantism. Freemasons constructed one of many characteristics of the Britishness or the Shanghailander's racial identity that separated them from the Chinese and other Europeans as shown in Maurice Tinkler's correspondence about his Masonic lodge in Shanghai.[44] F. M. Gratton listed 675 masons in Shanghai and northern China.[45]

Freemasonry in Shanghai adopted a racialized hierarchy and generally refused to admit Chinese masons except Chinese émigrés. John Fitzgerald and Mei-fen Kuo underline a Sydney-born Chinese Mason, William Yinson Lee (Li Yuanxin,1884–1965), who innovated charity in Shanghai from the 1920s through the 1940s, "participating actively in civic life . . . promoting trans-Pacific trade, and . . . recovering welfare sovereignty for modern China."[46] Freemasonry in Shanghai found a fertile soil to thrive in the early twentieth century because of the pre-existence and prevalence of Indigenous fraternities in Shanghai. However, Freemasonry is distinct from the Chinese Freemasons which is a misnomer referring to a Chinese fraternal entity *Tiandihui* (*Hongmen* or the Heaven and Earth Society) which has no connection with Freemasonry.

Christians and Judaism

Christians' encounters with Judaism in Shanghai have centered on drastically different approaches. Both Protestants and Catholics showed interest in investigating Judaism from a historical perspective. For instance, Bishop George Smith in Shanghai sent two Chinese Christians to Kaifeng to record inscriptions from the synagogue.[47] The Jesuits in the nineteenth century developed a much more scholarly interest in the Kaifeng Jews. A Jesuit sinologist from Spain, Jerónimo Tobar (1855–1917), was based in Shanghai for forty years. In 1900, Tobar published *Inscriptions juives de K'ai-fong-fou* (The Inscriptions of the Kaifeng Jews) in the Jesuit journal *Variétés sinologiques*.[48]

Jewish migration to Shanghai took on multiple waves. In the late 1840s, the first wave of migrating Sephardic Jewish businesspeople from Bombay and Baghdad took advantage of Shanghai as an open port and profited from the opium trade and real estate. The Sassoons from Baghdad migrated to Shanghai and used their fortune to invest more into buildings such as the Peace Hotel and a villa estate (now Cypress Hotel). The Kadoories, another Jewish family from Baghdad, built the Marble House on West Yan'an Road (now the Children's Palace).

Jewish synagogues numbered seven in Shanghai with Beth El in 1887 and She'erit Israel in 1900. The Shanghai Sephardic Jewish community centered their religious life around Ohel Rachel (House of Rachel), a synagogue built by Jacob Sassoon in honor of his mother Leah Sassoon in 1921. Rabbi Hirsch consecrated the synagogue with the sanctuary facing Jerusalem. Ohel Rachel also sprang into community life and provided a *mikveh* (ritual bath) and later the Shanghai Jewish School which enrolled students from many nationalities. A fourth Baghdadi synagogue is Beth Aharon built in 1927 with a large donation from Silas Aaron Hardoon. Maisie Meyer records the personal histories of Shanghai's Baghdadi Jews and states the marriage between a Jew and a non-Jew, or a Baghdadi Jew and an Ashkenazi, remained an anathema with some exceptions.[49] She also details how about 340 India-born Baghdadi Jews in Shanghai held British passports, thus were anglicized, but still suffered from British discrimination in Shanghai.[50]

Second, a Russian Jewish community also gradually formed in Shanghai. Russian Jewish soldiers settled in Shanghai after the Russo-Japanese War of 1904–5 and formally inaugurated the first Ashkenazi Russian synagogue in Shanghai in 1907.[51] The Bolshevik Revolution in 1917 generated the second wave of Russian Jews moving to Shanghai as refugees. Sam Moshinsky, a Russian Jew who was born in Shanghai, indicates that the Shanghai Ashkenazi Jewish Communal Association kept the birth certificates.[52] In 1926, Shanghai already had a Vladivostok Jewish community with Rabbi Meir Ashkenazi,[53] a friend of Moshinsky's parents, as the religious leader of the Russian Jewish congregation. After the Japanese invasion of Manchuria in 1931, the Russian Jews from Harbin sought safety in Shanghai.[54]

Although the Russian Jewish community first used the premise of the Baghdadi Jewish synagogue Sephardi She'erit Israel, the Russian Jews soon had their own building Ohel Moshe in 1927.[55] The Ohel Rachel Synagogue (Moxi Huitang, 1927), originally built by the Ashkenazi Jewish community, served as the social, cultural, and spiritual center of the Central Jewish refugees. For the minority ultra-orthodox Jews in Shanghai, Beth Aharon became a center for the study of the Torah. Rabbi Ashkenazi was responsible for the construction of the New Synagogue in the French Concession in 1941.[56] Mokinsky recalls the Russian Jewish community developing a school, a hospital, and a Talmud Torah study, a seniors' home, a ritual bathhouse for women called *mikveh*, a burial association known as the *Chevra Kadisha*, and a cemetery.[57]

The Russian Jews often suffered discrimination from the non-Jewish White Russians. White Russians in Shanghai generally earned a reputation for anti-semitism.[58] Diane Liu examines how the earlier history of the myth of Judeo-Bolshevism motivated Japan to send 70,000 troops in support of the White Russians in the Siberian Intervention (1918–22).[59] Furthermore, the Vichy government's anti-semitic policies impacted the French Concession in Shanghai in the 1940s. Following the reinforcement, the French-operated *École municipale* (Municipal School) ended the schooling of Jewish children.[60]

The third wave of Jews came from Central Europe fleeing Nazism, and Shanghai welcomed Jewish people who were stateless refugees. The 1938 Évian Conference held in France confirmed the refused entry of Jewish refugees to thirty-one countries except the Dominican Republic.[61] Latin America sought farmers, Australia claimed that any Jewish presence would disrupt racial uniformity, and other countries cited the labor market,[62] all viewing Jewish refugees as a problem which the international community was unwilling to solve. Japanese-controlled Shanghai and their initial benign attitude of accepting Jewish refugees may relate to their perceptions of the exaggerated myth of Jewish wealth.[63] Additionally, the influence and power the Sephardic Jews had established earlier had generated the openness of Japanese acceptance of Jewish refugees in Shanghai.

Between 1938 and 1940, Chinese consul-general Dr. Feng Shan Ho, based in Vienna at the time of the Anschluss, went against his superior's order and issued thousands of visas to Shanghai to Austrian Jews for them to escape from Nazi territory. After Adolf Hitler, Benito Mussolini, and Hideki Tojo signed

FIGURE 6.2 *Part of the surviving residential buildings in the Jewish quarter near Ohel Moshe Synagogue (1927) which served the Jewish community until the 1950s in Shanghai. Photo courtesy of Susangeline Patrick, 2008.*

the Tripartite Pact (the Berlin Pact) for military alliance in 1940, Japan shifted its attitude toward Jewish people in Japanese-controlled Shanghai. During the Japanese military invasion of Shanghai, Japan further collaborated with Germany, implemented the Final Solution of Shanghai (1943), and forced approximately 20,000 European Jews into living in designated ghettos. The European Jews who arrived in the 1930s and early 1940s did not live in the so-called Jewish Ghetto until 1943 when the Japanese authorities in Shanghai forcibly relocated the Jewish people into the 1.9 square kilometers. Irene Eber identifies the three Jewish groups not only as diverse in national origins, but also in their political and religious views, "especially within the Ashkenazi community . . . secular, observant, and ultra-religious."[64] Yaakov Libermann headed the *Betar* movement in Shanghai.

Apart from charitable works, Christians in Shanghai had little direct interaction with the approximately 20,000 Jewish refugees who escaped from concentration camps in Europe and found homes in Shanghai. Steve Hochstadt compares various reports on the number of Shanghai Jews and notes that Jewish refugees first came from Germany and Austria, and then Czechoslovakia, and Poland.[65] Jakob Rosenfeld (1903–52) was one of the more than four hundred doctors and dentists who fled to Shanghai. Originally from Lemberg in the Austro-Hungarian Empire (modern-day Lviv, Ukraine), Rosenfeld earned a doctorate in urology at the University of Vienna. He and his brother Joseph eventually fled to Shanghai. Rosenfeld joined the People's Liberation Army and served as a field doctor.[66]

Christians in Shanghai mainly encountered Jewish people in three different ways. First, Catholic schools accepted the children of Jewish refugees and several former Shanghai Jews have recorded their experiences in their memoirs. The Sisters of Sacré Cœur provided free tuition for fifteen Jewish refugee girls including Ursula Bacon.[67] While some Jewish parents sent their children to Catholic schools out of economic hardship, Nini Karpel recalls a nun offering her food in exchange for Karpel's conversion to Catholicism.[68] Christian universities in Shanghai enrolled a number of Jewish students as well.

Second, the suffering of the Jewish people compelled some Christians to wrestle with more profound philosophical and spiritual questions. Abraham Setsuzō Kotsuji (1899–1973), a Japanese Christian who descended from a long line of Shinto priests, later in his life converted to Judaism.[69] His life exemplified an extraordinary tri-religious conversation. Setsuzō became a Christian in his youth but became intrigued by Judaism when he read a Japanese translation of the *Tanach*[70] which led him to study Hebrew and Judaic studies at the American University in Washington DC. His fluency in Hebrew and expertise in Jewish studies made him a great asset to the Jewish community in Harbin, China. In 1940, Japan and Germany signed the Axis agreement and joined forces in their anti-semitism. Setsuzō refuted materials which defamed the Jewish character by publishing his *The True Character of the Jewish Nation*, advocating for Japan to shelter Jewish refugees.[71] In 1941, Professor Setsuzō made arrangements for Jewish refugees to escape from Germany to Kobe, Japan, with a two-week transit visa and then to be deported to Japanese-occupied Shanghai. Setsuzō wrote his memoir about his shift of religion to Judaism in *From Tokyo to Jerusalem*.[72]

Third, education and marriage bridged interreligious encounters among the Shanghai Jews. Robert Reuven Sokal, a Vienna-born Jew, attended St. John's College in Shanghai and married a Chinese wife who embraced Judaism.[73] However, for most Jewish refugees in Shanghai in the 1930s and 1940s, Catholicism emanated a temptation to convert or even a form of danger. Shanghai Jewish autobiographies articulate a posture of avoidance of other religions to preserve one's religious identity. Rabbi Walkin's eldest daughter Chaya Leah Walkin viewed the Catholic nuns' invitation to her to a Christian place of worship as a perceived means of proselytizing, and attributed the event as "her escape from the nuns to divine protection."[74] Therefore, Christian–Jewish interactions in Shanghai were marked by both compassion and caution. The Jewish communities also lived through the lingering threat of the German Nazis in Shanghai. The Glen Line Building next to the Bund housed the Gestapo headquarters and the Nazi swastika was a daily sight over the building rooftop in May 1945.

Nazism in Shanghai

A surprising chapter of Shanghai's global history is the early alliance of the Nationalist Party with the Third Reich in fighting against the Japanese in the 1930s prior to the German-Japanese alliance in the 1940s. Nazis arrived in Shanghai and promoted Nazi ideology among the Germans in Shanghai. Founder and editor Max Simon-Eberhard published the German-language newspaper *Deutsche Shanghai Zeitung* (renamed *Der Ostasiatische Lloyd* in 1936) spreading Nazi ideology in Shanghai, and Adolf Hitler's speeches were broadcast via XGRS in Shanghai.[75] Another significant German newspaper in Shanghai was *Ostasiatischer Beobachter*, which printed from 1933 through 1940, blaming the Jews as corrosive in creating all post-First World War separatist movements.[76]

Early Nazi officer (*Gauamtsleiter*) Franz Xaver Hasenöhrl spent three years in Shanghai (1932–4) developing a Ministry of Propaganda and the Foreign Press Bureau, promoting sympathy for Nazism among the German expatriates. Hasenöhrl became the first one to plant the Swastika in Shanghai.[77] German Nazi activities continued in Shanghai in the 1940s through six key personalities. Chief of Gestapo Gerhard Kahner spied on the Shanghai Jews from 1940 until 1943.[78] Josef Meisinger (known as the "Butcher of Warsaw"), a German colonel of police, oversaw all German activities in Shanghai from 1941 until 1947, for the purpose of maintaining loyalty to Hitler.[79] After Kahner, Franz Huber became Chief of the Gestapo in Shanghai in 1943 and crushed Free French resistance in Shanghai's French Concession.[80] Robert Neumann (known as the "Butcher of Buchenwald"), a former SS officer and physiologist, taught at the German-Chinese Medical School (*Deutsche Medizineschule für Chinesen*)[81] in Shanghai and was heavily involved with his research on race and instilling racism among his Chinese students during the period from 1940 to 1945. Lothar Eisenträger (also Ludwig Ehrhardt), Chief of Abwehr (Military Defense), conducted espionage on the Japanese and American navies from 1941 until his Tilanqiao imprisonment by the American military in 1947. Chief of Propaganda in Shanghai, Baron Jesco von Puttkamer, also attempted to seed the philosophy of the Third Reich among Germans in Shanghai from 1941 until 1947. Von Puttkamer even placed his bureau next to the German Church.[82]

The question is how German Christians in Shanghai dealt with Nazism. Kaiser Wilhelm School and its attendant church became the main Nazi centers in Shanghai which broadcasted Nazi propaganda and raised the SA "brownshirts." The *Hitlerjugend* (Hitler Youth) had a Shanghai chapter that brainwashed the German youth and raised them to be future leaders. German girls learned the definition of Nazi womanhood, "*Kinder, Küche, Kirche*" (Children, kitchen, church).[83] Hans Martin Wilhelm, an attendee at the German school, later recounted how his life was transformed from being a Hitler youth to becoming a Christian who was impacted by Chinese evangelist John Sung's sermon.[84] Han-Peter Cortum, a Shanghai-born German, attended the German School in the 1930s.[85] The school was next to the church which is now where the Hilton Hotel stands. The German School was shut down in 1945.

It is unclear whether the German Protestant Church abided with Nazi ideology in 1930s and 1940s Shanghai. The collaboration would be two-fold: one is the pro-Nazi stand and the other is anti-semitism. The Lutheran Church in China had primarily worked in Hubei, Hu'nan, and Guangdong, but Shanghai was never a center for the Lutheran mission. However, the German community in Shanghai began to expand and found themselves in need of a new church to replace the old church of 1901. From a 1909 postcard, the German consulate and a German church appeared to be located on Huangpu Road. After selling the old church, Pastor Ewald Krüger and congregation eventually purchased a new lot on Avenue Hudec (Huashan Road) and dedicated a new church in 1932. The Lutheran architect Hudec designed the church building. Pastor Krüger had begun to pastor the German Evangelical Church in Shanghai in 1925. Astrid Freyeisen suggests that Krüger was loyal to Hitler's government but his naive attitude about the struggles of the German church was due to his losing touch with reality.[86]

Other Religions and Sects in Shanghai

Other religions and sects such as Sikhism, Christian Scientism, and Shintoism also occupied spaces in Shanghai. Since 1885, the British Indian government administered the International Settlement and recruited Sikh Punjabis from India to serve as officers in the Shanghai Municipal Police. Sikh dairy farmers and watchmen were among other minority professions. The number of Sikhs rose so significantly that a Sikh temple called the Old Sikh Gurdwara was inaugurated in 1908. In 1935, the Sikh community numbered 2,389.[87] During the Second World War, Sikh officers in Shanghai sided with the Japanese and the Sikh police unit was disbanded in 1945.[88] Some Sikh families remained and married local people even after the Sino-India conflict in 1962. The Parsis also had a Fire Temple in Shanghai. The Talati family from Tianjin were also active members of the Freemasonry in Shanghai.

Additionally, the Christian Scientist Church and Shintoism occupied part of the early-twentieth-century religious landscape of Shanghai. The first Christian Scientist church in China was built in Shanghai in 1934 and the founder of the Christian Scientist Church, Mary Baker Eddy, was expected to lecture in Shanghai.[89] Japanese religious groups were active in Shanghai: Wen-Hsin Yeh states that the Higashi Honganji had a branch in Shanghai in 1874, Tenrikyô[90] and Shinto temples, shrines, and schools were present in Shanghai along with Japanese Christian churches.[91] Christian Scientism and Shintoism remained small but active in Shanghai prior to the 1950s.

Christians, Cults, and the Nonreligious

Shanghai has been a multireligious place, especially in the early twentieth and twenty-first centuries. According to the China Family Panel Studies 2012 sample of 2,362 people on religions in Shanghai, 86.7 percent are nonreligious, 10.4 percent are Buddhists, 1.9 percent are Protestant Christians, and 0.7 percent are Catholics.[92] Atheism and secularism in China have been systematically implemented via education since the early 1950s. However, atheism or nonreligious must be differentiated. French philosopher Michel Foucault's "knowledge is power" has long been translated as *Zhishi jiu shi liliang* and embraced as an authentically Chinese philosophy among intellectuals. Based on statistics of Christians around the world, Todd Johnson and Charles Tieszen identify personal contact between Christians and nonChristians as the *sine qua non* of Christian evangelism in the twenty-first century.[93]

Religions in Shanghai function in the context of government expectations of social harmony.[94] The Chinese government deems the value of harmony essential and integral; therefore, the government closely monitors any disturbance or threat of chaos. Religion, theoretically, becomes utilitarian and beneficial to society only when religious conditions and performance demonstrate charity and contribute to the primacy of the idea of social progress. Ye Xiaowen underlines Chinese cultural thinking of pluralistic harmony in Christian adaption and confrontation with the concept.[95]

Some Christian new religious movements have struggled not only with the government, but also with the house church. For the government-sanctioned churches in Shanghai, the city governance structurally protects them from new religious movements and cults. The house church is in a more vulnerable position for three reasons. First, house churches in Shanghai are not officially under the protection of the government and can easily be labeled as a cultic movement. The mistrust between the police and the house church perpetuates a further gulf and enforces the perceived or imagined danger of religion.

Second, some new religious movements originated from Chinese house churches because of a lack of theological education. Christian new religious movements are nontrinitarian, mixed with teachings of millennialism, and Chinese folk religious ideas and practices. Third, contrary to the popular perception of the lack of religious thought and freedom, the abundant activities of new religious movements in China have gained empathy in the North American media and, consequently, leaders of new religious movements have sought political asylum in the United States.

The most significant instance is the ongoing struggle between the Chinese government and *Dongfang shandian* (Eastern Lightning, known as the Church of the Almighty God). The Chinese government also banned another active group, Falun Gong, and regarded it as dangerous. The US-based group recruits members across the globe and tours with an ancient Chinese cultural-themed performance known as *Shen Yun* with a strong and explicit anti-communist message.[96] Juergensmeyer states the interaction as follows: "Although the group protested that it was being persecuted by the Chinese, there has been little bloodshed on either side."[97]

From a Western perspective, the repression of these new religious movements is religious persecution and a violation of human rights. From the Chinese government perspective, accusations about new religious movements are criminal and should be eradicated with the goal of safeguarding social harmony in a densely populated country. The house church, however, becomes a double victim. The Chinese government perceived house churches as potentially related to religious cults which were dangerous and disruptive to society. My interviewees Lee and Steve described this two-fold challenge when they worked with a house church in Shanghai. They spoke about the police taking Steve and six Christian teachers to the police station and questioning them until 4 a.m. Yet, another time, even when the police knocked on their apartment door and saw the Bible verses and cross, they simply dismissed them without any further action. Lee and Steve emphasized the importance of equipping Chinese Christians with biblical knowledge for discernment because of the abundance of cults.[98]

Ecumenism and *Humanitas*

Although Christian ecumenical movements in Shanghai have been sparse, some Christians have made efforts to work out major theological differences and sociopolitical conflicts. The Chinese Russian Orthodox priest Du Runchen made significant efforts to promote Chinese priesthood in Shanghai. Du also sought an ecumenical partnership with Protestantism. For example, Du invited a Protestant pastor Zhang Huaide to open Bible classes for the Shanghai Orthodox Seminary and to co-found the bi-weekly Chinese Orthodox magazine *Zhenguang* (Orthodox Light). Du also formed a friendship with the pastor of Moore Memorial Church. Interdenominational fellowship is evident among the five international churches in Shanghai. Some three-self churches and house churches have also attempted to peacefully co-exist.

Beyond Christian churches and fellowships, Christians in Shanghai are exploring and reorganizing the importance of *humanitas* in relating to other religions and wider society. The resurrection of Christian sites in Shanghai is not unique to Christianity. Daoist, Buddhist, Jewish, and other previously established religious sites are following the same trend of revival in twenty-first-century Shanghai. For example, the Ming Dynasty Hong Miao Temple was reopened as a Taoist study center as recently as 2016. The Shanghai Daoist Association rose to be the largest regional association in China. Different religious traditions are seeking to establish their unique identities, whose *raison d'être* is love and compassion while maintaining diversity.

Religions, philosophies, and ideologies in Shanghai inhabit not only the tension between diversity and uniformity, but also between postmodern secularization and religious revival. Peter van der Veer suggests that the political project and urban renewal have subdued the public manifestation of religions in large Chinese cities such as Shanghai and Beijing.[99] He argues: "Religion has not been gradually marginalized by an inescapable process of secularization, as assumed by modernization theory, but by anti-religious campaigns starting in the late nineteenth century and culminating in the Cultural Revolution of the 1960s."[100]

His tracing of anti-religious campaigns which disrupted the local structures and organizations of religions offers an important perspective for historians to reconsider two aspects of religion in a global city such as Shanghai. First, although the Cultural Revolution (1966–76) inflicted irreversible and serious damage on all religions in China, it cannot be considered the sole cause of religious oppression. Second, contrary to an evolutionistic projection of secularization of society that leads to the depletion of religiosity, religion as a movement does not simply disappear. Religious adherents reconstruct the manifestations of faith via newly adapted symbols, forms, and rituals.

A public Christian theology in Shanghai takes on a multifaceted collection of forms and structures. Religion in Shanghai, like most parts of China, must prove its utilitarian function and political benefits to society. An anthropological study of religion and charity in Chinese society identifies new forms of religious philanthropy and argues that alternative notions of social good act as influential forms of political merit-making and civic selfhood.[101] Religious democracy with its theoretical implications of religious freedom may not offer social and political salvific redemption for the complexities in Shanghai. Unique social and religious contexts necessitate and augment Shanghai Christians to strategically forge their own methods and pathways in a pluralistic global city.

7

Beyond the Borders

Transnational migration has linked Christians from Shanghai with the rest of the world. The evangelistic zeal and the Great Commission of Shanghai Christians often take them to unexpected places such as Jerusalem and Ethiopia. This chapter will highlight how Shanghai Christians have crossed social, political, and ethnic boundaries and formed friendships beyond the borders of China. Their active service and ministry worldwide shape the future of World Christianity.

Shanghai Christians Overseas

Chinese Catholics in the eighteenth century traveled to Europe and resided there, bridging China and Europe and their relations. Such an example was Fan Shouyi,[1] and multiple other Chinese Christians who lived in Italy and France, although none of them came from Shanghai or had any connection with the Catholics in Shanghai prior to the late nineteenth century. Macau's central location made it possible to train European and Asian Jesuits there. Several Chinese Catholics from Shanghai traveled to Macau and studied at Saint Paul's Seminary in the seventeenth century. Among them were Lu Xiyan (1631–1704) who joined Saint Paul's in 1682 and officially became a Jesuit priest in 1688. Lu also authored three major books titled *Yishuo* (Speaking of Oneness), *Xin ke zhubao dan* (the list of patron saints of the holy year), and *Aomen Ji* (Memory of Macau).[2]

Shanghai's early-twentieth-century cosmopolitan culture produced Christians who were fluent in many cultures and languages. Lu Zhengxiang (1871–1949) became the first Chinese titular abbot in Europe.[3] Born in Shanghai in a Protestant family, Lu was educated in a traditional Confucian style at a young age and then specialized in French at the School of Foreign Language in Shanghai. Under the influence of a Roman Catholic Chinese diplomat and reformer, Xu Jingcheng (1845–1900), Lu led a successful diplomatic career, gained fluency in Russian, and even married a Belgian woman, Bethe Bovy (1855–1926).

After Bovy's death, Lu withdrew from his active political life and became a Benedictine monk at the monastery of Sint-Andries in Belgium and eventually became an ordained priest in 1935. Lu became instrumental in educating the West about the Chinese war effort during the Japanese invasion of China during the Second World War. He also viewed the Christian faith as an answer to China's future in the 1940s and desired to return to China as a missionary. Although his dream was unfulfilled, his extensive writings in French bridged understandings of the Chinese church in the perception of the francophone world.

Shanghai Catholic Nuns Overseas (1912–54)

A new feature in Shanghai Catholicism is the evidential recognition of Shanghai-born Catholic nuns. Not only did some of them join the traditionally exclusive European and American Catholic orders, some of them also traveled outside of China and pursued a vibrant education or career. Antonella Marie Gutterres was the first Shanghai native to join the Sisters of Loretto (SL) in the United States.[4] In a US Congressional bill submitted to the House of Representatives, the report laid out that Gutterres had a Portuguese father and a Chinese mother and had studied in the US from 1938 to 1940.[5] After working in Shanghai for eight years, Gutterres pursued graduate studies at the University of St. Louis. The Congress bill detailed the potential deportation she faced as a Portuguese citizen to Portugal, Macau, or South America. The Dean at St. Louis petitioned for her, and Gutterres was granted permanent residency.[6] Gutterres authored *Lorettine Education in China, 1923–1952*[7] detailing the significant access the SL provided for Shanghai. After Gutterres left Shanghai, she taught at Loretto Heights College in Denver, Colorado.

Another Chinese Loretto Sister, Carlos Marie Lubeck (1920–1998), born Bertha, was the first Lorettine to receive an American degree. Two family memories tell the story related to Sister Lubeck. One is her father Carlos Borromeu Lubeck's Thanksgiving letter written in 1969, and the other one is the account of Anna Yang Lubeck (or Te-di, Teddy), the second wife of Carlos Lubeck in Albuquerque, New Mexico, in the spring and summer of 1994.[8] According to Lubeck and Yang, Bertha was the adopted Chinese daughter of Lubeck and his first Chinese wife, Lucy Zi (1892–1929). Bertha studied at the Loretto school in Shanghai from 1938 until 1940[9] and received training from the Novitiate of the SL in Kentucky from 1940. The *Denver Catholic Register* celebrated Lubeck on its front page as the first Chinese nun to receive the Bachelor of Arts from Loretto Heights College in 1945.[10] She returned to

Shanghai as a Loretto nun in 1946[11] and taught at the Loretto School in Shanghai for three years. In 1949, Lubeck's entire family migrated to the United States due to the uncertainty and fear of the new communist government in China. Very few activities of Lubeck were documented except that another Lorettine Patricia Anne Cullen's obituary mentioned that Lubeck had invited her to tutor at Rhodes Tutoring Center in the 1990s.[12] She later resided in Arapahoe, Colorado.

Many Catholic female orders contributed to the social wellbeing not only of Shanghai but also of other regions and overseas and the lives and work of Catholic nuns illustrate these important but often overlooked aspects of history. Sister Yin Yuan (1924–2017), a Shanghai native, had taught at *Xuhui Nüzhong*, a middle school for girls after her graduation from Xiaoming School for Girls and St. John's University in Shanghai. Yuan later joined the Society of Helpers in 1943 and dedicated her life to education, especially for girls. Approximately 169 nuns from the Society of Helpers served in Shanghai prior to their forced departure in the early 1950s. Yuan's calling had compelled her to Indonesia, where she and another Catholic nun, Zhaojuan Zhu, opened Nanyang *Nüzi Zhongxue* (Nanyang Girl's Middle School) in Makassar in 1953 where Yuan served as principal of the school for twenty-four years. She tirelessly gave herself to charity work and social welfare until her retirement in 2011.

Shanghai Christians in Exile

The early 1950s marked the first wave of Chinese Christian exiles. The founder of the Evangelize China Fellowship, Andrew Gih, took its work to Greater China, Southeast Asia, and later to the United States. Another significant Shanghai Protestant leader was Jiang Shoudao (Stephen Kaung, 1915–present). Jiang is the son of Jiang Changchuan, one of the earliest ordained Wesleyan ministers in Shanghai. In 1935, Jiang Shoudao had participated in Watchman Nee's ministries in Shanghai and other places. In 1950, Jiang and eleven other Christian evangelists published a document to prove Nee's innocence of charges of espionage, licentiousness, and stealing church funds. Jiang left China in the 1950s and ministered primarily in New York and San Francisco. He started the Christian Fellowship Publishers in Richmond, Virginia, and primarily published Watchman Nee's theological books. Peter A. Wu from Shanghai entered the Maryknoll Fathers in 1955 and was ordained in 1961. He served as a pastor and a teacher in Taiwan for fifty years from 1962 until his passing in Ossining, New York, in 2012.[13] Shanghai Christians carried a sense of global mission in their services.

Beyond Christian individuals, Christian institutions from Shanghai relocated to Taiwan on a large scale after the 1950s. The Jesuits from Shanghai opened two new dioceses in Taibei and Xinzhu by the end of 1951. Guangqi She, the Jesuit center in Xujiahui, closed its doors in 1953; however, it was reopened in Taibei in 1958, now known as the Kuangchi Program Service. Additionally, Catholic schools also found new life in Taiwan including the Xuhui School and Sacred Heart Girls' School. After the arrest of the Chinese Jesuit president Zhang Boda (1905–51) of Xuhui School (Saint Ignatius High School) in 1951, Xuhui School eventually moved to Xinbei City in Taiwan in 1963.

Interchurch communication has taken place between churches in Shanghai and Taiwan. A significant organization named the Chinese Christianity Cross-Strait Communication Association has made efforts to create mutual understanding and increase ministry opportunities for churches in mainland China and Taiwan. For instance, in 2016, a delegation from a Shanghai TSPM church visited churches in Taiwan and joined efforts in communicating ministry strategies and challenges.[14]

The second wave of Christian exiles arose after 1989, rebuilding their second physical and spiritual home in the United States. Among these scholars, a few of them came from Shanghai. Zhao Fusan (1926–2015), a graduate of St. John's College in 1944, became a high-profile figure in various Chinese government works from the early 1960s and the National Committee of the TSPM of Protestant churches in China in the 1980s. While at the UNESCO conference in Paris, Zhao publicly denounced Chinese government action against the student movement at Tian'anmen Square. He taught at Oklahoma University until his retirement and translated Feng Youlan's *A Short History of Chinese Philosophy* and other books related to Western philosophies. Shanghai Christian exiles in return contributed to Asian American Christianity in the late twentieth and early twenty-first centuries.

Additionally, Christian seminarians, priests, and women leaders also contributed to the intercultural and international exchange of faith and culture. In 1994, Bishop Jin Luxian of Shanghai initiated a policy which facilitated Catholic priests and seminarians to study in the United States, the Philippines, and Europe. The Missions Étrangères de Paris also invited Chinese Catholics to study in France.[15] Seminarians from Shanghai encounter opportunities and unique situations in other countries and such training can equip them to grow their intercultural intelligence and skills in cross-cultural missions.

Furthermore, Christians from Shanghai have been actively participating as missionaries to other countries and cultures. Wanbang Missionary Church in Shanghai has over twenty missionaries overseas.[16] The number may be small in comparison to large missionary-sending regions or cities; however, Chinese passport holders must overcome the increasing problem of visa limitation. It is incredible to see that some Shanghai individual Christians and churches are already mission-oriented, and they actively and sometimes quietly serve in diverse communities on different continents.

Christian Returnees: "Sea Turtles"

A principal theme among Shanghai Christians is that some overseas Shanghai students convert to Christianity while studying abroad. Some of them return to Shanghai as what the Chinese language dubs "sea turtles." Personal contact, social belonging, and friendship scaffold the journey of the Christian faith. Since the early twenty-first century, more Chinese students have studied in the United States. A personal encounter of faith and religious freedom is not the sole reason for students to join a Catholic or Protestant church. Ning Qian identifies social belonging as one of the reasons that many Chinese students in America would take on an institutionalized religion such as Catholicism in the United States.[17]

Another interesting movement is how Shanghai students become Christians in post-Christian Europe. The Pew Research Center identifies that the majority of Christians in Europe are non-practicing.[18] Countercultural to the trend of secularization, my interviewee Lee identifies a significant group of Shanghai students who studied in Europe and attended the Discipleship Training Program (DTC) of the Chinese Church in Europe.[19] Most of these new Shanghai Christian "sea turtles" are well-educated professionals who landed stable and high-paid jobs in Shanghai. The extensive network of DTC in Europe has also provided opportunities for Shanghai students such as "Adrienne"[20] to attend church discipleship training in the United Kingdom. With the intentional group training and ongoing formal and informal counseling, she shows steady spiritual growth.

Genuine friendship builds connections between Christians and oversea Shanghai students. The story of "G" demonstrates how friendship opened a way for her to become a Christian. G was a talented college volleyball player in California, then the Mid-America Nazarene University in Olathe, Kansas, recruited her to study. After almost four years of being connected with Christian friends, G decided to be baptized as a Christian at College Church in 2015. Upon graduation, she returned to Shanghai as a businesswoman.[21] Another interview I conducted features Joanna Gu, a Chinese professor in a Shanghai university, who encountered the Christian faith while being a visiting scholar in the United States. The local Chinese American church earned a reputation for helping overseas Chinese students and subsequently baptized Joanna and helped her connect with a Shanghai church consisting of returnees when she briefly went back to Shanghai for a few years. As an intellectual, she revealed that Christian ethics and her comparisons of Chinese and American societies served as an entry point for her to become a committed Christian.[22] G's and Joanna's faith journeys represent a phenomenon which has taken place in recent years. Yuqin Huang's interviews of returning Christians in Shanghai affirms such a trend in Shanghai Christianity as returnees often facilitate and operate transnationally.[23] Different from students who are already Christians when they begin to study overseas, nonreligious students may have options to explore life questions they have not previously considered.

Major Issues and Trends

Shanghai Christians share some commonalities with Christians who reside in global cities such as New York City, Cairo, Mexico City, and others, but the uniqueness of locating in the richest city in China also generates some unique challenges. Like other Chinese urban dwellers, Christians in Shanghai face three major issues. The first challenge is the dialogue of economy and faith. The second trend is Christians' attitude to and practices of family life. The third issue is that the aging population raises an important demand for caring for the elderly.

Economics and Faith

Economic changes impact how Christians participate and anticipate the implications for how faith functions in the marketplace, especially in a global city like Shanghai. When measuring the economic growth rate, China exhibits a supernormal economy along with rapid changes. Striking social advancement has produced positive outcomes as economists Lawrence Summers and Vinod Thomas stated in 1993: "A child born in Shanghai today has a smaller chance of dying in the first year of life, a longer life expectancy beyond one year, and a greater chance of learning to read than a child born in New York City."[24] Their predictions about economic growth and poverty reduction have been realized in Shanghai. Paradoxically, drastic changes have been reshaping society and people's lives, manifesting in the evidence of the largest number of domestic migrant workers, their children left in the care of extended families in their hometowns (*liushou ertong*), and the disparities of income.

In 2015, Chinese economist Jeffrey Zhengfu Shi proposed the figure of 300 to 400 million rural residents moving to Chinese urban areas in the next two or three decades.[25] Shi analyzes what he coined as China's "three-dimensional market system" and how the central government's empowerment of local government advances the development of enterprise,[26] balances out department bureaucracy, and therefore improves administrative efficiency.[27] The efficiency of the socioeconomic system in Shanghai exacerbates and dictates the changes residents experience. Two of my interviewees came from the nearby Anhui Province, both were Christians in their sixties. Seeking a better life, they moved to Shanghai about twenty years ago. The elderly man had been making a living by collecting cardboard and plastic bottles but the rise in living expenses in Shanghai made him decide to move back to his hometown with a small amount of government pension. The elderly woman had settled in Shanghai with family and children. Both commented on how the radical economic change had impacted their lives.[28]

Christians and Family in Shanghai

Shanghai Christians face marital pressure from their immediate and extended families. High anxiety about getting married has created the phenomenon of Chinese parental matchmaking. Jun Zhang and Peidong Sun argue that such a practice is not a direct revival of cultural tradition, but rather a re-articulation exacerbated by radical economic reform and social transformation via the one-child policy which have affected the Shanghai urbanites and their expectations for highly educated daughters.[29] The one-child policy beginning in the 1980s produced some unique challenges for the generation known as *baling hou* (people who were born during the 1980s). Social pressure, familial expectation, and economic stress have all contributed to a marriage culture with a minority rebelling from it.

My interviewees, Lee and her husband Steve, were born and raised in Taiwan but became Christians while studying in the United States. Lee recalls watching a documentary on the churches in China in 2006, which moved her. Six years later, Lee and Steve went to Shanghai through the For All Saints Team Ministry and they lived there for five years from 2012 to 2016 prior to their relocation to Hangzhou. Both Christian returnees from Europe and long-term local Shanghainese Christians attended their church and discipleship trainings.

Singleness for Christians is a serious challenge. One 35-year-old Christian woman, "Bee," from Lee and Steve's ministry, faced the pressure from family, frustration from blind dates, and temptation to give up. Bee instead blogged her journey of faith and singleness and encouraged other Christians who were facing similar challenges. Social and familial pressure to be married before a woman's late twenties is still a social norm. Family pressure does not simply come from one's parents. In China, the pressure is most vocally expressed by the aunts, the so-called *Qi dagu ba dayi* (literally, seven paternal aunts and eight maternal aunts). The pressure to marry is intensified especially when the celebration of Spring Festival or Lunar New Year takes place, a time nuclear or extended families would gather around the New Year's feast table. The marital pressure is so severe that a new business of renting a boyfriend came to the Chinese market. Filled with controversies and debates, loneliness is even commodified, as in the case of "butler cafés" called The Promise Land for women to rent companionship in Shanghai.

Although sexuality is generally a taboo topic in Chinese public life, Chinese society has gone through dramatic changes in the past thirty years. Huang Ping speaks of the "double identity" of homosexual Christians in China as the country sees an upsurge of gay and lesbian participation in Christianity. Ping states that, different from the United States, the conversation about homosexuality and faith in China has been a positive one.[30]

Varied aspects of Christian family life show importance in Shanghai Christians' daily and practical concerns. The issues of singleness, dating, marriage, and childbearing are all present. The wife in one Shanghainese Christian couple is a Christian returnee from the UK and a lawyer. She suffered postpartum depression. Then the couple's house caught fire and caused a complete loss of their possessions. DTC missionaries Lee and Steve highlighted the importance of providing "biblical advice" and counseling to church members on such issues and they observed transformations in Christians' lives. For example, one Shanghai returnee couple from the UK almost filed for divorce but decided to try out Christian counseling. After prayers and counseling sessions, they sobbed and asked each other for forgiveness. Another couple also struggled with parental conflict. The husband was a successful business consultant for many of the top 500 companies in Shanghai. Their unhappy marital stage drove the much younger wife to attempt suicide. DTC's three-folded foci on God's unconditional love, being dead to old habits, and becoming new creations in Christ motivated the couple to change. Their continuous efforts in studying the Bible aided their gradual change in acknowledging the worth and value of themselves and each other.

One Shanghainese Christian woman in her late fifties struggled with the guilt and shame complex imposed by her culture. When she was young, her brothers raped her, and the trauma followed her even after she had been a Christian for a long time. However, she was able to confide with Lee and felt freedom from the shame. She and her husband even renewed their marriage vows, which was quite unusual in China. Another Hangzhou-born Christian in Shanghai was in her sixties. Thirty years ago, she attempted suicide by jumping off the sixth floor when she discovered her husband's extramarital affair. Their marriage still had issues. Their daughter in Europe became a Christian and insisted that they find a church. The couple also experienced a major improvement as they worked through many counseling sessions and eventually joined one church in Shanghai.

Aging and Care

The third major issue is elderly care as the aging of China's population has emerged as an upcoming problem. Children who are impacted by the "one-child policy" are now in their late twenties and thirties and straddle two generations as they raise children and face the possibilities of caring for their elderly parents without much sibling support to share the responsibilities. China has begun to face a problem of an aging population in the past ten years. Although senior living facilities have thrived, many elderly people face challenges of loneliness and illness such as Alzheimer's. Additionally, urban development has altered the family structure as young people do not generally live near their parents. Accessibility to jobs provides the finances that young people depend on so they can care for grandparents and parents, therefore, elderly care relies on pension plans, social structures, and individual networks.

Christians in Shanghai have reached out to people who lack a social safety network or family support. Nearing death, one lady in a Shanghai nursing home, a professor from France, requested a visit from Lee and Steve. Upon hearing that God loved her, the former professor expressed her frustration and disappointment. When Lee quoted Romans 5:8 and affirmed that God still loved her regardless, the former professor decided to accept Christ's love and requested to be baptized one week later. The last couple of months of her life, she changed her disposition. Instead of refusing to go out of her room as she did before, she went out on her wheelchair and greeted people in the nursing home. Lee revealed that the former professor was a famous violinist in France emphasizing how much people need to be loved. Receiving the assurance of God's unconditional love comforted the lonely professor in the nursing home. To respond to the aging issue, churches in Shanghai have organized volunteer groups in caring for seniors.

Multiple Pathways to Faith

Christians in Shanghai have created innovative ways to express their faith and to witness to Christ through multiple pathways. Shanghai's Christian activities exercise influence on other countries. In the late nineteenth century, as Chinese and Japanese migration progressed and regressed in Canada, Chinese Rescue Home established a residence to save trafficked Chinese and Japanese girls and women in Victoria, British Columbia. Shelly Ikebuchi analyzes the moral and social foundation of such charitable societies.[31] In the United States, the Presbyterian mission concurrently ran a Chinese rescue home and Peggy Pascoe attributes the San Francisco rescue mission as being developed by the American Christian women who had long-term support of the rescue mission in Shanghai.[32]

Catholics, Protestants, and, to a lesser degree, Orthodox believers in Shanghai continue to navigate major changes of official state policies. Since 2018, churches in Shanghai, like many other places in China, have faced some new challenges under the new administration because religious affairs now are managed by the United Front Work Department. The structural change confines religious groups to a tightened watch.[33] As for the Catholic unregistered churches, in 2018, the Holy See and the Chinese government signed the *ad experimentum* (provisional agreement) which allowed communion among the bishops.[34] Both parties renewed the terms on October 22, 2022, and continued to foster a bilateral relation with the pastoral care of Chinese Catholics,[35] but Christoph Zimmer argues that divided loyalty among Chinese Catholics still continues despite such mitigating efforts.[36] We are yet to be able to fully analyze the impacts of the implementations of official rules on individuals, organizations, and churches in Shanghai. Christians in Shanghai have found alternative ways to communicate and express their faith through the digital space, books, the visual arts, and music.

Digital Space and Books

The internet is an important platform for people to encounter Christianity. Digital space online is able to transcend the limitations of time and space and presents nonconventional ways for people who are nonreligious or of other faith traditions. The accomplished Peking Opera Master Mei Baojiu, a Shanghai native, came to Christ through an overseas Chinese Christian friend's witness and friendship. Mei's friend pastors a Chinese church in Spain and has been writing a microblog as "Global Swallow" since 2010.[37]

FIGURE 7.1 *Bookstores like this one, nestled in a large shopping mall in Lujiazui, Pu Dong New Area, provide a place for people to dialogue with new ideas. Photo courtesy of Susangeline Patrick, 2020.*

Books written by Shanghai Christians cross boundaries and exert global influence. Dana Robert discusses how Watchman Nee's spiritual writings had spread through Chinese diasporas in other parts of Asia, North America, and Africa as his works were even read by a Shona Christian in rural Zimbabwe.[38] Another significant Shanghai Christian from the early twentieth century, Christiana Tsai's contemplation of being blind also reaches readers beyond the restraints of geographical boundaries and time.

The Arts as Witnesses

Art is not treated as a tool of evangelization, but as a voice dialoguing with others around faith or a space of hospitality. Art galleries, cafés, hotel conference rooms, theater stages, and computer/phone screens have become versatile spaces for people to see, discuss, hear, and even feel the Christian gospel. Memoire, the lives of Shanghai Christians, acts to communicate history and faith. In January 2022, the Shanghai Ruyi Yue Opera Company launched a Yue opera, *Guangqi in Shanghai*, to commemorate the 460th birthday of the seventeenth-century intellectual Xu Guangqi. The opera focuses on his scientific, technological, and political contributions. China has a long tradition of honoring intellectualism in public life which is deeply engrained in its educational system. Intellectual Christians and cultural Christians in Shanghai raise their voices in public discussions of ethics, morality, and other social concerns.

FIGURE 7.2 *Art galleries and public art have mushroomed in recent years in Shanghai. This giant sculpted person taking a drop of water from a faucet provokes the thoughts of the audience. Photo courtesy of Susangeline Patrick, 2020.*

Christmas has become a point of conversation or evangelic opportunity for churches to put on live performances and celebrations of dances and choirs in China despite its commercialization. Gamble's brief examination of "Shanghai Christmas" as a ritual indicates university students have been innovating and re-assembling symbols and meanings in unique ways since the re-emerging of Christmas in Shanghai in the 1980s.[39]

An unusual interaction between architecture and Christianity in Shanghai is the new construction of fake churches. Both preserved historical churches and government-sponsored decorative churches are commercialized through the cultural ideology of "consuming" churches in expressing the city's and individual participants' global identity. Tourists and newlyweds view churches as beautiful backdrops for photography and appropriate the theological and aesthetic qualities and meanings of the space. Leslie Sklair argues how the built environment relates to the cultural ideology of global consumerism within the network of capitalism. Sklair views the Urban Planning Institute in Shanghai's "One City, Nine Towns" as the most extraordinary case study for such consumerist ideology because of the envisaging of Gaoqiao as a Dutch town, Songjiang as an English town with Tudor- and Georgian-styled buildings and a Gothic church for wedding photos, Anting as a German town, Buzhen and Zhoupu as two Euro-American towns, the Spanish Fengcheng, Canadian Fengjing, Nordic Luodian, Italian Pujiang, and Chinese Zhujiajiao.[40] Young people in the past twenty years have enjoyed the aesthetic qualities of a church facade with or without profession of the Christian faith.

Faith and Music

In Shanghai, multiple forms of the arts are the media of the Christian message. One of the most extraordinary examples is the Shanghai-born Hong Kong singer and songwriter Gloria Tang Tsz-kei (1991–present) and her influence in music across the globe.[41] Tang, as a Christian, does not explicitly preach through her lyrics, but the influence from her faith is visible and impactful. In 2016, Forbes named Tang as one of the "30 under 30" list under the category of music.[42] On August 9, 2022, Warner Music China released the first single "Gloria" from her latest album title *Revelation.* As of August 16, 2022, her official music video had over 2.16 million views on YouTube.[43] The video for "Gloria" is set in a dark and grey wasteland where, as a young woman, Gloria waits for dawn. The lyrics reflect a yearning for light as she waits in the darkness. As the character Gloria narrates about her tears in the wilderness, she sees "deactivated" appearing on her left wrist. Then, she sings about the voice which speaks to her about unconditional love.

Some of the song's lyrics make direct references to scriptures in the Bible. The song directly quotes from part of 1 John 4:18. Other lyrics are innovative and reflective of God's faithful love and covenantal commitment to God's people. Parallels and paraphrases frequently appear in the lyrics. The renewal of one's strength alludes to Isaiah 40:31, "but those who wait for the LORD shall renew their strength, they shall mount up with wings like eagles, they shall run and not be weary, they shall walk and not faint." Another line about giving up one's burden is a paraphrase from Matthew 11:28, "Come to me, all you that are weary and are carrying heavy burdens, and I will give you rest."

Continuing from the music video, as Gloria breaks down in tears and dismay that the ocean in front of her leads to nowhere, she kneels and the ocean dramatically parts in two and forms a dry path for her to walk on. The scene mimics the Old Testament story of Exodus when Moses leads the Hebrew people out of Egypt and Yahweh delivers them by dividing the Red Sea into dry land (Exodus 14). Then in the music video, the mysterious voice repeats the refrain of ridding of her fear and trusting the eternal love. These lyrics illustrate an action of returning, reminiscent of the story of the Prodigal Son (Luke 15) and a returning of all creation to their eternal home.

The final scene depicts a door appearing in the pathway of the dry place between the divided ocean, and radiant light shining on the face of Gloria as the door slowly opens. "Gloria" ends on the raised ocean waves which almost resemble wings of angels and then the camera lens zooms in on the light from the other side of the door as if Gloria has crossed the threshold. The optic imagery is moving and powerful to the point of drowning out the lyrics although the music, imagery, and content of the lyrics all form an integral part of the music video. One of my interviewees "Samantha" describes "the images of shalom being brought about in chaos" in the creation narrative in Genesis 1 and the Exodus story.[44]

Tang's music piece is a brilliant interpretation of the Creator's love for the beloved creation. The song takes a personal narration approach but further points out to the grand theme of salvation history, from the Old Testament to the eschaton. The rich symbols and imageries have integrated much of biblical narrative and theology. Furthermore, the song relates to the global audience and the state of the world in 2022. Audiences who desire deliverance and relief from the chaos and pain in their personal lives or the suffering inflicted on the world could be uplifted with a sense of hope. The imagery also evokes what another interviewee, "Anna", speaks of as the work of fighting about institutional and systematic justice and interprets Gloria as "an icon of resistance and hope—doing the hard work, vulnerably walking towards the light."[45]

As a cosmopolitan and global city, Shanghai generates availability of diverse Christian theologies and praxis. Christians in Shanghai are expected to live differently from the rest of the consumerism-ridden city life. The Christian faith is not only an identity marker, but also Christian behaviors are to reflect a distinct difference in pragmatic ways. In Jos Gamble's 2003 ethnographic study of Shanghai in social and economic transition, his findings suggest that the reopened Christian churches offer an alternative and orderly place which contrasts with the morally ambiguous and chaotic rest of society.[46] Shanghai Christians around the world and world Christians in Shanghai work in partnership in aiming to bring transformations to the self, society, and healing of humanity and the world.

Conclusion

What Shanghai Christians Offer in World Christianity

Looking back at the diverse and fascinating history of Christians in Shanghai, three major instances of disruption and destruction have occurred: namely, the Taiping Rebellion in the mid-nineteenth century, the Japanese occupation of Shanghai from 1937 to 1945, and the regrettable Cultural Revolution (1966–76). Each of these three events is not merely restricted to the specific dates because they produce ripple effects and long-term consequences, but it is precisely in the devastation that we can see the resilience of Shanghai Christians. Some of them suffered, sacrificed, or even died as a result of these events, and survivors of these disruptions endeavor to recover, restore, and adapt to changes and new realities in Shanghai and beyond.

Disruptions and restrictions are circumstances Christians encounter and experience. Even though cultural contexts do not ultimately determine the ways Christians deal with situations, they present unique opportunities and challenges for Christians to embody their faith. What is striking about Shanghai Christians in the past four hundred years is the overwhelming diversity of Christian expression throughout all aspects of life. The diversity is also found in the inspirations, contradictions, paradoxes, and conflicts in Christian interpretations. Christian theologies motivated varied Christian expression. Some fervently fought for social justice, political activism, and compassion, while others excluded others and passionately disagreed with their rivals because they thought they were defending the truth. At the core of Christian history in Shanghai, no singular strand can represent the complexity of these stories.

The complexity of the history of Christianity reveals not only the past, but also how different people have chosen to remember differently. Social and political changes have informed the popular perceptions of Shanghai's relationship with Christianity and Christians in the twenty-first century are not exempt from disagreements and conflicts. Some Christians today tend to demonize the CCP as all evil and which generated persistent persecution and oppression of Christians in China. The "massive church destruction" after the communists took power only narrates part of the story. The exile of foreign missionaries and destruction of churches also occurred during the Japanese occupation and under the Nationalist government in the Republic of China prior to 1949. The claimed Christian faith of Chiang Kai-Shek did not prevent anti-Christian sentiment in Shanghai. Perhaps one version of democracy and freedom of religion cannot solve all our social illns.

We need to go beyond the binary vision of Christian history, especially what has taken place during the social and political rebirth of the early twentieth century. On the one hand, people who are outsiders to Shanghai or China are the ones who refuse to look closely and allow the narratives to speak of their nuances, complexity, and changes. The perception of China as a closed country hostile to the Christian faith prevents us from critically seeing its multifaceted history.

Another popular idea is the simplistic understanding of European and North American missionaries as imperialistic or colonial. This perspective is also problematic. In the history of Shanghai Christians, some of the individuals or communities exhibited such attitudes and behavior, but many of them endeavored to offer themselves and their services to the people of Shanghai. From the early Jesuit China mission in the seventeenth century, a pattern of simultaneous cultural exchange occurred as the Jesuit missionaries became the primary vehicles of Chinese knowledge and culture in Europe. Learned Jesuit missionaries acted in their varied roles of priests/laity, scientists, artists, diplomats, and scholars. Some other missionaries also followed the early Jesuits' footsteps and devoted themselves to learning and Christian services in the nineteenth and twentieth centuries. Mutual partnership, dialogue, and friendship with the Christians in Shanghai are part of the complex story.

Most importantly, the theme of resurrection ties together the strands of Shanghai Christian history. Chinese culture in general is both reflective and progressive and history provides the source for gleaning insight and wisdom for the future. Furthermore, studying and examining history plays a significant role in the historiographical tracing of Christianity in Shanghai. Christians in Shanghai have constantly noted and highlighted Christians who lived prior to their own time, desiring to draw strength. Lu Zhengxiang's 1934 publication *La Vie et les oeuvres du grand chrétien chinois* studies the life of seventeenth-century Shanghai Catholic Xu Guangqi[1] and other writings of biographies also attempt to increase our capacity to see past Christians not just as witnesses or inspirations, but also as complicated human beings who may be limited in their own bias and prejudices.

The act of remembering Shanghai Christians is not just to honor the past, but to realize and resonate with the fuller picture of Christians through the centuries, knowing that justice and mercy are recurring themes. The history of Shanghai Christians offers a window to see why and how Christians negotiated religious, social, political, and cultural identity. The historical landmarks further invite us to revive and renew faith with a global vision.

Notes

Preface

1 *The Courier-Journal*, Louisville, Kentucky, November 23, 1956, 8.

2 Ogle, *China Nurse*, 114–17. Special thanks to Heidi Campbell who generously provided the information.

Introduction

1 Johnson and Zurlo, *World Christian Encyclopedia*, 30.

Chapter 1

1 I use the term "semi-colonial" to describe the ambiguous status of Shanghai from the 1850s to 1945. As a port city, Shanghai had multiple foreign settlements which had commercial and political privileges, but Shanghai was not officially established as a foreign colony like Hong Kong or Macau. "Semi-colonial" is a more accurate term to describe Shanghai because the respective official governments of the Qing Empire and the governance during the Republic Era still maintained some social and political authorities.

2 Although the New China (*Xin Zhongguo*) dates to 1949, I have used 1954 to indicate the year when the last foreign Catholic mission left Shanghai.

3 Torr, *The Silk Roads*, 108.

4 Xu, *Silencing Shanghai*, 33–4.

5 *All about Shanghai*, 1–2. This 1934–5 guidebook describes Shanghai as the "Paris of the East" and the "New York of the West" which had its origin from a "fishing village on a mudflat which almost literally overnight became a great metropolis." It goes on: "There is nothing of outstanding importance to relate about Shanghai from the dawn of the 17th century down to 1843, when it was opened to foreign trade." The guidebook's assessment of Shanghai prior to 1843 is repeated by countless writers.

6 Wasserstrom, *Global Shanghai, 1850–2010*, 4–6.

7 Chinese Archaeology, Institute of Archaeology, "The Excavation of Qinglong Town Site in Shanghai," http://www.kaogu.cn/en/News/New_discoveries/2017/0306/57332.html.

8 Sidebotham, *Berenike and the Ancient Spice Route*, 3. Steven Sidebotham describes the "global economy" built through ancient maritime trade routes and the Maritime Spice Route that connected China to the Persian Gulf and the Mediterranean.

9 Futrell, "Shanghai," *Encyclopedia of World Trade*, 821.

10 The other six ports were Guangzhou, Quanzhou, Hangzhou, Qingyuan (Ningbo), Lanpu (Hanyan County in Jiaxing), and Wenzhou. At the end of the thirteenth century, Yuan rulers closed off some ports and only kept Qingyuan, Quanzhou, and Guangzhou open.

11 Futrell, "Shanghai," 821.

12 Futrell, "Shanghai," 821.

13 Merekina, "The Old Catholic Church," 275.

14 Huang, "Christian Communities," 142. Huang reported the chapel as "near" Xu's residence, but the chapel is part of the Xu family residence, and it still exists today.

15 "Li Tiangang: How did Xu Guangqi Completely Change the Lives of Chinese?" *Beijing News*.

16 Patrick, "Art as a Pathway," 66.

17 King, *"A Model for All Christian Women,"* 21.

18 Li Madou, *Yesu hui yu Tianzhu jiao jingru zhongguo shi*, 361. Li Madou is Matteo Ricci's Chinese name. Ricci did not record the names of Xu Guangqi's wife and father.

19 Zhong, *Xujiahui cang mingqing tianzhujiao wenxian xubian*, 147–57; Tang, *Li Madou*, 553.

20 Tang, *Li Madou*, 53.

21 Dong, "Lun Xu Guangqi de Xinyang" [Discourse of the Beliefs of Xu Guangqi], 64–6.

22 Wang, *Xu guangqi ji*, 531; Tang, *Li Madou*, 50–1.

23 Zhong, *Faguo guojia tushuguan cang mingqing tianzhujiao wenxian*, no. 4, 529–31; Tang, *Limadou*, 54–5.

24 Duceux, *La Introducción Del Aristotelismo*, 44.

25 Amsler, *Jesuits and Matriarchs*, 114.

26 Amsler, *Jesuits and Matriarchs*, 117–18.

27 Amsler, *Jesuits and Matriarchs*, 120–1.

28 King, *"A Model for All Christian Women,"* 90.

29 King, *"A Model for All Christian Women,"* 91.

30 King, *"A Model for All Christian Women,"* 91.

31 Merekina, "The Old Catholic Church," 276.

32 Merekina, "The Old Catholic Church," 276.

33 Amsler, *Jesuits and Matriarchs*, 115. It is unclear where the women's church is located.

34 Amsler, *Jesuits and Matriarchs*, 116.

35 Amsler, *Jesuits and Matriarchs*, 120.

36 King, *"A Model for All Christian Women"*, 87.

37 King, *"A Model for All Christian Women"*, 88.

38 King, *"A Model for All Christian Women"*, 89.

39 Huang, *Chuansha xianzhi* [Chuansha County Gazetteers], https://www.shtong.gov.cn/difangzhi-front/book/detailNew?oneId=1&bookId=4423&parentNodeId=48727&nodeId=35321&type=-1. The English translation is mine from the original Chinese text.

40 Huang, *Chuansha xianzhi*, 891.

41 Lefebvre, *A Guide to Catholic Shanghai*, 1.

42 Lefebvre, *A Guide to Catholic Shanghai*, 1.

43 Standaert, "Chinese Voices in the Rites Controversy," 50–1.

44 De Moidrey, "Ecclesiastical: The Roman Catholic Church," 322.

45 Witek, "Rocha, João da," 574.

46 Heirman, De Troia, and Parmentier, "Francesco Sambiasi," 32–40.

47 Meynard, *The Jesuit Reading of Confucius*, 12.

48 Couplet, *Histoire d'une Dame Chrétienne*, 38.

49 King, *"A Model for All Christian Women"*, 24.

50 King, *"A Model for All Christian Women"*, 25.

51 Weststejin, "'Intoxicated, We Listen to Warblers'," 295–6.

52 Rule, "François Noël," 139.

53 Aveiro, *The Far Eastern Catholic Missions*, 85.

54 King, *"A Model for All Christian Women,"* 51.

55 Amsler, *Jesuits and Matriarchs*, 71.

56 Thomas, *Catalogue of the Residences and Missions*, f. 408 e-r; Brockey, "The 'Portuguese' Jesuit Church in Seventeenth Century Peking," 70.

57 Huang, "Christian Communities and Alternative Devotions in China," 111. Huang documented that Songjiang and Suzhou Christians wrote to the Pope in 1835 and the Jiangnan Christians petitioned the Pope in 1840.

58 King, "The Xujiahui (Zikawei) Library," 458.

59 De la Servière, *Histoire de la mission du Kiangnan*, 12.

60 Mariani, "The Phoenix Rises from its Ashes," 300.

61 Huang, "Christian Communities," 124–5.

62 Clark, "Sealing Fate and Changing Course," 122.

63 Lefebvre, *A Guide to Catholic Shanghai*, 18.

64 Lu, *Beyond the Neon Light*, 278.

65 Lu, *Beyond the Neon Light*, 279.

66 Urrows, *François Ravary SJ and a Sino-European Musical Culture*, 36.

67 Mo, "The 'Roman Question' in Shanghai," 312–14.

68 Huang, "Christian Communities," 127.

69 Tiedemann, *Reference Guide to Christian Missionary Societies in China*, 60.

70 The General Hospital first treated foreign patients when it was initially founded in 1863.

71 Tiedemann, *Reference Guide to Christian Missionary Societies in China*, 62.

72 Sanneh, *Translating the Message*, 7.

73 Aleni, *Xingxue cushu*.

74 Reed, *Gutenberg in Shanghai*, 84.

75 One of the most outstanding publications is Manuel Dias's *Tang jingjiao beisong zhengquan* of 1878.

76 *Art Worlds*, 38; Kiong, *Quelques mots*, 35.

77 Rule, "Restoration or New Creation," 270.

78 Strong, *A Call to Mission*, 59.

79 Tiedemann, *Reference Guide to Christian Missionary Societies in China*, 21.

80 Huang, *Shanghai Filmmaking*, 1, 133.

81 Xu, "Liu Na'ou nianbiao," 159–69.

82 Mungello, *Drowning Girls in China*, 77; *Annales de l'Oeuvre de la Sainte-Enfance* 1 (1846–9): 419.

83 Mungello, *Drowning Girls in China*, 10.

84 Mungello, *Drowning Girls in China*, 56.

85 Mungello, *Drowning Girls in China*, 59.

86 Mungello, *Drowning Girls in China*, 82–3.

87 Lefebvre, *A Guide to Catholic Shanghai*, 18.

88 Clark, "Recovering China's Past," in the Whitworth Digital Commons, 11, https://digitalcommons.whitworth.edu/cgi/viewcontent.cgi?article=1015&context=historyfaculty.

89 Moshinsky, *Goodbye, Shanghai*, 121–2.

90 Strong, *A Call to Mission*, Vol. 2, 296.

91 Ristaino, *The Jacquinot Safe Zone*, 1–2.

92 Tiedemann, *Reference Guide to Christian Missionary Societies in China*, 39.

93 Tiedemann, *Reference Guide to Christian Missionary Societies in China*, 6.

94 Tiedemann, *Reference Guide to Christian Missionary Societies in China*, 74.

95 Tiedemann, *Reference Guide to Christian Missionary Societies in China*, 84.

96 Tiedemann, *Reference Guide to Christian Missionary Societies in China*, 281.

97 Tiedemann, *Reference Guide to Christian Missionary Societies in China*, 83.

98 *The Far East*, 14.

99 The Legion of Mary, an international Marian movement, had a branch in Shanghai. Although Frank Duff first established the lay organization in Dublin in 1921, the group aimed to serve God under Mary and revitalized spiritual activities such as prayers and acts of mercy.

100 The Sisters of Loretto was originally organized in 1812 by three women who sought guidance from Belgian priest Charles Nerinckx (1761–1824). The founder of the Irish Columban priests, Edward Galvin (1882–1956) in Hanyang, China, invited six Loretto Sisters to China in 1923. The Loretto Sisters purchased a property and formed a girls' school first in Hanyang, and later in Shanghai.

101 Lefebvre, *A Guide to Catholic Shanghai*, 10.

102 Tiedemann, *Reference Guide to Christian Missionary Societies in China*, 78.

103 Lefebvre, *A Guide to Catholic Shanghai*, 10.

104 Loretto Community, https://www.lorettocommunity.org/sr-grace-clare-shanley-in-china/.

105 Clark, *China's Saints*, 55.

106 McGrath, *From Navan to China*.

107 Mariani, *Church Militant*.

108 "Columban – It was like a miracle: Fr. Aedan McGrath," Missionary Society of St. Columban, September 8, 2008, https://www.youtube.com/watch?v=A5E9_1naVnQ.

109 Michelle Qiao, "Restoration Retains Original Look of Seminary," *Shanghai Daily*, July 15, 2016.

110 A plenary indulgence is a Catholic practice of remitting temporal punishment of sins due to a believer's prayers or pious actions.

Chapter 2

1 In this chapter, I use the term "Chinese" to include all ethnicities in China. I will specify the name of the ethnic group when it is necessary.

2 I put these two historical periods together because of the significant continuity and overlap in various themes and missional activities. Although the year of 1949 was the official date of when the new Chinese government took power, the 1950s was the time when Protestant missionaries were gradually expelled from mainland China.

3 Smith, *A Narrative of an Exploratory Visit*, 466.

4 Smith, *A Narrative of an Exploratory Visit*, 466.

5 Smith, *A Narrative of an Exploratory Visit*, 466.

6 Lockhart, *The Medical Missionary*, 280.

7 *Church Missionary Society Periodicals*, 172. The other four port cities are Canton (Guangzhou), Amoy (Xiamen), Fuzhou, and Ningbo. The treaty also forced Qing China to cede the territory of Hong Kong.

8 Lu, *Beyond the Neon Lights*, 29.

9 The Old City is coterminous with Nanshi (literally the southern market), part of today's Huangpu District.

10 Morrison, *A Grammar of the Chinese Language*; Morrison, *A Dictionary of the Chinese Language*.

11 Smith, *A Narrative of an Exploratory Visit*, 467.

12 Lutz, "Attrition among Protestant Missionaries," 22.

13 Campbell, "Drs. Bertha and Arthur Selmon," 87. Adventist missionaries in Shanghai experienced similar issues of returning home due to health reasons.

14 These verses are from the New Revised Standard Version of the New Testament.

15 *The China Mail*, Hong Kong, May 7, 1923, 8. Manley and Madar were the paternal grandparents of Alexandra Christina Manley, the former spouse of Prince Joachim of Denmark.

16 Bickers, "Shanghailanders," 194–6.

17 Lutz, *Chinese Politics and Christian Mission*, 264–5.

18 Chen, *A Short Biography of John Shaw Burdon*, 17–18.

19 Smith, *A Narrative of an Exploratory Visit*, 467.

20 Bai, *Fusion of East and West*, 20. Bai discusses how Protestant missionaries prioritized evangelism and utilized education and medical services as ways to serve evangelistic goals.

21 Wong, *In Remembrance of Martyrs a Century Ago*, 6.

22 Flora Clover was the wife of fellow CIM missionary Archibald Edward Glover, author of *A Thousand Miles of Miracles*.

23 Wong, *In Remembrance of Martyrs a Century Ago*, 275.

24 *Directory of Protestant Missionaries in China, Japan, and Corea*, 5.

25 Goforth and Goforth, *Miracle Lives of China*, 127–9.

26 *Directory of Protestant Missionaries in China, Japan, and Corea*, 6.

27 Huntington, *Accounts of the American Church*, 13.

28 I have obtained the information from Richard Doss, a great grandnephew of John Oss, Wilmore, Kentucky, June 27, 2022.

29 Heidi Olson Campbell, "Oss, Olga Bertina (Osnes) (1897–1977)," in *Encyclopedia of Seventh-Day Adventists*, November 28, 2021, https://encyclopedia.adventist.org/article?id=FJEY&highlight=y#fn50.

30 *Directory of Protestant Missionaries in China, Japan, and Corea*, 7.

31 *Directory of Protestant Missionaries in China, Japan, and Corea*, 8.

32 *Directory of Protestant Missionaries in China, Japan, and Corea*, 14.

33 DeBernardi, "Circulations," 64.

34 Taylor, *A Retrospect*, 40; Taylor, *China, Its Spiritual Need*, 85. Taylor arrived in Shanghai in 1854.

35 Taylor, *A Retrospect*, 73. Taylor reported about meeting with Rev. R. Lechler from the Basel Missionary Society.

36 Taylor, *China, Its Spiritual Need*, 20. Taylor compared the number of ministers in Guangdong, Great Britain, and Scotland and showed the scarcity of missionaries in the area.

37 Smith, *The Christian's Secret of a Happy Life*.

38 *Directory of Protestant Missionaries*, 10.

39 The first name of Mrs. Hykes is not listed.

40 *Directory of Protestant Missionaries*, 3.

41 Church Missionary Society, *Proceedings*, xxxviii.

42 *Directory of Protestant Missionaries*, 19.

43 *Directory of Protestant Missionaries*, 14.

44 Huskey, "The Cosmopolitan Connection," 227.

45 *Directory of Protestant Missionaries*, 19.

46 Tiedemann, *Reference Guide to Christian Missionary Societies in China*, 156.

47 黄光域：基督教传行中国纪年, 332.

48 Austin, "Women and Guangdong Native-Place," 179.

49 Iap, "Bernt Berntsen," 93.

50 Iap, "Bernt Berntsen," 92.

51 Anderson, "Pentecostalism in India and China," 125.

52 Zhao, "The True Jesus Church," 3–4.

53 Sheng Xuanhuai (1844–1916), a philanthropist and business person who made his fortune out of shipping, mining, telegram, and weaving production, founded *Nanyang Gongxue* (Nan Yang Public School) in 1896, one of the earliest universities in modern Chinese history.

54 Cochran, *The Lius of Shanghai*, 14.

55 T. B. Ray, *Southern Baptist in China*, 14.

56 T. B. Ray, *Southern Baptist in China*, 15.

57 *Directory of Protestant Missionaries*, 15.

58 *Directory of Protestant Missionaries*, 17.

59 Tiedemann, *Reference Guide to Christian Missionary Societies in China*, 154.

60 The United Christian Mission Society, *They Went to China*, 16.

61 The United Christian Mission Society, *They Went to China*, 16.

62 The United Christian Mission Society, *They Went to China*, 42.

63 The United Christian Mission Society, *They Went to China*, 16.

64 The United Christian Mission Society, *They Went to China*, 26; *The Missionary Intelligencer*, 512.

65 Campbell, "Drs. Bertha and Arthur Selmon," 89.

66 Bridgman, "Defying Tradition," 55.

67 Bridgman, "Defying Tradition," 57.

68 Liu, *The Changing Face*, 23–4.

69 Georgia Historical Society, https://georgiahistory.com/marker-monday-wesleyan-college-worlds-first-college-chartered-to-grant-degrees-to-women/.

70 Liu, *The Changing Face*, 55.

71 Xu, "Religion and Education," 19.

72 Tsu, *Friends of Fisherman*.

73 Cochran and Xie, *The Lius of Shanghai*, xii.

74 MacGillivray, *A Century of Protestant Missions*, 12.

75 "Obituaries," *Quarterly Journal*, 221.

76 Handasyde, "Anzac Theology," 20.

77 Ray, *Southern Baptist in China*, 10.

78 H. C. E. Liu, *The Baptist Quarterly*, 208.

79 Wei, *My Revolutionary Years*, 88.

80 Ray, *Southern Baptist in China*, 4.

81 Ray, *Southern Baptist in China*, 7.

82 Ray, *Southern Baptist in China*, 11.

83 Huntington, *Account of the American Church*, 11.

84 Gong, "The Case of Julia B. Mateer," 102.

85 Gong, "The Case of Julia B. Mateer," 103.

86 Gong, "The Case of Julia B. Mateer," 107.

87 Gong, "The Case of Julia B. Mateer," 108.

88 Gong, "The Case of Julia B. Mateer," 113.

89 Gong, "The Case of Julia B. Mateer," 113.

90 Lockhart, *The Medical Missionary*, 116.

91 Lockhart, *The Medical Missionary*, 117.

92 Lockhart, *The Medical Missionary*, 119.

93 Nakajima, "Health, Medicine and Nation," 38–9.

94 *Church Missionary Society Periodicals*, 170.

95 Lockhart, *The Medical Missionary*, 227.

96 King, "Women's Christian Medical College," 756.

97 King, "Women's Christian Medical College," 757.

98 Huntington, *Account of the American Church*, 13.

99 *Directory of Protestant Missionaries*, 14.

100 *Directory of Protestant Missionaries*, 14.

101 *Directory of Protestant Missionaries*, 15.

102 Tiedemann, *Reference Guide to Christian Missionary Societies in China*, 226.

103 Ray, *Southern Baptist in China*, 21.

104 Ray, *Southern Baptist in China*, 21.

105 Walshe, *"Ways that are Dark"*, 23–4.

106 Inouye, "Charismatic Moderns," 21.

107 Inouye, "Charismatic Moderns," 22–6.

108 Tiedemann, *Reference Guide to Christian Missionary Societies in China*, 253.

109 Wylie, *Memories of Protestant Missionaries*, 101–2.

110 Wylie, *Memories of Protestant Missionaries*, 219. Wylie did not provide the first name of Mrs. Cunningham.

111 Wylie, *Memories of Protestant Missionaries*, 219–20.

112 Hershatter, "Prostitution and the Market in Women," 267.

113 Bonnell, "Inside and Outside the Wall," 288–9.

114 Bonnell, "Inside and Outside the Wall," 289.

115 Henriot, *Prostitution and Sexuality*, 340.

116 Bonnell, "Inside and Outside the Wall," 291.

117 Hershatter, *Dangerous Pleasures*, 248.

118 Gronewold, "A New Family," 298.

119 Gronewold, "A New Family," 282.

120 Bollback, *To China and Back*, chapter 6.

121 Tiedemann, *Reference Guide to Christian Missionary Societies in China*, 152.

122 Tiedemann, *Reference Guide to Christian Missionary Societies in China*, 150.

123 Scully, "Prostitution as Privilege," 855.

124 Bickers, "Shanghailanders," 190.

125 Bickers, "Shanghailanders," 191.

126 The United Christian Mission Society, *They Went to China*, 24.

127 The United Christian Mission Society, *They Went to China*, 69.

128 Xiong, *Shanghai Urban Life*, 370–1.

129 The United Christian Mission Society, *They Went to China*, 57.

130 The United Christian Mission Society, *They Went to China*, 60.

131 Pritchard, *Methodists and Their Missionary Societies*, 38.

132 Gillespie, *Around the World*, 64. James Gillespie recalls his Baptist missionary father's imprisonment.

133 Carter, "Lanneu, Sophie Stevens," 18–19.

134 Carter, "Lanneu, Sophie Stevens," 19.

135 Grypma, *China Interrupted*, 5–6.

136 Stark and Wang, *A Star in the East*, 44.

137 Bays, *A New History of Christianity*, 186.

Chapter 3

1 Widmer, *The Russian Ecclesiastical Mission*, 4.

2 Widmer, *The Russian Ecclesiastical Mission*, 4; Aldrich, *The Search for a Vanishing Beijing*, 177. Both Widmer and Aldrich reported that the Kangxi Emperor allowed the Russian Orthodox priest to convert an old Buddhist prayer house into an Orthodox chapel.

3 Aldrich, *The Search for a Vanishing Beijing*, 177.

4 Widmer, *The Russian Ecclesiastical Mission*, 4.

5 Widmer, *The Russian Ecclesiastical Mission*, 5.

6 *Accounts of the Martyrs in Beijing* [no page number available]. First published in Russian in 1906, the book provided 222 accounts of Orthodox martyrs.

7 Witek, "Christianity and China," 22.

8 Lourié, "Russian Christianity," 286. The names of the Chinese assistants are unknown.

9 Knyazeva, "High and Low," 23; Wang, *Istoriia russkoi*, 19.

10 Biryukova, "Russian Orthodox Mission in Korea," 153.

11 Biryukova, "Russian Orthodox Mission in Korea," 154.

12 Wang, *Istoriia russkoi*, 81.

13 Mikkonen, "Shanghai Russians," 62.

14 Eber, *Wartime Shanghai*, 25.

15 Christensen, *The Making of the New Martyrs*, 42.

16 Hubbs, *Mother Russia*, 208.

17 Mikkonen, "Shanghai Russians," 77.

18 Knyazeva, "The Scribe of Russian Shanghai," 178.

19 Knyazeva, "The Scribe of Russian Shanghai," 178.

20 Knyazeva, "The Scribe of Russian Shanghai," 179.

21 Adamek, "Unworthy to Be Quoted," 30.

22 Gamsa, *Harbin: A Cross-Cultural Biography*, 193.

23 Adamek, "Unworthy to Be Quoted," 31.

24 Adamek, "Unworthy to Be Quoted," 31.

25 Adamek, "Unworthy to Be Quoted," 32.

26 Adamek, "Unworthy to Be Quoted," 32.

27 Chashchin, *Russians in China*, 54–185.

28 Knyazeva, "The Scribe of Russian Shanghai," 164–5.

29 Knyazeva, "The Scribe of Russian Shanghai," 165.

30 Knyazeva, "The Scribe of Russian Shanghai," 167.

31 Knyazeva, "The Scribe of Russian Shanghai," 167.

32 Knyazeva, "The Scribe of Russian Shanghai," 167.

33 Russian Collection at the University of Hawai'i at Mānoa Library.

34 Grescoe, *Shanghai Grand*, 114.

35 Zhiganov, *Russians in Shanghai*.

36 Knyazeva, "The Scribe of Russian Shanghai," 163.

37 Knyazeva, "High and Low," 24.

38 Knyazeva, "The Scribe of Russian Shanghai," 184–5.

39 Knyazeva, "The Scribe of Russian Shanghai," 184.

40 Knyazeva, "The Scribe of Russian Shanghai," 186.

41 Minasyan, "Socio-Economic Activity," 63.

42 Halton and Constantine, "Rise and Shine: An Active Armenian Community in Hong Kong," 24.

43 Henry, "Occupational Mobility," 35.

44 Sergoyan, *The Gathering Place*, 10.

45 Noravank Foundation, "'Don't Fall Off the Earth': The Armenian Communities in China from the 1880s – 1950s," http://www.noravank.am/eng/articles/detail.php?ELEMENT_ID=15513.

46 Sergoyan, *The Gathering Place*, 74.

47 Sergoyan, *The Gathering Place*, 79.

48 Meltickian Collection: Armenians in China, 1915–1953, Armenian Studies Program, Fresno State University.

49 Henry, "Occupational Mobility," 41. Sheila Henry speculates that the terminology may relate to how the term "Oriental" stands in contrast to "Caucasian."

50 Armenian Immigration Project, http://markarslan.org/ArmenianImmigrants/Public-ViewDetail-ArmenianImmigrants-Naturalizations.php?submit=View&Staging=&SourcePage=Public-ViewSummary-ArmenianImmigrants-Combined-ByOriginPlace&SelectOriginCountry=China&SelectOriginVSP=all&SelectOriginTown=all&SelectSortOrder=ByName&argument1=USA-WA-Spokane-Spokane-District-EasternDistrictofWA-D-15485.

51 Bays, *A New History*, 212; Adamek, "Unworthy to be Quoted," 26.

52 Knyazeva, "The Scribe of Russian Shanghai," 187.

53 Norman, "Eastern Christianity in China," 288.

54 Baker, "The Orthodox Churches in China," 445.

55 Knyazeva, "The Scribe of Russian Shanghai," 191.

56 Adamek, "Unworthy to Be Quoted," 26.

57 Geraldine Fagan, "China: Will Orthodox Christians Soon be Allowed Priests?" in *Forum 18 News Service*, Oslo, Norway.

58 "Metropolitan Anthony of Chersonesus and Western Europe Visits Shanghai," The Russian Orthodox Church, Department for External Church Relations, October 21, 2019.

59 "Metropolitan Anthony."

60 "Orthodoxy in China," http://orthodox.cn.

61 OFASC, http://www.orthodox.cn/ofasc/ofascbrochure_en.htm.

Chapter 4

1 McLean, *Dr. Li Yuin Tsao*, 3.

2 It is unclear if the adoption was formal. However, Tsao maintained a lifelong relationship with the Lambuths.

3 McLean, *Dr. Li Yuin Tsao*, 5.

4 McLean, *Dr. Li Yuin Tsao*, 6.

5 McLean, *Dr. Li Yuin Tsao*, 6.

6 McLean, *Dr. Li Yuin Tsao*, 8.

7 Hanan, "The Bible as Chinese Literature," 224.

8 Henriot, " '*From a Throne of Glory*'," 134.

9 Henriot, " '*From a Throne of Glory*'," 136.

10 Mungello, *The Great Encounter*, 117.

11 Mungello, *The Great Encounter*, 119.

12 Mungello, *The Great Encounter*, 121–2.

13 Mungello, *The Great Encounter*, 140.

14 Mungello, *The Great Encounter*, 140.

15 International Mission Photography Archive, ca.1860–ca.1960, University of Southern California Digital Library, https://calisphere.org/item/cf6bf7a7789b51b55cac54e9b43c39b4/.

16 Qian, *Chinese Students Encounter America*, 248; Lin, *Zhongguo liuxue jiaoyushi*, 273–4.

17 Bays, "Boone, William Jones," 77.

18 Banister, "The Anglican Communion," 328.

19 Hood, "Gibson, John Campbell," 241.

20 Chen, *A Brief History of Foreign Debt in China*, 52–3.

21 Klein, "Anti-imperialism at Grassroots," 291. Klein dates the anti-Christian movement launched in Shanghai and Beijing as 1922.

22 Junio, *Patriotic Cooperation*, 28.

23 Lee, *Pioneers of Modern China*, xiv.

24 Tillman, "Mediating Modern Motherhood," 120–1.

25 Bonhomme and Boivin, *Milestone Documents*, 1301.

26 Carradice, *Shanghai Massacre*, 84.

27 Fernandez, *Mao's Prey*, 61.

28 Fernandez, *Mao's Prey*, 61.

29 Cochran, *The Lius of Shanghai*, 194.

30 Cochran, *The Lius of Shanghai*, 205.

31 Jiang, *Women Playing Men*, 144.

32 Tsao, *Shanghai Bride*, 51.

33 Wang, "The Chinese Home Missionary Society," 88.

34 Wang, "The Chinese Home Missionary Society," 91–3.

35 Liao, *God is Red*, xvi.

36 Liao, *God is Red*, xix.

37 Liao, *God is Red*, xvii–xviii.

38 Chan, "Mission Movement," 69.

39 Jin, *The Memoirs*, 22–3.

40 Jin, *The Memoirs*, 113–16.

41 Jin, *The Memoirs*, 151.

42 Jin, *The Memoirs*, 169.

43 Martin, *The Shanghai Green Gang*, 69.

44 Martin, *The Shanghai Green Gang*, 69–70.

45 Wei, "News as Weapon," 118.

46 "Dong Jing'an: Exemplary Chinese Christian Educator in East China," *Biographical Dictionary of Chinese Christianity*.

47 Barwick, "Wang Liming: Promoting a Protestant Vision of the Modern Chinese Woman," 136–57.

48 Ray, *Southern Baptist in China*, 22.

49 Ray, *Southern Baptist in China*, 22. Shanghai was part of the Central China field.

50 Tang, "Identity and Marginality–Christianity in East Asia," 86.

51 Due to the war in 1937, the seminary moved to Hong Kong in 1938, Guizhou in 1941, then briefly to Shanghai for a year in 1946, and finally moved again to Hong Kong in 1947.

52 MacInnis, "Gih, Andrew (Ji Zhiwen)," 241.

53 Lin, *Shanghai Faithful*, 132.

54 The whole Wendeli neighborhood has been replaced by shopping malls.

55 Meng, "The Spirituality of Watchman Nee," 15.

56 Anderson, "Pentecostalism and Charismatic Movements in Asia," 163.

57 Inouye, *China and the True Jesus*, 162.

58 O'Brian, *An American Editor in Early Revolutionary China*, 192. O'Brian only listed Mary Barret as the author of the article. Barret and Kiang, "What's Happening at Christian Colleges," 131–3.

59 O'Brian, *An American Editor in Early Revolutionary China*, 192.

60 "Hongde Church," China Christian Council National Committee of Three-Self Patriotic Movement of the Protestant Churches in China, https://en.ccctspm.org/churchinfo/355.

61 Wen, "7 Building Up the Church," 113–14.

62 Li, *Shanghai Homes: Palimpsests of Private Life*, 14.

63 Li, *Shanghai Homes: Palimpsests of Private Life*, 122–3.

64 "Review Meeting of a New Hymnal Held in Shanghai," https://en.ccctspm.org/newsinfo/15632.

65 Kelly Rodriguez, "Notes from the Underground: One Student Navigates Her Faith within the Undercurrent of Shanghai," *Pepperdine University Graphic*, April 13, 2016. Rodriguez speaks of a guest speaker to her class being an anonymous Shanghai Christian woman who sees proper training as a major issue.

Chapter 5

1 Laird, *From Shanghai to the Burma Railway*, 1.

2 Lefebvre, *A Guide to Catholic Shanghai*, 8.

3 Gilbert and Lo, *Performance and Cosmopolitics*, 8.

4 Kato, "Through the Kaleidoscope," 34–5.

5 Fogel, *Maiden Voyage*, 101.

6 Fogel, *Maiden Voyage*, 98–9.

7 Henriot, *The Population of Shanghai*, 148.

8 Shan, *Japanese Accounts of Shanghai*, 113.

9 Kato, "Through the Kaleidoscope," v.

10 Uchiyama, *Sonhe Ohe: Shanhai Seikatsu Sanjugonen*, 17.

11 Tanizaki studied at the Tokyo First Middle School where the Japanese Quaker Nitobe Inazō (1862–1933) was the headmaster in the 1910s.

12 Shan, *Japanese Accounts of Shanghai*, 116; Tanizaki, "Shanghai Friends," 75.

13 Kato, "Through the Kaleidoscope," 23.

14 Kato, "Through the Kaleidoscope," 48; Ibukiyama, *Mato No Minato*, 200.

15 Yang, "Bookstore Frequented by Revolutionaries Reopens in Tianjin," https://www.chinadaily.com.cn/a/202107/11/WS60ea8b7fa310efa1bd6610d5.html.

16 *The New Glories of the Catholic Church*, 106–18.

17 Kleiner, *Korea, A Century of Change*, 7. Pope Paul John II canonized the Korean martyrs on commemorating Korea's 200th anniversary of Christianization.

18 "Shanghai Church Draws Korean Pilgrims," in *PIMA Asianews*, July 21, 2005. https://www.asianews.it/news-en/Shanghai-church-draws-Korean-pilgrims-3758.html, accessed June 1, 2022.

19 Seo, *Korean Nationalism Betrayed*, 30.

20 Kleiner, *Korea, A Century of Change*, 39.

21 Seo, *Korean Nationalism Betrayed*, 31.

22 Bonhomme and Boivin, *Milestone Documents*, 1175.

23 Bonhomme and Boivin, *Milestone Documents*, 1175.

24 Fields, *Foreign Friends*, 3.

25 Bonhomme and Boivin, *Milestone Documents*, 1175.

26 Fields, *Foreign Friends*, 71.

27 Fields, *Foreign Friends*, 70–2.

28 Fields, *Foreign Friends*, 72–3.

29 Fields, *Foreign Friends*, 42.

30 Seo, *Korean Nationalism Betrayed*, 102.

31 Kim, *Project Eagle: The American Christians of North Korea*, 34.

32 Kim, *Project Eagle: The American Christians of North Korea*, 38.

33 Kim, *Project Eagle: The American Christians of North Korea*, 44.

34 Park, *Maria Kim*.

35 Kuo, "*The 'Invisible Work' of Women*," 168.

36 *North China Herald*, December 28, 1932, 494.

37 Kuo, "*The 'Invisible Work' of Women*," 168.

38 Fitzgerald, "Building Trust," 200.

39 Austin, *"Kingdom-Minded" People*, 185–6.

40 Smedley, "The Dedicated," 13.

41 Smith, "The Chinese Church, Labour, and Elites," 100.

42 Hershatter, "Prostitution and the Market," 263. Hershatter attributed the cause of the Cantonese migration and establishment of companies to warlords from the 1920s in the Canton area. However, Sincere and Wing On were from Cantonese who migrated from Australia to Shanghai, not from Canton to Shanghai.

43 Henriot, " '*From a Throne of Glory*'," 149.

44 Wang, *Portuguese in Shanghai*.

45 Wang, *Portuguese in Shanghai*, 67–8.

46 An Archimandrite is an honorific title for a celibate priest.

47 Lefebvre, *A Guide to Catholic Shanghai*, 20.

48 Lefebvre, *A Guide to Catholic Shanghai*, 20.

49 Martin, *The Shanghai Green Gang*, 69; Zhu, *Zhu Zhiyao*, 9. Martin traces Zhu's and Lu's Catholic heritage to the seventeenth century. Zhu Wenwei traces Zhu Zhiyao's Catholic roots to the 1720s on the paternal side of the family. Zhu Zhiyao's Catholic mother Ma'erda Ma came from Dantu in Jiangsu Province, so the maternal side of the family would not have been Catholic in seventeenth-century Shanghai. Lu's family moved from Dantu in Jiangsu to Dongjia Du after the Taiping Rebellion in the mid-nineteenth century.

50 Ding's letters are located at Mount Holyoke College Archives and Special Collections in South Hadley, Massachusetts.

51 McLean, *Dr. Li Yuin Tsao*. McLean published a biography of Li in 1925.

52 Littell-Lamb, "Caught in the Crossfire," 135.

53 Littell-Lamb, "Caught in the Crossfire," 141.

54 United Presbyterian Church, *Minutes*, 68.

55 *Christian Advocate*, 576.

56 Cornwell, *Ruth, A Portrait*, 42.

57 The United Christian Mission Society, *They Went to China*, 16.

58 Bridgman, "Defying Tradition," 41.

59 "John G. Oss Dies in California," *Newman Grove Reporter*, August 4, 1948, 1.

60 Isabel, "Faith Tends to Grow When We are Out of Our Comfort Zone." Isabel's testimony comes from Madrid, Spain, on March 18, 2018.

61 Yumei, "My Eyes were Restrained like the Two Men on Their Road to Emmaus," https://www.columban.org.au/media-and-publications/articles/faith-stories/shanghai-faith-stories/my-eyes-were-restrained-like-the-two-men-on-their-road-to-emmaus.

62 Moon, "The Korean Diaspora Models," 97.

63 Cho, "Korean Diaspora and Christian Mission," 270.

64 Shanghai Municipal Bureau of Statistics.

65 Eiko, "The City as a Contact Zone," 146.

66 Participant observation via online worship services in 2021–2.

67 Flynn, "Mission Continues," https://www.maryknollmagazine.org/2016/09/mission-continues/.

68 Grace Zhi, "Nick Vujicic Speaks of Being Your Best in Shanghai," in *China Christian Daily*, August 4, 2016.

69 Yang, *Atlas of Religion in China*, 114.

70 Zhi, "Shanghai Churches Collectively Hold Bazaars to Aid Poor Sick Children."

71 Cui, "Story of Shanghai Church Co-worker's Voluntary Service," http://chinachristiandaily.com/news/china/2022-05-19/story-of-shanghai-church-co-worker--voluntary-service-_11467.

72 Chou, "Churches in Shanghai are Stepping Up during the Latest Lockdowns."

73 Sun, "Testimony: A Shanghai Christian's Experience."

74 Zhong, "Easter in Shanghai."

75 Sander, *Passing Through Shanghai*, 172.

76 Turner, "Studying the Tensions of Transnational Engagement," 1052.

77 Sander, *Passing Through Shanghai*, 172.

78 Reilly, *Saving the Nation*, 8.

79 Bays, "Chinese Protestant Christianity Today," 496–7.

Chapter 6

1 Although it is an important question to ask how different religious adherents in Shanghai perceived Christianity and interacted with Christians, I have narrowed the discussion because it would involve more space to discuss the question.

2 Brook, "Xu Guangqi," 94.

3 Zürcher, "Xu Guangqi and Buddhism," 159–60.

4 Ferrão, "Dreams, Visions and a Taoist-Christian 'Saint'," 110–11.

5 Ferrão, "Dreams, Visions and a Taoist-Christian 'Saint'," 117–18.

6 Ferrão, "Dreams, Visions and a Taoist-Christian 'Saint'," 112.

7 Ferrão, "Dreams, Visions and a Taoist-Christian 'Saint'," 108.

8 Patrick, "Art as a Pathway," 119–20.

9 King, *"A Model for All Christian Women": Candida*, 80–1.

10 King, *"A Model for All Christian Women": Candida*, 81.

11 Xu Guangqi, "Pi shishi zhuwang," in *Xujiahui cangshulou ming qing tianzhujiao wenxian*, I: 62; Zhang, "About God, Demons, and Miracles," 19.

12 Li Madou, *Yesu hui yu Tianzhu jiao jingru zhongguo shi*, 338, 339; Tang, *Limadou* [Matteo Ricci], 51.

13 Zhang, "About God, Demons, and Miracles," 16–17.

14 Patrick, "Art as a Pathway," 129.

15 Tsao, *Shanghai Bride*, 45.

16 Tsao, *Shanghai Bride*, 125, 157, 208.

17 Tsao, *Shanghai Bride*, 206.

18 Tsao, *Shanghai Bride*, 188–9. Tsao's husband Liankui represented the adopted Chinese sons of the Hardoon-Luo family in a bitter legal battle over inheritance.

19 Nedostup, "Religion, Superstition and Governing Society," 210.

20 Interview, January 4, 2023.

21 Interview, January 4, 2023.

22 Smith, *Chinese Characteristics*, 313.

23 Yates, *Ancestral Worship*, 31.

24 Yates, *Ancestral Worship*, 36.

25 Yates, *Ancestral Worship*, 36–7.

26 Yates, *Ancestral Worship*, 37.

27 Yates, *Ancestral Worship*, 46.

28 Yates, *Ancestral Worship*, 46.

29 Yates, *Ancestral Worship*, 47.

30 Faber, *Problems of Practical Christianity in China*, 6–7.

31 Faber, *Problems of Practical Christianity in China*, 17.

32 Faber, *Problems of Practical Christianity in China*, 41–122.

33 Faber, *Problems of Practical Christianity in China*, 113.

34 Mungello, *The Great Encounter*, 41–3.

35 Standaert, *Yang Tingyun*, 211.

36 Ahmad, "Chinese Muslims in Taipei, Nanjing, and Shanghai," 178.

37 Juergensmeyer, *Global Rebellion*, 54.

38 Juergensmeyer, *Global Rebellion*, 95.

39 Interview, January 3, 2023.

40 Gladney, *Muslim Chinese*, 113–15.

41 Juergensmeyer, *Global Rebellion*, 4–5.

42 Gratton, *Freemasonry in Shanghai*, 2–4.

43 Gratton, *Freemasonry in Shanghai*, 5–7.

44 Bickers, "Shanghailanders," 186.
45 Gratton, *Freemasonry in Shanghai*, 152–61.
46 Fitzgerald and Kuo, "Diaspora Charity," 72.
47 Clarke, "From Kaifeng to Shanghai via Rome and Paris," 142–3.
48 Clarke, "From Kaifeng to Shanghai via Rome and Paris," 142.
49 Meyer, "Recollections of Shanghai's Baghdadi Jews," 33.
50 Meyer, "Recollections of Shanghai's Baghdadi Jews," 38–41.
51 Moshinsky, *Goodbye, Shanghai*, 54.
52 Moshinsky, *Goodbye Shanghai*, 9.
53 Moshinsky, *Goodbye Shanghai*, 17.
54 Moshinsky, *Goodbye Shanghai*, 55.
55 Eber, *Wartime Shanghai and the Jewish Refugees from Central Europe*, 77.
56 Moshinsky, *Goodbye Shanghai*, 56.
57 Moshinsky, *Goodbye Shanghai*, 56.
58 Meyer, "Recollections of Shanghai's Baghdadi Jews," 33; Moshinsky, *Goodbye Shanghai*, 71.
59 Liu, "Myths that Shaped the Exile," 56.
60 Moshinsky, *Goodbye Shanghai*, 63.
61 Liu, "Myths that Shaped the Exile," 53.
62 Liu, "Myths that Shaped the Exile," 53.
63 Liu, "Myths that Shaped the Exile," 70.
64 Eber, *Wartime Shanghai and the Jewish Refugees from Central Europe*, 77.
65 Hochstadt, "Introduction: How Many Shanghai Jews Were There?," 7.
66 Kaminski, "Dr. Jakob Rosenfeld: Mensch und Mythos," 461–78.
67 Bacon, *Shanghai Diary*, 37.
68 Buxbaum and Gesellschaft, *Transit in Shanghai*, 79.
69 Schwarcz, *In the Crook of the Rock*, 63.
70 Schwarcz, *In the Crook of the Rock*, 63.
71 Setsuzō, *The True Character of the Jewish Nation*.
72 Setsuzō, *From Tokyo to Jerusalem*.
73 Schwarcz, *In the Crook of the Rock*, 143.
74 Schwarcz, *In the Crook of the Rock*, 197.
75 Grescow, *Shanghai Grand*, 114.
76 Liu, "Myth that Shaped the Exile," 57.
77 McKale, "The Nazi Party in the Fast East," 294.
78 Spang, "The German East Asiatic Society," 53.
79 Roberts, "Relative Resistance," 245.
80 Ristaino, *Port of Last Resort*, 178.
81 A German doctor Erich Paulun founded the medical school in 1907.

82 Freyeisen, Astrid, *Shanghai und die Politik*, 272.

83 Wilhelm, *China Hans*, 44–8.

84 Wilhelm, *China Hans*, 25.

85 Cortum's memoir in Chinese can be found at: http://www.cqvip.com/qikan/Detail.aspx?gch=83098X&years=2010&num=03.

86 Freyeisen, *Shanghai und die Politik des Dritten Reiches*, 177.

87 Xiong, *Shanghai Urban Life*, 27.

88 Cao, *From Policemen to Revolutionaries*, 141–62.

89 *The North-China Herald*, November 7, 1934.

90 Tenrikyô is a Japanese new religion that is based on the teaching of Nakayama Miki (1798–1887).

91 Yeh, *Wartime Shanghai*, 40.

92 Lu, "Dangdai zhongguo zongjiao zhuangkuang baogao," 13.

93 Johnson and Tieszen, "Personal Contact," *Missio Nexus*, October 1, 2007.

94 Vermander, Hingley, and Zhang, *Shanghai Sacred*, 3–4.

95 Ye, *Pluralism and Harmony*, 41–6.

96 Participant observation, Kansas City, Missouri, October 9, 2021.

97 Juergensmeyer, *Global Rebellion*, 258.

98 Interview, April 2022.

99 Van der Veer, "Urban Planning and Secular Atheism," 47.

100 Van der Veer, "Urban Planning and Secular Atheism," 47.

101 Weller, Huang, Wu, and Fan, *Religion and Charity*, 60.

Chaper 7

1 Meynard, "Fan Shouyi," 25.

2 Tang, *Li Madou*, 60.

3 Clark, "Sealing Fate and Changing Course," 137.

4 Cross, "Old School in China Holds Reunion in Kentucky," 4.

5 United States Congress House, "83d Congress 2d Session, House of Representatives, Report No. 2226," in *Report*.

6 "Sister Antonella Marie Gutterres (Thereza Maria Gutterres)," in *Congressional Record—House*, 1954, 13294.

7 Gutterres, *Lorettine Education in China, 1923–1952*.

8 https://www.genealogy.com/ftm/n/o/e/Christi-A-Noel-CA/FILE/0001page.html.

9 Carlos Borromeu Lubeck, "Autobiography of Carlos Borromeu Lubeck: To My Children." Letter collected at the Macanese Library, https://www.macaneselibrary.org/pub/uiExtFiles/Biographies/Misc/LubeckAutobiography.htm. Lubeck's letter also reveals that his wife was Yang Te-di, who came from a Catholic family among the boat people of Wusih area near Tai Lake. Judging

from the location, Yang came from Wuxi in nearby Jiangsu Province, an area where Catholics maintained a strong presence since the late Ming Dynasty in the early seventeenth century.

10 "Heights Gives 1st U.S. Degree to Chinese Nun," in *Denver Catholic Register*, Vol. XL, No. 49. Denver, Colorado, Thursday, August 9, 1945.

11 Sister Lubeck's father did not mention her getting a degree in his family letter.

12 Loretto Community, https://www.lorettocommunity.org/remembrance-of-the-life-of-sister-patricia-anne-formerly-sister-mary-richelle-cullen/.

13 "Father Peter A. Wu, M.M.," in *Catholic New York*, May 21, 2020.

14 Yi Yang, "Shanghai Church Visits Taiwan Church to Discuss Ministry Development," in *China Christian Daily*, July 8, 2016.

15 Charbonnier, "The MEP in China," 268.

16 Luedi, "Finding God in Africa," https://www.asiabyafrica.com/point-a-to-a/chinese-in-africa-christianity-religion.

17 Qian, *Chinese Students Encounter America*, 80.

18 Pew Research Center, "Being Christian in Western Europe," May 29, 2018, https://www.pewresearch.org/religion/2018/05/29/being-christian-in-western-europe/.

19 Interview, April 2022.

20 Pseudonym.

21 Interview of D W, a friend of G, September 4, 2022.

22 Interview of Joanna Gu (Pseudonym), January 4, 2023.

23 Huang, "Western-Educated Chinese Christian Returnees," 6–9.

24 Summers and Thomas, "Recent Lessons of Development," 242–3.

25 Shi, *Supernormal Growth*, 104.

26 Shi, *Supernormal Growth*, 34.

27 Shi, *Supernormal Growth*, 49.

28 Interview, Shanghai, January 5, 2019.

29 Zhang and Sun, "When Are You Going to Get Married," 118–20.

30 Huang, "Homosexuality in China: An Emergent Social and Religious Controversy," Berkley Center for Religion, Peace, and World Affairs, Georgetown University, April 25, 2013.

31 Ikebuchi, *From Slave Girls to Salvation*, 35–6.

32 Pascoe, *Relations of Rescue*, 13.

33 Wang Zhicheng, "Goodbye to the Religious Affairs Bureau: Religions are Now under the Direct Control of the Party," *PIME Asia News*, March 22, 2018.

34 "Holy See and China Renew Provisional Agreement for 2 Years," *Vatican News*, October 22, 2020.

35 "Holy See–China: Provisional Agreement on Nomination of Bishops Renewed for Second Time," *Vatican News*, October 22, 2022.

36 Zimmer, "Disrupted Loyalties? 21st-Century Sinicization of the Catholic Other," 147–63.

37 Wang, "Peking Opera Master Mei Baojiu Dies at 82," http://chinachristiandaily.com/news/china/2016-04-26/peking-opera-master-mei-baojiu-dies-at-82--his-christian-friend-witnesses-his-conversion-to-christianity-_1090.

38 Robert, *Christian Mission*, 174.

39 Gamble, *Shanghai in Transition*, 167.

40 Sklair, "Towards an Understanding of Architectural Iconicity," 41.

41 The example of popular singer Gloria Tang Tze Kei is unique. I have not found any other Shanghai-related Christian singers with the same level of influence.

42 "Forbes 30 Under 30," https://www.forbes.com/30-under-30-2016/music/#5c38096f5c0f.

43 "G.E.M. Official Music Video, Chapter 01 Revelation," https://www.youtube.com/watch?v=stGUpMav1sc.

44 Interview, August 16, 2022.

45 Interview, August 16, 2022.

46 Gamble, *Shanghai in Transition*, 139.

Conclusion

1 Lu, *La Vie et les oeuvres du grand chrétien chinois*, 10–15.

Appendices

Appendix A: Names of Places, Institutions, and Events

Albazinian 阿尔巴津人
An Laohui 安老会
Anpin xiao zimei hui (Congregation of the Little Sisters of the Poor) 安贫小姊妹会
Baoshan 宝山
Changning 长宁
Chongming 崇明岛
Chuansha xianzhi (Chuansha County Gazatteers) 川沙县志
Cimu Tang 慈母堂
Dafo chang 大佛厂
Dianhu 佃户
Difang zhaohui yundong 地方召会运动
Dongjia du 董家渡
Du'en Shuyuan 度恩书院
Fengxian 奉贤
Fuxing Road 复兴路
Gongji Hospital (General Hospital) 公济医院
Guandi Miao (Guandi Temple) 关帝庙
Guangci yiyuan (Saint Marie Hospital) 光慈医院
Guangqi She 光启社
Harbin 哈尔滨
Hengshan Road 衡山路
Hongkou 虹口
Huaihai East Road 淮海东路
Huangpu 黄浦
Huating 华亭
Huimin Road 惠民路
Jiading 嘉定
Jiangnan 江南
Jiaowu zazhi (The Chinese Recorder) 教务杂志
Jidu tu 基督徒
Jinjiaxiang 金家巷
Jinshan 金山
Jing'an 静安
Jingjiao 景教
Jinhui shuju (Baptist Publishing) 浸会书局
Jiujian lou (Nine-room Building) 九间楼

Jushi 居士
Liuhe congtan 六合丛谈
Liujia Harbor 刘家港
Liushou ertong (Left behind children) 留守儿童
Meihua shuguan (The American Presbyterian Mission Press) 美华书馆
Minhang 闵行
Mohai shuguan 墨海书馆
Moxi huitang 摩西会堂
Nanjing jiaoan 南京教案
Nügonghui (Women's Union Missionary Society) 女公会
Peiya Shuyuan 培雅书院
Pu 谱
Putuo 普陀
Qin Tianjian 钦天监
Qinglong zhen 青龙镇
Qingpu jiaoan (Qingpu religious case) 青浦教案
Qingpu District 青浦区
Ren'ai xiunü Hui (Daughters of Charity) 仁爱修女会
Ruose Shuyuan 若瑟书院
Shandong 山东
Shanghai 上海
Shanmu xiunü hui (Sisters of the Good Shepherd) 善牧修女会
Shanghai Puqiao 上海葡侨
Sheshan Xiuyuan (Sheshan Seminary) 佘山修院
Sheng Yuehan Shuyuan (St. John's College) 圣约翰书院
Shi 史
Songjiang District 松江区
Tianjin 天津
Tianzhu jiao 天主教
Tilanqiao 提篮桥
Tushanwan 土山湾
Wenyan wen 文言文
Xianxian 献县
Xilei Middle School 天主教锡类中学
Xin Yesu de 信耶稣的
Xinjiang 新疆
Xinle Road 新乐路
Xuhui zhongxue (Xuhui High School) 徐汇中学
Xujiahui 徐家汇
Yangjingbang 洋泾浜
Zhangjialou 张家楼
Zhangjiawan 张家湾
Zhangpuqiao 张朴桥
Zhendan daxue (Aurora University) 震旦大学
Zhenguang dalou (True Light Building) 真光大楼
Zhennü xiantang hui 贞女献堂会
Zhengwang hui (Society of the Helpers of the Holy Souls) 拯望会
Zhi 志
Zhonghua guonei budao hui 中华国内布道会

Zhonghua sheng gonghui 中华圣公会
Zhuxiang 诸巷

Appendix B: Names of Churches

Andelie Tang 安得烈堂
Beishi Tang 北市堂
Cimu Tang 慈母堂
Eguo nüzhong shengmu Tang 俄国女中圣母堂 Holy Mother Church at the Russian Girls' School
Fujia meiguo shengmu Tang (The Fu Family Rose Our Lady Church) 傅家玫瑰圣母堂
Fuyin Tang 福音堂
Heping Tang 和平堂
Hongde Tang (Fitch Memorial Church) 鸿德堂 (formerly 思娄堂 Silou Tang)
Huxi libai Tang (West Shanghai Church) 沪西礼拜堂
Jinglian Tang 景莲堂
Jinglin Tang 景林堂 (After 1981, known as Jingling Tang 景灵堂 Adoring the Holy Spirit)
Jingyi Tang 敬一堂 (The same as Shichun Tang 世春堂)
Jiuzhu Tang 救主堂
Junwang Tang 君王堂 (The same as Diwang Tang 帝王堂)
Lanfen Tang 兰芬堂
Ling'en Tang 灵恩堂
Lude shengmu Tang (Church of Our Lady of Lourdes) 露德圣母堂
Shengmu Tang 圣母堂
Shengmu wuran yuanzui Tang (The Immaculate Conception Church) 圣母无染原罪堂
Shanghai deguo libai tang (Shanghai German Church) 上海德国礼拜堂
Shanghai guoji libai tang (Community Church) 上海国际礼拜堂
Shanghai zhanglao hui diyi hui Tang (First Presbyterian Church of Shanghai) 上海长老会第一会堂
Shanghai zhusheng Tang (Christ All Saints Church) 上海诸圣堂
Sheng Boduolu Tang (Saint Peter's Church) 圣伯多禄堂
Sheng nigula Tang (Saint Nicholas Church) 圣尼古拉堂
Sheng nigula junren xiaojiao Tang (Saint Nicholas Military Chapel) 圣尼古拉斯军人小教堂
Tian'en Tang 天恩堂
Tihuan Tang 提唤堂
Wu yuanzui shitai Tang (Immaculate Conception Church, Jinjiangxiang) 无原罪始胎堂
Xiyan Tang 息焉堂 Xiyan Hall (formerly 圣母升天堂)
Xin'en Tang (New Grace Church) 新恩堂
Yangsi jidu fuyin Tang 杨思基督福音堂
Yesu shengxin Tang (Sacred Heart of Jesus) 耶稣圣心堂
Zhuxian Tang (Epiphany Church) 主显堂

Appendix C: Names of People

Ai Fangji (François Estève) 艾方济
An Duo (Antoine Thomas) 安多
Bai Yingli (Philip Couplet) 柏应理
Bao Zhaoqi (George E. Partch) 包兆祺
Bi Fangji (Francesco Sambiasi) 毕方济
Bi Xueyuan (Bishop Cayetano Pires Pireira) 毕学源
Du Ruolan (Desjacques Marin) 杜若兰
Elias Wen Zizheng 文子正
Geng Lishu (Talitha Gerlach) 耿丽淑
Gong Peng 龚澎
Guo Jujing (Lazzaro Cattaneo) 郭居静
Han Sen 韩森
He Gengbo (Alphonse De Moerloose) 和羹柏
Hui Jiliang (Auguste Haouissée) 惠济良
Jiang Shixu 蒋时叙
Jin Luxian 金鲁贤
Le Lingsheng (Frank Joseph Rawlinson) 乐灵生
Li Ningshi (Pedro Ribeiro) 黎宁石
Li Ruihe 李瑞和
Li Xiufang (Benjamin Brueyre) 李秀芳
Liu Na'ou 刘呐欧
Liu Yunde 刘云德
Lou Liren 娄理仁
Lu Xiyan 陆希言
Luo Boji (Louis de Besi) 罗伯济
Luo Weilin (William Lockhart) 雒魏林
Luo Wenzao (Gregory Lopez) 罗文藻
Ma Jianshu 马健淑
Ma Liyao (Léon Mariot) 马力耀
Ma Xiangbo 马相伯
Mai Dusi (Walter Henry Medhurst) 麦都思
Mai Ganlin (Cameron Farquhar McRae) 麦甘霖
Martina Xu 玛尔第纳
Mu Weilian (William Muirhead) 慕维廉
Nan Gelu (Claude Gotteland) 南格禄
Pan Guoguang (Francesco Brancati) 潘国光
Pan Yaona 潘尧纳
Peter Joseph Fan Xuanyan 范学淹
Shen Que 沈榷
Simon Zhu Kaimin 朱开敏
Sun Yuanhua 孙元化
Tang Ruowang (Johann Adam Schall von Bell) 汤若望
Wang Ruowang 王若望
Wei Fangji (François Noël) 卫方济
Wu Li 吴历 (Wu Yushan) 吴渔山
Xu Chengbin (Francis Hsu Cheng-ping) 徐诚斌
Xu Candida 徐甘第大

Xu Guangqi 徐光启
Xu Kesheng 徐可升
Xu Sicheng 徐思诚
Yan Yongjing 颜永京
Yang Shaotang 杨绍唐
Yao Zongli (Próspero París) 姚宗李
Ye Zhaochang (François-Xavir Diniz) 叶肇昌
Yu Qiaqing 虞洽卿
Zhang Boda 张伯达
Zhang Jingqiao 张景乔
Zhang Ruogu 张若谷
Zhang Ximan 张西满
Zhang Yujing 张宇敬
Zheng He 郑和
Zhu Shude 朱树德
Zhu Zhiyao 朱志尧

Appendix D: List of Major Christian Hospitals

1844–present: founded by British medical missionary as Renji Hospital in 1844. Now it is part of the Renji Hospital attached to Jiaotong University.

1863–present: founded as General Hospital by the French Jesuits. Changed into Gongji Hospital in 1878. Shanghai City Government took it over in 1953 and changed its name into the First Hospital of Shanghai. Now attached to Jiaotong University in Shanghai.

1866–present: founded as St. Luke's Hospital by the American Anglicans. It was part of the Medical College of St. John's University. Expanded in 1880 and renamed as Tongren Hospital. Taken over by the city government in 1955. Restored its original name in 1979. Still known as Tongren Hospital.

1884–present: founded as Furu Hospital (Women and Children's Hospital) by American missionary Margaret Williamson in 1884. Local patients warmly named it "the Red House Hospital" because of its red roof. Expanded to the Women's Medical College in Shanghai, the only one of its kind in the Republic Era. Now known as the Women's Hospital attached to Fudan University.

1906–present: built as a clinic by Ningbo-born Christian businesspeople in Shanghai (*Siming huisuo*). Moved to the French Concession as Siming Hospital in 1922. Taken over by the city government in 1954. Now known as Shuguang Hospital.

1907–present: built as Saint Maria Hospital by the French Catholics in 1907. Also known as Guangci Hospital. Taken over by the city in 1951. Now known as Ruijin Hospital.

Appendix E: List of Christian Schools in Shanghai

1850–1949; 1953–present: Xuhui School, built by the French Jesuits. Originally a boys' boarding school. The city took it over in 1949 and changed it into a nonreligious school for boys and girls.

1850–1953; 1953–present: Biwen Girls' School, opened by American Episcopalian missionary Eliza Jane Bridgeman. The city took it over in 1953 and changed it into co-educational in 1969. Now known as No. 9 Middle School.

1851–1952; 1952–present: Fangde Primary School, built by the Catholic Church in Dongjiadu. State-owned since 1952. Relocated to Yaojianong in 2010. Known as No. 2 Primary School of Dujiadu.

1855–1950s; 1950s–present. Jingyan Primary School, Chongde Girls' School, and Xuhui Girls' School and Qiming Girls' School all formed into Huiming Girls' Middle School, and then renamed as No. 4 Middle School.

1857–1953; 1953–present: Leisi Primary School, built as the church school of Saint Joseph's Catholic Church. Renamed as Sichuan South Road Elementary School in Huangpu District.

1859–1953; 1953–present: Leisi xuetang, built by the Catholic Church in Chongming. Taken over by the Chongming County government in 1953. Relocated in 1984 and known as Ganyan Elementary School of Chongming.

1861–1953; 1953–present: Qingxin Girls' School, built by American Presbyterian missionary. The Shanghai city government took it over in 1953 and changed it into a co-educational school in 1969. Known as No. 8 Middle School.

1861–1950s; 1950s–present: Qingxin Middle School, built by American Presbyterian missionary. Took over by the government in the 1950s, now known as Shinan Middle School.

1868–1952; 1952–present: Chejia Public School, built by the Catholic Church. Renamed as Dayi Public School in 1898. Took over by the government in 1952 and now known as Tangzhen Middle School.

1874–1950s; 1950s–present: Saint Francis Xavier Academy, built by French Catholic priest. State-owned since the 1950s. Divided into two schools, known as Beihong Middle School and Shidai Middle School.

1876–1950s; 1950s–present: Gezhi Academy, co-founded by Xu Shou and British missionary John Fyer. Known as Gezhi Middle School.

1881–1952; 1952–present: Saint Maria Girls' School, built by American Anglicans in 1881; Zhongxi Girls' School, built by American Methodist (South) in 1892. The government merged the two schools in 1952 and renamed it as No. 3 Girls' School.

1884–1950s; 1950s–present: Leixi Elementary School, built as a church school by the French Catholics at Immaculate Concept Church on Puxi Road.

Became Huishi Elementary School in 1934. State-owned since 1950s. Its name was restored as Huishi Elementary School in 1998.

1889–1951; 1951–present: Huizhong Middle School, built by American Seventh Day Baptist. State-owned since 1951 and renamed as Li Huili Middle School and Wuai High School.

1893–1950s; 1950s–present: church school. State-owned and known as No. 5 Middle School.

1893–1950s; 1950s–present: Shaodao Girls' Middle School and Elementary School, founded by the French Catholics. State-owned since the 1950s and known as No. 1 Elementary School on Haining Road, Hongkou District.

1897–1950s; 1950s–present: Dayi Public School, originally founded in the church building of Tangzhen Catholic Church. State-owned in the 1950s. Relocated in 1987 and now known as Tangzhen Elementary School.

1898–1953; 1953–present: Yinghua shuyuan/Mailun Middle School, built by LMS in 1898. State-owned since 1953 and known as Jiguang Middle School.

1901–1950s; 1950s–present: YMCA Middle School. State-owned and now known as Puguang Middle School.

1905–50; 1950–present: Fudan Public School, founded by Chinese Jesuit Ma Xiangbo. The university section moved in 1922. Renamed as Fudan Middle School since 1944.

1908–49; 1949–present: Zhendan Academy, founded by Chinese Jesuit Ma Xiangbo. Renamed as Xiangming Middle School in the 1950s.

Appendix F: List of Churches on a Timeline

- 1608–? Xu residential chapel in Jiuge Lou. Xu Guangqi constructed the private chapel for the initial Catholics to celebrate mass with Cattaneo.
- Between 1628 and 1644 until 1937; 1949; 2004–present: Shengmu wuran yuanzui Tang/The Immaculate Conception Church (Catholic), built in the late Ming Dynasty. Korean Saint Andrew Kim received his ordination here in 1845. New church building in 1872. Bombed in 1937 and new church of 1949 bombed within a month. New CPA church built in 2004.
- 1630s–1730; 1862–1960s: Jingyi Tang/Worship the One Hall. Xu Guangqi's granddaughter Martina purchased a residential building from the Pan family and gifted it to the Catholic Church as Jingyi Tang, No. 137 Wutong Street. After 1730, the Qing government converted the church to *Shenjiang shuyuan*, a private school, and a Taoist Guandi temple. The church was restored in 1862 and was confiscated in the 1960s. It is currently part of the seniors' activity center, used for exhibitions and calligraphy classes.
- Late seventeenth century–1966; 1983–present: Fujia meigui shengmu Tang/The Fu Family Rose Our Lady Church (Catholic).

- 1744–1960s; 2003–present: Yesu shengxin Tang/Sacred Heart of Jesus Church in Zhangjialou (Catholic). Built by Zhang Yujing as Xunhuo shizijia Tang. Added a second building in 1843 and completed in 1865. Torn down in 2000. New building since 2003. Added Mass in English since 2005.
- 1847–1966: Saint Francis Xavier's Church (Dongjiadu Cathedral).
- 1860–1966; 1986–present: Saint Joseph's Church/Sheng ruose Tang. As part of the treaty compensation, the church was built in the French Concession. Briefly closed during the Cultural Revolution. CPA since 1986.
- 1863–1960s; ?–present: Sheshan Basilica, Songjiang District.
- 1869–present: Holy Trinity Cathedral (Church of England), Huangpu District, No. 219 Jiujiang Road. Still in use as a church.
- 1874–present: Mu'en Tang/Moore Memorial Church (American Methodist Episcopal, South), No. 316 Middle Xizang Road, Huangpu District. TSPM since 1958.
- 1890–1934: Shanghai deguo libai tang/Shanghai German Church/Deutsch-evangelische Kirche Shanghai (Lutheran), Huangpu Road, Hongkou District. Renovated in 1911 along with William School. Torn down between 1932 and 1934.
- 1898–1958; 1992–present: Lude shengmu Tang/Church of Our Lady of Lourdes (Catholic), No. 3310 Tanglu Highway, Tang Town, Pudong District. Major pilgrimage site in May. Closed in 1958 and reopened as CPA in 1992.
- 1905–32: Zhuxiang Tang/Epiphany Church (Eastern Orthodox). First Orthodox church in Shanghai. Zhabei District, No. 43 North He'nan Road. Destroyed during the January 28 incident in 1932.
- 1910–37; 1948–66: Beishi Tang, American missionary George E. Partch began the church on Caojia Road. Destroyed during the Sino-Japanese war. Rebuilt in 1948 as Tiandao Tang and destroyed in 1966.
- 1910–1950s; 1980–present: Huaien Tang/Grace Church (American Southern Baptist), Jing'an District, No. 375 North Shaanxi Road. TSPM since 1980.
- 1916–1950s; Huibei huitang/Church in North Shanghai (Seventh Day Adventist), No. 183 Wujin Road. TPSM property and rented as a hotel and a restaurant.
- 1922–1950s; 1981–present: Jinglin Tang (Methodist Episcopal Church, South), Hongkou District, No. 135 Kunshan Road. TSPM since 1981 and changed its name into Jingling Tang.
- 1922–34: Nicholas Military Chapel (Eastern Orthodox), No. 13, Lane 583, East Huanghai Road. Closed in 1934.
- 1922–57; 1980–present: Chongdao Church (American Methodist Episcopal Church, South), Xiaogang Villiage, Zhoujia Lane, Chengqiao Town, Chongming County. Reopened as TSPM church in 1980. New church building in 1991 and renamed as Chongzhu Church.
- 1923–1950s; 1979–present: Qingxin Tang/Pure Heart Church (American Presbyterian), Huangpu District, No. 30 Dachang Street. TSPM church since 1979.
- 1924–48: Tihuan Tang (Eastern Orthodox), No. 1, Lane 737, Hengshan Road. Closed in 1948.

- 1925–66; 1980–present: Zhusheng Tang/Christ All Saints Church (the American Episcopal Church). Became a united church in 1958. Reopened as TPSM in 1980. Worship for the blind since 1985.
- 1926–56: Jiuzhu Tang (Eastern Orthodox), No. 5, Lane 120, Huimin Road. Closed in 1956.
- 1927–36: Shengmu Tang (Eastern Orthodox), No. 1233, Fuxing Road. Closed in 1936.
- 1928–1950s; 1992–present: Hongde Tang/Fitch Memorial Church (American Presbyterian), Hongkou District, No. 59 Duolun Road. TSPM church since 1992.
- 1928–54; 1990–present: Heping Tang, built by French Jesuits to accommodate factory workers. No. 692 Huimin Road, Yangpu District. The Spanish Jesuits took over the church in 1936. Joined CPA in 1954. New building since 1990.
- 1930–48: Shengmu Tang at the Russian Girls' School (Eastern Orthodox), South Maoming Road. Closed in 1948.
- 1931–1950s; 2008–present: Xiyan Tang/Xiyan Church (Chinese Catholics) Changning District No. 1 Kele Road. Resumed as a Catholic church since 2008.
- 1931–66; 1993–present: Shengnü xiao deliesa Tang/St. Teresa Church (Catholic), No. 370, Datian Road (formerly Datong Road), Jing'an District. CPA since 1993.
- 1931–48: Andelie Tang (Eastern Orthodox), Huoshan Road (later No. 13, Lane 220 Nanchang Road). Closed in 1948.
- 1932–Cultural Revolution: the second Shanghai German Church. No. 30, Huashan Road, Jing'an District. Hilton Hotel and Crystal Hotel were built on the site in 1990.
- 1933–1960s; 1995–present: Saint Peter's Church (Catholic), Huangpu District. The Byzantine-styled church was the chapel for Aurora University. The church was rebuilt in 1995 as a modern church.
- 1934–1950s: Sheng nigula Tang/Saint Nicholas Church (Eastern Orthodox), Huangpu District, No. 16 Gaolan Road. Bookstore since 2019.
- 1935–48: Shengmu xiudaoyuan Church (Eastern Orthodox), No. 1229, Middle Fuxing Road. Closed in 1948.
- 1935–1950s: Jinglian Tang (Methodist Episcopal Church, South), Changning District, No. 155 Jiangsu Road. Now auditorium at No. 3 Girls' High School since 1981.
- 1936–62: Shengmu da Tang/Notre Dame Cathedral (Eastern Orthodox), No. 55 Xinle Road. Stopped religious activities in 1962.
- 1939–1950s; 1989–present: Xin'en Tang/New Grace Church (CIM), Jing'an District, No. 25 North Wulumuqi Road. TSPM church since 1989.
- 1943–66: Yangsi jidu fuyin Tang. Built by Gu Wenda from the Gospel Tour of the Mu'en Church and a local Christian Wang Linsheng. Destroyed in 1966.
- 1996–present: Shanghai Community Fellowship (Interdenominational), two groups of expatriates who previously gathered at the Holiday Inn and the Portman Hotel. Use the Hengshan Community Church space, 53 Hengshan Road, Xuhui District.

Appendix G: Interview Questions

1 Name (or a pseudonym), Gender, Age group (25–45; 45–65; 65 and above), Education?

2 Would you tell me something about your upbringing and your faith journey, please?

3 What motivated you to become a missionary to Shanghai? Why Shanghai?

4 How long were you in Shanghai? Are you still connected with the friends you made in Shanghai?

5 How would you describe five friends or disciples you worked with?

6 What kinds of mission work did you do in Shanghai?

7 What are the three most unique and unforgettable experiences you had as a missionary in Shanghai?

8 How would you summarize and evaluate your mission experience?

9 What are the most challenging issues you faced in your mission work?

10 What kind of future do you envision for Christians in Shanghai? What are your concerns and hopes?

11 Anything else you would like to share?

Bibliography

Accounts of the Martyrs in Beijing in 1900. Translated by Nina Tkachuk Dimas [unknown place of publication], 2004.

Adamek, Piotr. "'Unworthy to Be Quoted among the Believers—Worthy to Be Quoted among the Martyrs': Women in the Orthodox Church in China." *Religions and Christianity in Today's China*, Vol. VII, No. 4 (2017): 25–33.

Ahmad, Ahmad Atif. "Chinese Muslims in Taipei, Nanjing, and Shanghai." *Macalester International*, Vol, 18, Chinese Worlds: Multiple Temporalities and Transformations, Art. 15. Spring 2007, 175–83.

Aldrich, M. A. *The Search for a Vanishing Beijing: A Guide to China's Capital through the Ages*. Hong Kong: Hong Kong University Press, 2006.

Aleni, Giulio. *Xingxue cushu.* [A General Introduction of the Human Nature.] Woodblock edition. Shanghai: Shanghai Cimutang, 1873.

All about Shanghai and Environs: The 1934–1935 Standard Guide Book. Foreword by Peter Hibbard. Hong Kong: Earnshaw Books (Reprint from Shanghai: Shanghai University Press), 2008.

Amsler, Nadine. *Jesuits and Matriarchs: Domestic Worship in Early Modern China*. Seattle: University of Washington Press, 2018.

Anderson, Allan Heaton. "Pentecostalism and Charismatic Movements in Asia." In *The Oxford Handbook of Christianity in Asia*, edited by Felix Wilfred, 158–70. New York: Oxford University Press, 2014.

Anderson, Allan Heaton. "Pentecostalism in India and China in the Early Twentieth Century and Inter-Religious Relations." In *Global Pentecostalism: Encounters with Other Religious Traditions*, edited by David Westerlund, 117–36. London: I.B. Tauris, 2009.

Annual report of *Missionary Intelligencer*, 1918.

Austin, Denise A. "Women and Guangdong Native-Place Charity in Chinese Australian Pentecostalism: 'The Miracle of Grace'." *Chinese Diaspora Charity and the Cantonese Pacific, 1850–1949.* Crossing Seas Series, edited by John Fitzgerald and Hon-ming Yip, 173–92. Hong Kong: Hong Kong University Press, 2020.

Austin, Denise A. *"Kingdom-Minded" People.* Leiden: Brill, 2011.

Aveiro, Maria Guadalupe de Lencastre. *The Far Eastern Catholic Missions 1663–1771: The Original Papers of the Duchess D'aveiro: [Descriptive Catalogue]*. Vol. 2. Tenri: Tenri Central Library, 1975.

Bacon, Ursula. *Shanghai Dairy: A Young Girl's Journey from Hitler's Hate to War-Torn China*. Milwaukie, OR: Milestone Books, 2004.

Bai, Limin. *Fusion of East and West: Children, Education and a New China, 1902–1915*. Leiden: Brill, 2019.

Baker, Kevin. "The Orthodox Churches in China, Japan and Korea." In *Eastern Christianity and Politics in the Twenty-First* Century, edited by Lucian N. Leustean, 439–52. New York: Routledge, 2014.

Banister, [William]. "The Anglican Communion." In *Twentieth Century Impressions of Hongkong, Shanghai, and Other Treaty Ports of China: Their History, People, Commerce, Industries, and Resources*, edited by Arnold Wright, 326–31. London: Lloyd's Greater Britain, 1908.

Barret, Mary, and Chun-chang Kiang. "What's Happening at Christian Colleges." *China Weekly Review*. October 29 (1949): 131–3.

Barwick, John. "Wang Liming: Promoting a Protestant Vision of the Modern Chinese Woman." In *Salt and Light 3: More Lives of Faith that Shaped Modern China*, edited by Carol Lee Hamrin and Stacey Bieler, 136–57. Eugene, OR: Pickwick, 2011.

Bays, Daniel H. "Boone, William Jones, Sr." In *Biographical Dictionary of Christian Missions*, edited by Gerald H. Anderson, 77. Grand Rapids: William B. Eerdmans, 1999.

Bays, Daniel H. *A New History of Christianity in China*. Malden, MA: Wiley-Blackwell, 2012.

Bays, Daniel H. "Chinese Protestant Christianity Today." *The China Quarterly*, No. 174 (June 2003): 488–504.

Bickers, Robert. "Shanghailanders: The Formation and Identity of the British Settler Community in Shanghai 1843–1937." *Past & Present*, No. 159 (May 1998): 161–211.

Biryukova, Kristina V. "Russian Orthodox Mission in Korea until 1917." *Pacific Science Review* 16 (2014): 148–55.

Bollback, Anthony G. *To China and Back*. Chicago: WingSpread, 2014.

Bonhomme, Brian, and Cathleen Boivin, eds. *Milestone Documents in World History: Exploring the Primary Sources That Shaped the World*. Dallas: Schlager Group, 2010.

Bonnell, Cornelia. "Inside and Outside the Wall." *Vassar Miscellany*, Vol. XLIII, No. 4, February 1 (1914): 287–90.

Bridgman, David F. "Defying Tradition: Eliza Bridgman, Foreign Feminist and the Wakening of Women in China." *Journal of Royal Asiatic Society China*, Vol. 78, No. 1 (November 2018): 41–70.

Brockey, Liam Matthew. "Flowers of Faith in an Emporium of Vices: The 'Portuguese' Jesuit Church in Seventeenth-Century Peking." *Monumenta Serica* 53 (2005): 45–71.

Brook, Timothy. "Xu Guangqi in His Context: The World of the Shanghai Gentry." In *Statecraft and Intellectual Renewal in Late Ming China: The Cross-Cultural Synthesis of Xu Guangqi (1562–1633)*, edited by Catherine Jami, Peter Engelfriet, and Gregory Blue, 72–98. Leiden: Brill, 2001.

Buxbaum, Elisabeth, and Armin Berg Gesellschaft. *Transit Shanghai: Ein Leben Im Exil*. Vienna: Edition Steinbauer, 2008.

Campbell, Heidi Olson. "Oss, Olga Bertina (Osnes) (1897–1977)." *Encyclopedia of Seventh-Day Adventists*, November 28, 2021.

Campbell, Michael. "Drs. Bertha and Arthur Selmon: Case Study in the Formation of Early Adventist Mission Identity in China." *Journal of Adventist Mission Studies*, Vol. 17, No. 2 (2021): 76–96.

Cao, Yin. *From Policemen to Revolutionaries: A Sikh Diaspora in Global Shanghai, 1885–1945*. Leiden: Brill, 2017.

Carradice, Phil. *Shanghai Massacre: China's White Terror, 1927.* Barnsley: Pen & Sword Military, 2018.

Carter, Carolyn Howard. "Lanneu, Sophie Stevens." In *Dictionary of North Carolina Biography*, Vol. 4 L-O, edited by William S. Powell, 18–19. Chapel Hill: The University of North Carolina Press, 1991.

Chan, Kim-kwong. "Mission Movement of the Christian Community in Mainland China: The Back to Jerusalem Movement." *Seoul Consultation*, Study Commission IX, Edinburgh (2010): 67–82.

Charbonnier, Jean-Pierre. "The MEP in China: A Chronology from the 17th Century to the Present." In *Missions Étrangères de Paris (MEP) and China from the Seventeenth Century to the Present.* Studies in the History of Christianity in East Asia, Vol. 6, edited by Ji Li, 245–68. Leiden: Brill, 2021.

Chashchin, Kirill. *Russians in China: Shanghai D–917 Police Applicants 1930–1942.* New York: South Eastern, 2017.

Chen, Ruiwen. *A Short Biography of John Shaw Burdon, Bishop of Hong Kong.* Hong Kong: Zongjiao jiaoyu zhongxin (Religious Education Resource Center), 2018.

Chen, Zhengping. *A Brief History of Foreign Debt in China.* Translated by Mirong Chen and edited by Alastair Robert Wilson. [Beijing]: Social Sciences Academic Press, 2014.

Cho, Sam. "Korean Diaspora and Christian Mission." In *Korean Diaspora and Christian Mission*, edited by Sŭng-hun Kim and Wonsuk Ma, 264–80. Oxford: Regnum Books International, 2011.

Chou, Eva. "Churches in Shanghai are Stepping Up during the Latest Lockdowns." *Christianity Today*, translated by Sean Cheng, April 13, 2022.

Christensen, Karin Hyldal. *The Making of the New Martyrs of Russia: Soviet Repression in Orthodox Memory.* New York: Routledge, 2018.

Christian Advocate, Vol. 86. J. B. M'Ferrin for the Methodist Episcopal Church, South, April 17, 1925.

Church Missionary Society. *Proceedings of the Church Missionary Society for Africa and the East: Ninety-Seventh Year, 1895–1896.* London: Church Missionary House, 1896.

Clark, Anthony. "Recovering China's Past: Missionary Photographs of Late-Imperial and Republican China in Western Archives." History Faculty Scholarship. Paper 12. Whitworth University, 2012.

Clark, Anthony. "Sealing Fate and Changing Course: French Catholicism and Chinese Conversion." In *China's Christianity: From Missionary to Indigenous Church*, edited by Anthony E. Clark, 121–40. Leiden: Brill, 2017.

Clark, Anthony. *China's Saints: Catholic Martyrdom during the Qing (1644–1911).* Bethlehem, PA: Lehigh University Press, 2011.

Clarke, Jeremy. "From Kaifeng to Shanghai via Rome and Paris: Jesuits and the History of Judaism in China." In *"The Tragic Couple": Encounters between Jews and Jesuits*, edited by James William Bernauer and Robert A. Maryks, 125–44. Leiden: Brill, 2014.

Cochran, Sherman, and Zhengguang Xie. *The Lius of Shanghai.* Cambridge, MA: Harvard University Press, 2013.

Confucius and Thierry Meynard. *The Jesuit Reading of Confucius: The First Complete Translation of the Lunyu (1687) Published in the West.* Leiden: Brill, 2015.

Cornwell, Patricia. *Ruth, A Portrait: The Story of Ruth Bell Graham*. Colorado Springs: Waterbrook, 1997.

Couplet, Philippe. *Histoire d'une dame chrétienne de la Chine, où par occasion les usages de ces peuples, l'établissement de la religion, les manières des missionnaires, & les exercises de pieté des nouveaux chrétiens sont expliquez*. [History of a Christian Lady of China, Whereby Occasion the Usages of these People, the Establishment of Religion, the Manners of the Missionaries, and the Exercises of Piety of the New Christians are Explained]. Paris, 1688.

Cross, Al. "Old School in China Holds Reunion in Kentucky." *The Courier-Journal*. Louisville, KY, October 9 (1983): 4–5.

Cui, Mark. "Story of Shanghai Church Co-worker's Voluntary Service." *China Christian Daily*, translated by Stephen Huang, May 19, 2022.

De la Servière, Joseph. *Histoire de la mission du Kiangnan: Jesuites de la province de France (Paris) (1840–1898)*. Vol. 1. Shanghai: Catholic Mission Press, 1914.

De Moidrey, J. "Ecclesiastical: The Roman Catholic Church." In *Twentieth Century Impressions of Hongkong, Shanghai, and Other Treaty Ports of China: Their History, People, Commerce, Industries, and Resources*, edited by Arnold Wright, 321–5. London: Lloyd's Greater Britain, 1908.

DeBernardi, Jean. "Circulations: Evangelical and Pentecostal Christianity in Nineteenth-Century Singapore and Penang." In *The Anthropology of Global Pentecostalism and Evangelism*, edited by Simon Coleman and Rosalind I. J. Hackett, 57–74. New York: New York University Press, 2015.

Dias, Manuel. *Tang jingjiiao beisong zhengquan*. [The Annotated Explanation of the Nestorian Stele of the Tang Dynasty.] Shanghai: Cimu Tang, 1887.

Directory of Protestant Missionaries in China, Japan, and Corea. Hong Kong: The "Daily Press" Office, 1903.

Dong, Shaoxin. "Lun Xu Guangqi de xinyang yu zhengzhi lixiang—yi Nanjing jiaoan wei zhongxin." [Discourse of the Beliefs and Political Visions of Xu Guangqi, with a Special Reference to the Nanjing Case.] *Shilin*, No. 1 (2012): 60–70.

Duceux, Isabelle. *La Introducción Del Aristotelismo En China a Través Del De Anima: Siglos XVI–XVII*. [The Introduction of Aristotelianism in China through *On the Soul*, Sixteenth and Seventeenth Centuries.] 1st ed. El Colegio de Mexico, 2009.

Dunlop, John B. *Exodus: St John Maximovitch Leads His Flock Out of Shanghai*. Yonkers, NY: St. Vladimir's Seminary Press, 2017.

Eber, Irene. *Wartime Shanghai and the Jewish Refugees from Central Europe: Survival, Co-Existence, and Identity in a Multi-Ethnic City*. Berlin: De Gruyter, 2012.

Eiko, Hasegawa. "The City as a Contact Zone: Shanghai as a Crossroad between China and Japan." In *Recentring Asia: Histories, Encounters, Identities*, edited by Jacob Edmond, Henry Johnson, and Jacqueline Leckie, 130–48. Leiden: Global Oriental, 2011.

Faber, Ernst. *Problems of Practical Christianity in China*. Translated by Franklin Ohlinger and edited by John Stevens. Shanghai: Office of "The Celestial Empire" and "The Shanghai Mercury", 1897.

"Father Peter A. Wu, M.M." *Catholic New York*, May 21, 2020.

Fernandez, Jeannette Ford. *Mao's Prey: The History of Chen Renbing, Liberal Intellectual*. New York: Routledge, 2001.

Fields, David P. *Foreign Friends: Syngman Rhee, American Exceptionalism, and the Division of Korea*. Lexington, KY: University Press of Kentucky, 2019.

Fitzgerald, John. "Building Trust: Private Charity (cishan 慈善) and Public Benefit (gongyi 公益) in the Associational Life of the Cantonese Pacific, 1850–1949)." *Chinese Diaspora Charity and the Cantonese Pacific, 1850–1949*. Crossing Seas Series. Edited by John Fitzgerald and Hon-ming Yip, 193–210. Hong Kong: Hong Kong University Press, 2020.

Fitzgerald, John, and Mei-fen Kuo. "Diaspora Charity and Welfare Sovereignty in the Chinese Republic: Shanghai Charity Innovator William Yinson Lee (Li Yuanxin, 1884–1965)." *Twentieth-Century China*, Vol. 42, No. 1 (2017): 72–96.

Flynn, Lawrence. "Mission Continues." *Maryknoll Magazine*, September 1, 2016.

Fogel, Joshua A. *Maiden Voyage: The Senzaimaru and the Creation of Modern Sino-Japanese Relations*. Berkeley: University of California Press, 2014.

Freyeisen, Astrid. *Shanghai und die Politik des Dritten Reiches* [Shanghai and the Politics of the Third Reich]. Würzburg: Würzburg Königshausen und Neumann, 2000.

Futrell, W. Chad. "Shanghai." In *Encyclopedia of World Trade: From Ancient Times to the Present*. Vols. 1–4, edited by Cynthia Clark Northrup, 821–3. New York: Routledge, 2015.

Gamble, Jos. *Shanghai in Transition: Changing Perspectives and Social Contours of a Chinese Metropolis*. London: Routledge, 2003.

Gamsa, Mark. *Harbin: A Cross-cultural Biography*. Toronto: University of Toronto Press, 2020.

Gilbert, Helen, and Jacqueline Lo. *Performance and Cosmopolitics: Cross-Cultural Transactions in Australasia*. New York: Palgrave Macmillan, 2009.

Gillespie, James P. *Around the World and Headed South: Growing up a Twin and a Missionary Kid*. 3rd ed. Morrisville, NC: Lulu Press, 2013.

Gladney, Dru. *Muslim Chinese: Ethnic Nationalism in the People's Republic*. Cambridge, MA: Harvard University Press, 1991.

Goforth, Rosalind, and Jonathan Goforth. *Miracle Lives of China*. London: Marshall, Morgan & Scott, 1931.

Gong, Hong-yu. "The Case of Julia B. Mateer: Protestant Missionaries and School Music Education in Late Qing China." *Chime 18–19* (2010): 101–34.

Gratton, F. M. *Freemasonry in Shanghai and Northern China*. 2nd ed. Shanghai: the "North-China Herald" Office, 1900.

Grescoe, Taras. *Shanghai Grand: Forbidden Love and International Intrigue in a Doomed World*. New York: St. Martin's Press, 2016.

Gronewold, Sue. "A New Family: Domesticity and Sentiment among Chinese and Western Women at Shanghai's Door of Hope." In *Divine Domesticities: Christian Paradoxes in Asia and the Pacific*, edited by Hyaeweol Choi and Margaret Jolly, 281–98. Canberra: Australian National University Press, 2014.

Grypma, Sonya. *China Interrupted: Japanese Internment and the Reshaping of a Canadian Missionary Community*. Waterloo, ON: Wilfrid Laurier University Press, 2012.

Gutterres, Antonella Marie. *Lorettine Education in China, 1923–1952: Educational Activities of the Sisters of Loretto in China, Hanyang and Shanghai*. [Taipei]: United Publishing Center, 1961.

Halton, Dan, and Laura Constantine. "Rise and Shine: An Active Armenian Community in Hong Kong is Making Its Mark across Asia." *AGBU*, August 2019.

Handasyde, Kerrie. "Anzac Theology and Women Poets under the Southern Cross." *Colloquium: The Australian & New Zealand Theological Review*, Vol. 49, No. 1 (2017): 17–30.

Hanan, Patrick. "The Bible as Chinese Literature: Medhurst, Wang Tao, and the Delegates' Version." *Harvard Journal of Asiatic Studies*, Vol. 63, No. 1 (June 2003): 197–239.

"Heights Gives 1st U.S. Degree to Chinese Nun." *Denver Catholic Register*, Vol. XL, No. 49. Denver, Thursday, August 9, 1945.

Heirman, Ann, Paolo De Troia, and Jan Parmentier. "Francesco Sambiasi, a Missing Link in European Map Making in China?" *Imago Mundi*, Vol. 61, No. 1 (2009): 29–46.

Henriot, Christian, Lu Shi, and Charlotte Aubrun. *The Population of Shanghai (1865–1953): A Sourcebook*. Boston, MA: Brill, 2019.

Henriot, Christian. "'From a Throne of Glory to a Seat of Ignomity': Shanghai Prostitution Revisited (1849–1949)." *Modern China*, Vol. 22, No. 2 (April 1996): 132–63.

Henriot, Christian. *Prostitution and Sexuality in Shanghai: A Social History, 1849–1949*. Cambridge: Cambridge University Press, 2001.

Henry, Sheila Eileen. "Occupational Mobility and the Ethnic Community: A Comparative Study of Armenians and Japanese-Americans in Los Angeles." PhD diss., University of California, Los Angeles, 1973.

Hershatter, Gail. *Dangerous Pleasures: Prostitution and Modernity in Twentieth-century Shanghai*. Berkeley: University of California Press, 1997.

Hershatter, Gail. "Prostitution and the Market in Women in Early Twentieth-Century Shanghai." In *Marriage and Inequality in Chinese Society*. Edited by Joint Committee on Chinese Studies (U.S.), Conference on Marriage and Inequality in Chinese Society, Rubie S. Watson, and Patricia Buckley Ebrey, 256–85. Berkeley: University of California Press, 1991.

Hochstadt, Steve. "Introduction: How Many Shanghai Jews Were There?" In *A Century of Jewish Life in Shanghai*, edited by Steve Hochstadt, 3–26. New York: Touro University Press, 2019.

Hoffman, Paul. *Witness to History: From Vienna to Shanghai: A Memoir of Escape, Survival and Resilience*. Hong Kong: Earnshaw, 2021.

Hood, George A. "Gibson, John Campbell." In *Biographical Dictionary of Christian Missions*, edited by Gerald H. Anderson, 241. Grand Rapids: William B. Eerdmans, 1999.

黄光域：基督教传行中国纪年. [Huang, Guangyu, ed. *The History of Christian Missions in China, 1807–1949*.] Guilin, Guangxi: Guangxi Normal University Press, 2017.

Huang, Xiaojuan. "Christian Communities and Alternative Devotions in China, 1780–1860." PhD diss., Princeton University, 2006.

Huang, Xuelei. *Shanghai Filmmaking: Crossing Borders, Connecting to the Globe, 1922–1938*. Leiden: Brill, 2014.

Huang, Yanpei, ed. *Chuansha xianzhi* [Chuansha County Gazatteers]. Shanghai: Shanghai guoguang shuju [originally published in 1937], 2001.

Huang, Yuqin. "Western-Educated Chinese Christian Returnees, Nationalism, and Modernity: Comparison between the Pre-1949 Era and the Post-1978 Era." *Sage Open*, No. 1 (2021): 1–12.

Hubbs, Joanna. *Mother Russia: The Feminine Myth in Russian Culture*. 1st Midland book edition. Bloomington: Indiana University Press, 1993.

Huntington, M. C., and A. G. Barbour. *Account of the American Church Mission in Shanghai and the Lower Yangtse Valley*. New York: E. & J.B. Young, 1898.

Huskey, James. "The Cosmopolitan Connection: Americans and Chinese in Shanghai during the Interwar Years." *Diplomatic History*, Vol. 11, No. 3 (Summer 1987): 227–42.

Ibukiyama, Shirō. *Mato No Minato/魔都の港*. Tokyo: Bungeisha/文芸社, 2006.

Ikebuchi, Shelly. *From Slave Girls to Salvation: Gender, Race, and Victoria's Chinese Rescue Home, 1886–1923*. Vancouver: The University of British Columbia Press, 2015.

Inouye, Melissa Wei-Tsing. "Charismatic Moderns: Pluralistic Discourse within Chinese Protestant Communities, 1905–1926." *Twentieth-Century China*, No. 42 (2017): 26–51.

Inouye, Melissa Wei-Tsing. *China and the True Jesus: Charisma and Organization in a Chinese Christian Church*. New York: Oxford University Press, 2018.

Isabel [unknown family name]. "Faith Tends to Grow When We are Out of Our Comfort Zone." *Shanghai Faith Stories*, St. Columbans Mission Society, June 21, 2018.

Jiang, Jin. *Women Playing Men: Yue Opera and Social Change in Twentieth-century Shanghai*. Seattle: University of Washington Press, 2009.

Jin, Luxian. *The Memoirs of Jin Luxian: Volume One: Learning and Relearning 1916–1982*. Translated by William Hanbury-Tenison. Hong Kong: Hong Kong University Press, 2012.

"John G. Oss Dies in California," *Newman Grove Reporter*, August 4, 1948.

Johnson, Todd M., and Gina A. Zurlo. *World Christian Encyclopedia*. 3rd ed. Edinburgh: Edinburgh University Press, 2019.

Juergensmeyer, Mark. *Global Rebellion: Religious Challenges to the Secular State, from Christian Militias to Al Qaeda*. Rev. ed. Berkeley: University of California Press, 2008.

Junio, Diana. *Patriotic Cooperation: The Boarder Services of the Church of Christ in China and Chinese Church–State Relations, 1920s to 1950s*. Religion in Chinese Societies Series, Vol. 12. Boston, MA: Brill, 2017.

Kaminski, Gerd. "Dr. Jakob Rosenfeld: Mensch und Mythos." In *From Kaifeng to Shanghai: Jews in China*, edited by Roman Malek, 461–78. Sankt Augustin, Germany: Routledge, 2000.

Kaplan, Marion A. *Between Dignity and Despair: Jewish Life in Nazi Germany*. New York: Oxford University Press, 1998.

Kato, Naoko. "Through the Kaleidoscope: Uchiyama Bookstore and Sino-Japanese Visionaries in War and Peace." PhD diss., University of Texas, 2013.

Kim, Robert S. *Project Eagle: The American Christians of North Korea in World War II*. Lincoln, NE: Potomac Books, 2017.

King, Frances W. "Women's Christian Medical College, Shanghai." *Chinese Medical Journal*, Vol. 40, No. 8 (1926): 756–8.

King, Gail. *"A Model for All Christian Women": Candida Xu, A Chinese Christian Woman of the Seventeenth Century*. Collectanea Serica, New Series 2. New York: Routledge, 2021.

King, Gail. "The Xujiahui (Zikawei) Library of Shanghai." *Libraries and Culture* (1997): 456–69.

Kiong, Simon. *Quelques mots sur la politesse chinoise*. [A Few Words on Chinese Politeness.] Shanghai: Imprimerie de la Mission Catholique [The Catholic Mission Printing Press], 1906.

Klein, Thoralf. "Anti-Imperialism at Grassroots: Christianity and the Chinese Revolution in Northeast Guangdong, 1919–1930." In *The Chinese Revolution in the 1920s: Between Triumph and Disaster*, edited by Mechthild Leutner, 289–306. New York: Routledge, 2002.

Kleiner, Jürgen. *Korea, a Century of Change*. River Edge, NJ: World Scientific, 2001.

Knyazeva, Katya. "The Scribe of Russian Shanghai: Vladimir Zhiganov and His Perennial Masterpiece." *Journal of the Royal Asiatic Society China*, Vol. 77, No. 1 (2017): 162–95.

Knyazeva, Katya. "High and Low: The Material Culture of the Russian Diaspora in Shanghai, 1920–1950s." *Global Histories*, Vol. 3, No. 2 (Oct 2017): 21–42.

Kuo, Mei-fen. "The 'Invisible Work' of Women: Gender and Philanthropic Sociability in the Evolution of Early Chinese Australian Voluntary Organizations." *Chinese Diaspora Charity and the Cantonese Pacific, 1850–1949*. Crossing Seas Series, edited by John Fitzgerald and Hon-ming Yip, 154–72. Hong Kong: Hong Kong University Press, 2020.

Laird, Rory. *From Shanghai to the Burma Railway: The Memoirs and Letters of Richard Laird, A Japanese Prisoner of War*. Barnsley: Pen & Sword Military, 2020.

Lee, Khoon Choy. *Pioneers of Modern China: Understanding the Inscrutable Chinese*. River Edge, NJ: World Scientific, 2005.

Lefebvre, Peter. *A Guide to Catholic Shanghai*. Shanghai: T'ou-sè-wè Press, 1937.

Li, Jie. *Shanghai Homes: Palimpsests of Private Life*. New York: Columbia University Press, 2015.

Li, Madou. *Yesu hui yu Tianzhu jiao jingru zhongguo shi*/耶稣会与天主教进入中国史. Translated by Wen Zheng and edited by Mei Oujin. Beijing: Shangwu yinshu guan/The Commercial Press, 2014.

"Li Tiangang: How did Xu Guangqi Completely Change the Lives of Chinese?" *Beijing News*, October 26, 2021.

Liao, Tony Hongyue. "Shang and Shan: The Philanthropy of Shanghai's Four Great Companies." PhD diss., Swinburne University, Melbourne, 2017.

Liao, Yiwu. *God is Red: The Secret Story of How Christianity Survived and Flourished in Communist China*. New York: HarperOne, 2011.

Lin, Jennifer. *Shanghai Faithful: Betrayal and Forgiveness in a Chinese Christian Family*. Lanham, MD: Rowman & Littlefield, 2017.

Lin, Zixun. *Zhongguo liuxue jiaoyushi, 1847–1975*. [A History of Chinese Overseas Education]. Taipei: Hwa Kang Press, 1976.

Littell-Lamb, Elizabath. "Caught in the Crossfire: Women's Internationalism and the YWCA Child Labor Campaign in Shanghai, 1921–1925." *Frontiers: A Journal of Women Studies*, Vol. 32, No. 3 (2011): 134–66.

Liu, Diane. "Myths that Shaped the Exile Experience of Central European Jewish Refugees in Japanese-Occupied Shanghai." In *Myth: German and*

Scandinavian Studies, edited by Evan Torner and Victoria Lenshyn, 51–73. Newcastle upon Tyne: Cambridge Scholars Press, 2009.

Liu, Xiaoyan. *The Changing Face of Women's Education in China: A Critical History of St. Mary's Hall, McTyeire School and Shanghai No. 3 Girls' Middle School*. Zurich: Lit Verlag, 2017.

Lockhart, William. *The Medical Missionary in China: A Narrative of Twenty Years' Experience*. London: Hurst and Blackett, 1861.

Lourié, Basil. "Russian Christianity." In *The Blackwell Companion to Eastern Christianity*, edited by Kenneth Parry, 207–30. Malden, MA: Blackwell, 2007.

Lu, Hanchao. *Beyond the Neon Lights: Everyday Shanghai in the Early Twentieth Century*. Berkeley: University of California Press, 1999.

Lu, Yunfeng. "Dangdai zhongguo zongjiao zhuangkuang baogao." *The World Religious Cultures*, Vol. 1 (2014): 11–25.

Lu, Zhengxiang. *La Vie et les oeuvres du grand chrétien chinois Paul Siu Koang-k'i*. [The Life and Works of the Great Chinese Christian Paul Xu Guangqi.] Apostolat Monastique et Missionnaire, Abbaye de Saint-André, Lophem-lez-Bruges, 1934.

Luedi, Jeremy. "Finding God in Africa: How Chinese Expats are Changing Christianity." *Asia by Africa*, July 1, 2018.

Lutz, Jessie Gregory. *Chinese Politics and Christian Mission: The Anti-Christian Movements of 1920–28*. Notre Dame, IN: Cross-Cultural Publications, 1988.

Lutz, Jessie Gregory. "Attrition among Protestant Missionaries in China, 1807–1890." *International Bulletin of Missionary Research*, Vol. 36, No. 1 (2012): 22–7.

MacGillivray, Donald, ed. *A Century of Protestant Missions (1807–1907): Being the Centenary Conference Historical Volume*. Shanghai: The American Presbyterian Mission Press, 1907.

MacInnis, Donald. "Gih, Andrew (Ji Zhiwen)." In *Biographical Dictionary of Christian Missions*, edited by Gerald H. Anderson, 241. Grand Rapids: William B. Eerdmans, 1999.

Manion, Patricia Jean. *Venture into the Unknown: Loretto in China, 1923–1998*. St. Louis, MO: Independent, 2006.

Mariani, Paul Philip. *Church Militant: Bishop Kung and Catholic Resistance in Communist Shanghai*. Cambridge, MA: Harvard University Press, 2011.

Mariani, Paul. "The Phoenix Rises from its Ashes: The Restoration of the Jesuit Shanghai Mission." In *Jesuit Survival and Restoration: A Global History, 1773–1900*, edited by Robert A. Maryks, and Jonathan Wright, 299–314. Boston, MA: Brill, 2014.

Martin, Brian G. *The Shanghai Green Gang: Politics and Organized Crime, 1919–1937*. Berkeley: University of California Press, 1996.

McGrath, Aedan W., Eamonn McCarthy, and Michael Walsh. *From Navan to China: The Story of a "Chinese Irishman"*. Dublin: [Eamonn McCarthy/Michael Walsh], 2008.

McKale, Donald M. "The Nazi Party in the Fast East, 1931–45." *Journal of Contemporary History*, Vol. 12, No. 2 (April 1977): 291–311.

McLean, Mary H. *Dr. Li Yuin Tsao: Called and Chosen and Faithful*. St. Louis, MO: M. H. McLean, 1925.

Meng, Jin. "The Spirituality of Watchman Nee from a Neo-Confucian Perspective." PhD diss., The University of Western Ontario, 2018.

Merekina, Olga. "The Old Catholic Church in Shanghai: A 350-Year-Old Treasure." *Ming Qing Studies* (2013): 275–84.

Meyer, Maisie. "Recollections of Shanghai's Baghdadi Jews." In *A Century of Jewish Life in Shanghai,* edited by Steve Hochstadt, 27–72. New York: Touro University Press, 2019.

Meynard, Thierry. "Fan Shouyi, A Bridge Between China and the West under the Rite Controversy." *Annales Missiologici Posnanienses* 22 (2017): 21–32.

Mikkonen, Simo. "Shanghai Russians: Negotiating Cultural Heritage in a Far East Metropolis." In *Transcending the Borders of Countries, Languages, and Disciplines in Russian émigré Culture*, edited by Christoph Flamm, Roland Marti, and Ada Raev, 59–80. Newcastle upon Tyne: Cambridge Scholars Press, 2018.

Minasyan, I. D. "Socio-Economic Activity of Armenians in China." In *ТЕОРИЯ И ПРАКТИКА ИНСТИТУЦИОНАЛЬНЫХ ПРЕОБРАЗОВАНИЙ В РОССИИ* [Theory and Practice of Institutional Transformation in Russia], edited by B. H. Yerznkyan, 61–68. Moscow: CEMI Russian Academy of Sciences, 2011.

Mo, Wei. "The 'Roman Question' in Shanghai: A Gendered Perspective to Approach the Conflicts between the French Jesuits and the Evolution of Papal Diplomacy in Modern China." In *Exchanges and Parallels between Italy and East Asia*, edited by Gaoheng Zhang and Mario Mignone, 304–26. Newcastle upon Tyne: Cambridge Scholars Press, 2020.

Moon, Steve Sang-cheol. "The Korean Diaspora Models of a Missional Church." In *Korean Diaspora and Christian Mission*, edited by Sŭng-hun Kim and Wonsuk Ma, 84–100. Oxford: Regnum Books International, 2011.

Morrison, Robert. *A Grammar of the Chinese Language*. Serampore: Mission Press, 1815.

Morrison, Robert. *A Dictionary of the Chinese Language, in Three Parts*. Macao, China: P. P. Thoms, 1815–23.

Mungello, David E. *The Great Encounter of China and the West, 1500–1800*. 2nd ed. Lanham, MD: Rowman & Littlefield, 2005.

Mungello, David E. *The Great Encounter of China and the West, 1500–1800*. 3rd ed. Lanham, MD: Rowman & Littlefield, 2009.

Mungello, David E. *Drowning Girls in China: Female Infanticide Since 1650*. Lanham, MD: Rowman & Littlefield, 2008.

Nakajima, Chieko. "Health, Medicine and Nation in Shanghai, ca. 1900–1945." PhD diss., University of Michigan, 2004.

Nedostup, Rebecca Allyn. "Religion, Superstition and Governing Society in Nationalist China." PhD diss., Columbia University, 2001.

Norman, Jeremias. "Eastern Christianity in China." In *The Blackwell Companion to Eastern Christianity*, edited by Kenneth Parry, 280–90. Malden, MA: Blackwell, 2007.

"Obituaries." *Quarterly Journal of the Royal Astronomical Society*, Vol. 26, No. 2 (1985): 219–28.

O'Brien, Neil L. *An American Editor in Early Revolutionary China: John William Powell and the China Weekly/monthly Review*. New York: Routledge, 2003.

Olge, Mary S. *China Nurse: The Life Story of Elisabeth Redelstein*. Mountain View, CA: Pacific Press, 1974.

박용옥. 《김마리아: 나는 대한의 독립과 결혼하였다》. 서울: 홍성사, 2003. [Park, Yongok. *Maria Kim: I Married the Independence of Korea*]. Seoul: Hong Seongsa, 2003.

Pascoe, Peggy. *Relations of Rescue: The Search for Female Moral Authority in the American West, 1874–1939*. New York: Oxford University Press, 1993.

Patrick, Susangeline. "Art as a Pathway to God: A Historical-Theological Study of the Jesuit Mission to China, 1552–1773." PhD diss., Asbury Theological Seminary, Kentucky, 2019.

Pritchard, John. *Methodists and Their Missionary Societies 1900–1996*. New York: Routledge, 2016.

Qian, Ning. *Chinese Students Encounter America*. Translated by T. K. Chu. Seattle: University of Washington Press, 2002.

Ray, T. B. *Southern Baptist in China*. Richmond, VA: Foreign Mission Board Southern Baptist Convention, 1924.

Reed, Christopher A. *Gutenberg in Shanghai: Chinese Print Capitalism, 1876–1937*. Vancouver: The University of British Columbia Press, 2004.

Reilly, Thomas H. *Saving the Nation: Chinese Protestant Elites and the Quest to Build a New China, 1922–1952*. New York: Oxford University Press, 2020.

Ribeiro, António Vitor. "Dreams, Visions, and a Taoist-Christian 'Saint' in the Seventeenth-Century Jesuit Records of the China Mission." *Archivum Historicum Societatis Iesu*. Vol. LXXXVIII, Fasc. 175 (2019-I): 103–33.

Ristaino, Marcia R. *Port of Last Resort: The Diaspora Communities of Shanghai*. Redwood City, CA: Stanford University Press, 2001.

Ristaino, Marcia R. *The Jacquinot Safe Zone: Wartime Refugees in Shanghai*. Redwood City, CA: Stanford University Press, 2008.

Robert, Dana. *Christian Mission: How Christianity Became a World Religion*. Malden, MA: Wiley-Blackwell, 2009.

Roberts, Lee M. "Relative Resistance: Fascist Aryanization Practices and the Bond of Victimhood in the Antifascist Animation *A Jewish Girl in Shanghai*." In *The History of the Shanghai Jews: New Pathways of Research*, edited by Kevin Ostoyich and Yun Xia, 237–71. London: Palgrave Macmillan, 2022.

Rule, Paul. "Restoration or New Creation? The Return of the Society of Jesus to China." In *Jesuit Survival and Restoration: A Global History, 1773–1900*, edited by Robert A. Maryks and Jonathan Wright, 261–77. Boston, MA: Brill, 2014.

Rule, Paul. "François Noël, SJ, and the Chinese Rites Controversy." In *The History of the Relations between the Low Countries and China in the Qing Era (1644–1911)*. Leuven Chinese Studies XIV, edited by W. F. Vande Walle and Noël Golvers, 137–66. Leuven/Louvain, Belgium: Leuven University Press, 2003.

Sander, Marie. *Passing Through Shanghai: Ethnographic Insights into the Mobile Lives of Expatriate Youths*. Heidelberg: Heidelberg University Publishing, 2016.

Sanneh, Lamin. *Translating the Message: The Missionary Impact on Culture*. 2nd ed. Maryknoll, NY: Orbis Books, 2009.

Schwarcz, Vera. *In the Crook of the Rock: Jewish Refuge in a World Gone Mad: The Chaya Walkin Story*. Boston, MA: Academic Studies Press, 2018.

Scully, Eileen P. "Prostitution as Privilege: the 'American Girl' of Treaty-Port Shanghai, 1860–1937." *The International History Review*, Vol. 20, No. 4 (1998): 855–83.

Seo, Joong-Seok. *Korean Nationalism Betrayed*. Folkestone: Global Oriental, 2007.

Sergoyan, E. G. *The Gathering Place: Stories from the Armenian Social Club in Old Shanghai*. Seattle: Coffeetown Press, 2012.

Setsuzō, Kotsuji. *From Tokyo to Jerusalem*. Jerusalem: Random House, 1964.

Shan, Lianying. "Japanese Accounts of Shanghai in the Late Nineteenth and Early Twentieth Centuries." In *Revealing/Reveiling Shanghai: Cultural Representations from the Twentieth and Twenty-first Centuries*, edited by Lisa Bernstein and Chu-chueh Cheng, 103–22. Albany, NY: State University of New York Press, 2020.

"Shanghai Church Draws Korean Pilgrims." *PIMA Asianews*, July 21, 2005.

上海统计局. 上海统计年鉴：1990 - 2013 年. 北京：中国统计出版社，1990 - 2013. [Shanghai Municipal Bureau of Statistics. *Shanghai Statistics Yearbook 1990–2013*]. Beijing: China Statistics Press, 1990–2013].

Shi, Jeffrey Zhengfu. *Supernormal Growth: China's Economy 1979–2049.* Hackensack, NJ: World Century, 2015.

Sidebotham, Steven E. *Berenike and the Ancient Maritime Spice Route.* Berkeley: University of California Press, 2011.

Sklair, Leslie. "Towards an Understanding of Architecture Iconicity." In *Aspects of Urbanization in China: Shanghai, Hong Kong, Guangzhou*, edited by Gregory Byrne Bracken, 27–46. [Amsterdam]: Amsterdam University Press, 2012.

"Sister Antonella Marie Gutterres (Thereza Maria Gutterres)." *Congressional Record–House*, 1954, 13294.

Smedley, Agnes. "The Dedicated." *Bulletin of Concerned Asian Scholars*, Vol. 7, No. 1 (1975): 12–18.

Smith, George. *A Narrative of an Exploratory Visit to Each of the Consular Cities of China, and to the Islands of Hong Kong and Chusan, in [on] Behalf of the Church Missionary Society, in the Years 1844, 1845, 1846.* New York: Harper and Brothers, 1847.

Smith, H. Arthur. *Chinese Characteristics.* New York: Fleming H. Revell Company, 1894.

Smith, Carl T. "The Chinese Church, Labour and Elites and the Mui Tsai Question in the 1920's." *Journal of the Hong Kong Branch of the Royal Asiatic Society*, Vol. 21 (1981): 91–113.

Society of the Holy Childhood. *Annales de l'Œuvre de la Sainte-Enfance.* Paris: Bureau du Conseil Central de Œuvre, 1846–9.

Spang, Christian W. "The German East Asiatic Society (OAG) in Shanghai, 1931–1945." In *The History of the Shanghai Jews: New Pathways of Research*, edited by Kevin Ostoyich and Yun Xia, 43–74. London: Palgrave Macmillan, 2022.

Standaert, Nicolas. *Yang Tingyun, Confucian and Christian in Late Ming China: His Life and Thought.* Leiden: Brill, 1988.

Standaert, Nicolas. "Chinese Voices in the Rites Controversy: The Role of Christian Communities." In *The Rites Controversies in the Early Modern World.* Studies in Christian Mission, Vol. 53, edited by Ines G. Županov and Pierre Antoine Fabre, 50–67. Leiden: Brill, 2018.

Stark, Rodney, and Xiuhua Wang. *A Star in the East: The Rise of Christianity in China.* West Conshokocken, PA: Templeton Press, 2015.

Strong, David. *A Call to Mission: A History of the Jesuits in China 1842–1954.* Vol. 1: The French Romance. Hindmarsh, SA: ATF Press, 2018.

Strong, David. *A Call to Mission: A History of the Jesuits in China 1827–1957.* Volume 2: The Wider European and American Adventure. Hindmarsh, SA: ATF Press, 2018.

Summers, Lawrence H., and Vinod Thomas. "Recent Lessons of Development." *The World Bank Research Observer*, Vol. 8, No. 2 (July 1993): 241–54.
Sun, Steve. "Testimony: A Shanghai Christian's Experience, Takeaway after Recovering from Covid-19." *China Christian Daily*, translated by Shuya Wang, April 27, 2022.
Tang, Edmond. "Identity and Marginality: Christianity in East Asia." In *The Oxford Handbook of Christianity in Asia*, edited by Felix Wilfred, 80–97. New York: Oxford University Press, 2014.
Tang, Kaijian, ed. *Li Madou: Mingqing zhongwen wenxian ziliao quanshi* [Matteo Ricci: Chinese Texts and Documentations and Annotations from the Ming-Qing Period]. Shanghai: Shanghai guji chuban she [Shanghai Chinese Classics Publishing House], 2017.
Tanizaki, Jun'ichirō. "Shanghai Friends." *Chinese Studies in History*, Vol. 30, No. 4 (1997): 71. [Armonk, NY: M. E. Sharpe].
Taylor, James Hudson. *China, Its Spiritual Need and Claims: With Brief Notices of Missionary Effort, Past and Present.* London: James Nisbet, 1865.
Taylor, James Hudson. *A Retrospect.* London: Morgan and Scott, 1905.
The China Mail, Hong Kong, May 7, 1923.
The Far East. Vol. XIX, No. 4, April 1936. St. Columbans, NE: St. Columban's Foreign Mission Society.
The Missionary Intelligencer, Vol. 30. Cincinnati: Foreign Christian Missionary Society, 1917.
The New Glories of the Catholic Church. Translated by the Fathers of the London Oratory. London: Richardson and Son, 1859.
The United Christian Mission Society. *They Went to China: Biographies of Missionaries of the Disciples of Christ.* Indianapolis: Stone-Campbell Books, 1948.
Thomas, Antoine. *Catalogue of the Residences and Missions of the Vice-Province of China of the Society of Jesus for 1703.* Peking, September 25, 1703, ARSI Jap.-Sin. 134.
Tiedemann, R. G. *Reference Guide to Christian Missionary Societies in China: From the Sixteenth to the Twentieth Century.* London: Routledge, 2016.
Tillman, Margaret Mih. "Mediating Modern Motherhood: The Shanghai YWCA's 'Women's Work for Women,' 1908–1949." In *Spreading Protestant Modernity: Global Perspectives on the Social Work of the YMCA and YWCA, 1889–1970*, edited by Harald Fischer-Tiné, Stefan Huebner, and Ian R. Tyrrell, 119–44. Honolulu: University of Hawai'i Press, 2021.
Torr, Geordie. *The Silk Roads: A History of the Great Trading Routes between East and West.* Canterbury: Arcturus, 2021.
Tsao, Christina Ching. *Shanghai Bride: Her Tumultuous Life's Journey to the West.* Hong Kong: Hong Kong University Press, 2005.
Tsu, Andrew Yu-Yue. *Friends of Fisherman.* Ambler, PA: Trinity Press, 1966.
Turner, Simon. "Studying the Tensions of Transnational Engagement: From the Nuclear Family to the World-Wide Web." *Journal of Ethnic and Migration Studies*, Vol. 34, No. 7 (2008): 1049–56.
Uchiyama, Kanzō. *Sonhe Ohe: Shanhai Seikatsu Sanjugonen.* Tokyo: Iwanami Shinsho, 1949.

United Presbyterian Church in the U.S.A. General Assembly. *Minutes of the General Assemblies of the Presbyterian Church in the U.S.A.* Philadelphia: The University of Pennsylvania, 1925.

United States Congress House. "83d Congress 2d Session, House of Representatives, Report No. 2226." *Report.*

Urrows, David Francis. *François Ravary SJ and a Sino-European Musical Culture in Nineteenth-Century Shanghai.* Newcastle upon Tyne: Cambridge Scholars Press, 2021.

Van der Veer, Peter. "Urban Planning and Secular Atheism in Shanghai, Beijing and Singapore." In *Religion and the Global City*, edited by David Garbin and Anna Strhan, 47–61. London: Bloomsbury Academic, 2017.

Vermander, Benot, Liz Hingley, and Liang Zhang. *Shanghai Sacred: The Religious Landscape of a Global City.* Seattle: University of Washington Press, 2018.

Walshe, W. Gilbert. *"Ways that are Dark": Some Chapters on Chinese Etiquette and Social Procedure.* Shanghai: Kelly and Walsh, *c.* 1890.

Wang, Chongmin. *Xu guangqi ji* [A Collection of Xu Guangqi's Writings], Vol. 12. Shanghai: Shanghai guji chuban she, 1984.

Wang, Marina. "The Chinese Home Missionary Society: An Early Attempt at Shaping an Interdenominational and Indigenised Chinese Christianity." In *Yearbook of Chinese Theology*, edited by Paulos Z. Huang, 75–96. Boston, MA: Brill, 2017.

Wang, Ruth. "Peking Opera Master Mei Baojiu Dies at 82, His Christian Friend Witnesses His Conversion to Christianity." *China Christian Daily*, April 26, 2016.

Wang, Zhicheng. *Portuguese in Shanghai.* Macau: Aomen Jijin Hui [unknown date of publication].

Wang, Zhicheng. *Istoriia russkoi emigratsii v Shankhae* [History of Russian Emigration to Shanghai]. Moscow: Russkii out, 2008.

Wasserstrom, Jeffrey N. *Global Shanghai, 1850–2010: A History in Fragments.* New York: Routledge, 2009.

Wei, Shuge. "News as a Weapon: Hollington Tong and the Formation of the Guomindang Centralized Foreign Propaganda System, 1937–1938." *Twentieth-Century China*, Vol. 39, No. 2 (2014): 118–43.

Wei, Yu-hsiu. *My Revolutionary Years: The Autobiography of Madame Wei Tao-ming.* New York: Scribner's Sons, 1943.

Weller, Robert P., C. Julia Huang, Keping Wu, and Lizhu Fan. *Religion and Charity: The Social Life of Goodness in Chinese Societies.* New York: Cambridge University Press, 2018.

Wen, Ge. "7 Building Up the Church in a Socialist Country: An Examination of Bishop K.H. Ting's Chinese Social Theology." In *Yearbook of Chinese Theology 2017*, edited by Paulos Z. Huang, 113–38. Leiden: Brill, 2017.

Weststeijn, Thijs. "'Intoxicated, We Listened to Warblers and Swallows Chattering in the Spring Wind': Art in the Friendship between François de Rougemont and Wu Li." *Netherlands Yearbook for History of Art/Nederlands Kunsthistorisch Jaarboek Online*, Vol. 70, No. 1 (2020): 294–309.

Widmer, Eric. *The Russian Ecclesiastical Mission in Peking during the Eighteenth Century.* Cambridge, MA: Harvard University Press, 1976.

Wilhelm, Hans M. *China Hans: From Shanghai to Hitler to Christ.* Victoria, BC: Trafford, 2009.

Witek, John W. "Christianity and China: Universal Teaching from the West." In *China and Christianity: Burdened Past, Hopeful Future*, edited by Stephen Uhalley Jr. and Xiaoxin Wu, 11–28. New York: M. E. Sharpe, 2001.

Witek, John W. "Rocha, João da." In *Biographical Dictionary of Christian Missions*, edited by Gerald H. Anderson, 573–4. Grand Rapids: William B. Eerdmans, 1999.

Wong, Sik Pui. *In Remembrance of Martyrs a Century Ago: Last Words and Letters from the Missionary Martyrs of the 1900 Boxer Incident*. Petaluma, CA: CCM, 2009.

Wue, Roberta. *Art Worlds: Artists, Images, and Audiences in Late Nineteenth-century Shanghai*. Honolulu: University of Hawai'i Press, 2014.

Wylie, Alexander. *Memorials of Protestant Missionaries to the Chinese: Giving a List of Their Publications, and Obituary Notices of the Deceased*. Shanghai: American Presbyterian Mission Press, 1867.

Xiong, Yuezhi. *Shanghai Urban Life and Its Heterogeneous Cultural Entanglements*, translated by Lane J. Harris and Chun Mei. Leiden: Brill, 2022.

Xu, Edward Yihua. "Religion and Education: St. John's University as an Evangelizing Agency." PhD diss., Princeton University, 1994.

Xu, Fang. *Silencing Shanghai: Language and Identity in Urban China*. Lanham, MD: Lexington Books, 2021.

Xu Guangqi, "Pi shishi zhuwang." In *Xujiahui cangshulou ming qing tianzhujiao wenxian* [Documents concerning Ming and Qing Catholicism at the Xujiahui Library], edited by Zhong Mingdan (Nicolas Standaert), 389–528. Taipei: Fuda Theological Seminary, 1996.

Xu, Qinzhen. "Liu Na'ou nianbiao." In *Modeng, Shanghai, xin ganjue*, edited by Qinzhen Xu, 159–69. Taipei: Xiuwei zixun keji, 2008.

Yang, Cheng. "Bookstore Frequented by Revolutionaries Reopens in Tianjin." *China Daily*, July 11, 2021.

Yang, Fenggang. *Atlas of Religion in China: Social and Geographical Contexts*. Boston, MA: Brill, 2018.

Yates, M. T. *Ancestral Worship: A Revised Edition of an Essay*. Shanghai: American Presbyterian Mission Press, 1878.

Ye, Xiaowen. *Pluralism and Harmony in the Religions of China*. Beijing: Foreign Language Press, 2018.

Yeh, Wen-Hsin. *Wartime Shanghai*. New York: Routledge, 1998.

Yumei [family name unknown]. "My Eyes were Restrained like the Two Men on Their Road to Emmaus." *Shanghai Faith Stories*, St. Columbans Mission Society [undated].

Zhang, Jun, and Peidong Sun. "When are You Going to Get Married? Parental Matchmaking and Middle-Class Women in Contemporary Urban China." In *Wives, Husbands, and Lovers: Marriage and Sexuality in Hong Kong, Taiwan, and Urban China*, edited by Deborah Davis and Sara Friedman, 118–44. Redwood City, CA: Stanford University Press, 2014.

Zhao, Pan. "The True Jesus Church and the Bible in Republican China." *Religions*, Vol. 11, No. 2 (2020): 89.

Zhang, Qiong. "About God, Demons, and Miracles: The Jesuit Discourse on the Supernatural in Late Ming China." *Early Science and Medicine*, Vol. 4, No. 1 (1999): 1–36.

Zhi, Grace. "Nick Vujicic Speaks of Being Your Best in Shanghai." *China Christian Daily*, August 4, 2016.

Zhi, Grace. "Shanghai Churches Collectively Hold Bazaars to Aid Poor Sick Children." *China Christian Daily*, translated by Karen Luo, November 5, 2018.

Zhiganov, V. D. *Russians in Shanghai*. Shanghai [unknown publisher], 1936.

Zhong, Mijia. "Easter in Shanghai: Christians' Life, Faith, Love under Covid-19 Lockdown." *China Christian Daily*, translated by Charlie Li, April 20, 2022.

Zhong, Mingdan, ed. *Xujiahui cang mingqing tianzhujiao wenxian xubian*, Vol. 14. Taibei: Lishi xueshe, 2013.

Zhong, Mingdan, Du Dingke, and Meng Xi. 法国国家图书馆明清天主教文献/*Faguo guojia tushuguan cang mingqing tianzhujiao wenxian* [Ming-Qing Catholic Texts from the National Library of France], No. 4. Taibei: Taibei Lishi xueshe, 2009.

Zimmer, Christoph. "Disrupted Loyalities? 21st-Century Sinicization of the Catholic Other." In *Religious Othering: Global Dimensions*, edited by Mark Juergensmeyer, Kathleen Moore, and Dominic Sachsenmaier, 147–63. New York: Routledge, 2023.

Zürcher, Erik. "Xu Guangqi and Buddhism." In *Statecraft and Intellectual Renewal in Late Ming China: The Cross-Cultural Synthesis of Xu Guangqi (1562–1633)*, edited by Catherine Jami, Peter Engelfriet, and Gregory Blue, 155–69. Leiden: Brill, 2001.

Index